ISAAC NEWTON'S

OBSERVATIONS ON THE PROPHECIES OF DANIEL AND THE APOCALYPSE OF ST. JOHN

MELLEN CRITICAL EDITIONS AND TRANSLATIONS

EDITORIAL DIRECTOR

Maurice Hindle

Mellen Critical Editions and Translations is a new series that makes historically
significant but neglected texts available to the research
community in a fully annotated scholarly form. Each
work, which will have originated usually before
1900, is prepared and presented by
scholarly specialists.

EDITORIAL POLICY

Proposals for volumes in this series, which are invited from
scholars working in any field of the humanities and the human
sciences, should be submitted for consideration to:
Dr Maurice Hindle c/o The Edwin Mellen Press, Mellen House,
Unit 17 Llambed Ind. Est., Lampeter, Ceredigion,
Wales, United Kingdom SA48 8LT.

Isaac Newton's
Observations on the Prophecies of Daniel and the Apocalypse of St. John
A Critical Edition
Prophecy as History

Edited by

S.J. Barnett

With Preface and Biblical Studies Notes by

Mary E. Mills

Mellen Critical Editions and Translations
Volume 2

The Edwin Mellen Press
Lewiston•Queenston•Lampeter

BS
1556
. N36
1999

Library of Congress Cataloging-in-Publication Data

Newton, Isaac, Sir, 1642-1727.
  [Observations on the prophecies of Daniel and the Apocalypse of
St. John]
  Isaac Newton's observations on the prophecies of Daniel and the
Apocalypse of St. John / edited by S.J. Barnett ; with preface and
biblical studies notes by Mary E. Mills.
      p. cm. -- (Mellen critical editions and translations ; v. 2)
  Includes bibliographical references and index.
  ISBN 0-7734-8155-9 (hardcover)
  1. Bible. O.T. Daniel--Prophecies--Early works to 1800.
  2. Bible. O.T. Revelation--Prophecies--Early works to 1800.
  I. Barnett, S. J., 1960-   . II. Mills, Mary E.   III. Title.
  IV. Series.
  BS1556.N36   1999
  224'.5015--dc21   99-13609
                                                                  CIP

This is volume 2 in the continuing series
Mellen Critical Editions & Translations
Volume 2 ISBN 0-7734-8155-9
MCET Series ISBN 0-7734-8292-X

A CIP catalog record for this book is available from the British Library.

Copyright © 1999   The Edwin Mellen Press

The Edwin Mellen Press   The Edwin Mellen Press
        Box 450   Box 67
  Lewiston, New York   Queenston, Ontario
  USA 14092-0450   CANADA L0S 1L0

The Edwin Mellen Press, Ltd.
Lampeter, Ceredigion, Wales
UNITED KINGDOM SA48 8LT

Printed in the United States of America

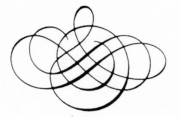

Table of Contents.

Acknowledgements

My thanks to Mary Mills (St Mary's University College, Twickenham) for her learned, diligent and invaluable contribution to this edition, not least her translation and especially insightful interpretation of Newton's Hebrew and Greek phrases. I am also grateful to Christine Hallet (University of Manchester) for her continued interest and encouragement in the preparation of this volume, especially for her ever-sharp eye for errors. I am also grateful to Penny Gouk - of the University of Manchester's Centre for the History of Science, Technology and Medicine – for one of my first discussions on Newton's religious thought. Finally, I am indebted to Nick Croft for the very generous donation of his skill and time, without which the final manuscript would not have fared well.

Preface

Isaac Newton is a name which, for many students, represents the flourishing of early modern science, endorsing a rational and reflective approach to the universe. However, this perspective highlights only one of Newton's interests. His Observations on Daniel and the Apocalypse reveal his deep-seated concern with traditional Christianity. Newton here shows himself to have been a committed believer in Jesus Christ, possessed of a faith founded on the Christian Scriptures. Yet Newton's Christianity was itself but one facet of the diverse world of early modern European religion. His outlook was based on dissent from Anglicanism and on a Unitarian approach to God, which Newton discerned as already present in the Jewish tradition within which Christianity was emerging in late antiquity.

This present volume makes Newton's religious views available to those with an interest in cultural matters, but who do not have a sufficient knowledge of Latin and Greek to be able to follow Newton's original text unaided. The editor sets out to make Newton's text accessible and to provide an introduction to his life and thought, which stresses the fact that his religious works are not now peripheral or outdated, but rather provide the twentieth-century student with vital evidence of seventeenth- and early eighteenth-century religious thought.

This initiative is of significance for contemporary students not only because Newton's religious texts may be less well read than his scientific works, but because the biblical books which Newton examines are themselves obscure and not infrequently regarded as peripheral to the Old and New Testaments. The core of Christian teaching is often placed in the Gospels or in the Pauline Letters and apocalyptical material is discarded as reflecting fringe views. But Newton regarded the Apocalypse genre as essential to the Christian tradition and as the heart of Christian teaching, out of which other texts such as Gospel books emerge. For Newton the apocalyptic texts are prophetic revelations of the true nature and destiny of European society. In this approach there is no separation between religion and culture: in order to achieve a true understanding of the concept of Europe the reader must also have a true appreciation of the nature of Christianity. Newton's religious endeavours, then, were no fringe activity but a serious and sober evaluation of his cultural environment.

Newton's religious interests included the Millennium and - as this volume amply demonstrates - he dwelt upon the historical face that may be given to the idea of a thousand year reign of Christ found in the book of Revelation. In this setting, Newton may be considered not only for the individuality of his thought, or its seventeenth-century background, but may also be viewed as part of a chain of millennial thinking which stretches from the book of Revelation in the first century to the present day. Investigation into European history reveals a series of movements, often separate from the religious status quo of the day (if not actively hostile to its values) which took as their focus the theory of a thousand year reign of grace in a society cleansed of corruption and evil. One may note here the millenarianism of Joachim of Fiore (c. 1132-1202) in the medieval period and its effect on St Francis of Asissi (1181/2-1226). In this case millenarianism, as a `dissenting' influence was absorbed into the mainstream Church of the time. Likewise, in Cromwellian England, millennial concern is evident in the letters of Cromwell himself. But, moving from opposition to the centre of authority, Cromwell and his supporters became an establishment force suppressing other radical millennial elements such as the Fifth Monarchists. Just as with Newton, the millenarianism of such sects reveals a mixture of religion and politics in a contest for power and influence within society. Newton, indeed, combined the essence of that diversity in his own situation, being in a position of social authority in the status quo culture of Anglicanism, but at the same time personally siding with Dissent.

It is clear that Newton's religious texts are of considerable value for a number of contemporary students both for those interested in the history of the seventeenth century and for those concerned with the nature of religious theory within the Christian tradition. It is in this broad context of scholarship that the present edition of Newton's Observations takes its place, making accessible to readers material which has not recently been published, or at all in contemporary critical form.

Mary E. Mills, St Mary's University
College, August 1998.

INTRODUCTION

The last of the Babylonians and Sumerians?

Isaac Newton is of course widely renown for his path-breaking studies of gravity, the laws of motion, the nature of light and the development of calculus. As a consequence of his monumental achievements, many have justly regarded him as the father of modern science. The following discussion, however, relates almost exclusively to Newton's other great endeavours: his religious studies. The aim of this edition of *Newton's Observations upon the Prophecies of Daniel and the Apocalypse of St John* (1733) is to make available to students of late seventeenth- and eighteenth-century history the other, religious half of the mind of Isaac Newton. This discussion is not, therefore, intended as a study of biblical prophecy *per se*, or to note how supposedly correct or incorrect was Newton's understanding of biblical prophecy. Rather the goal is to set Newton's thinking on the Old Testament prophecy of Daniel and the New Testament prophecy of John within the general early modern politico-religious context of England. Mary Mills, however, has below provided some guidance for the non-specialist readers who might wish to compare today's conceptions those of the prophecies of Daniel and John with those of early modern thinkers.

To students of late seventeenth-century history, the fact that Isaac Newton (1642-1727),[1] the most famous of all English scientists, was also a millennialist

---

[1]   For a treatment of the life of Newton see Frank Manuel's A *Portrait of Isaac Newton*, (Cambridge Mass., 1968); Richard Westfall's *The Life of Isaac Newton* (Cambridge, 1994); Rupert Hall's *Adventurer in Thought*; and Michael White's, *Isaac Newton, The Last Sorcerer* (London, 1997).

consumed with an intense piety and wrote more than one million words[2] on religious matters should be no surprise. Indeed, the great philosopher and friend of Newton, John Locke (1632-1704), remarked that he knew few who could equal Newton for his knowledge of Scripture.[3] Happily, the notion that seventeenth-century scientific developments were all, in themselves, 'modern' challenges to religion and biblical concepts of the world has for some time now been dismissed as fundamentally misleading. Thus, in recent decades, the religious endeavours of Newton have been somewhat retrieved from the embarrassed gloom into which they had been cast for more than 200 years. As Amos Funkenstein has illustrated, in the lifetime of Isaac Newton there was an unprecedented fusion of scientific reasoning and religious thought.[4] The complex and seemingly endless wonders of the material world and their hidden laws indicated by scientific investigation were usually deemed self-evident proofs of an awesome, ineffable creator.

An understanding of the religious perspective of Newton cannot but be central in the endeavour to reveal some of the various influences at play in the development of late seventeenth- and eighteenth-century intellectual thought: of the mentalities behind the unintentionally often blinkered and sometimes sensationalist headlines of history. To study the prophetic aspect of Newton's religious views[5] is to remind ourselves that the role of science in the origins of the

---

[2]   F. Manuel, *The religion of Isaac Newton* (Oxford, 1974), p. 8..

[3]   Hall, *Adventurer in Thought*, p. 236.

[4]   A. Funkenstein, *Theology and the Scientific Imagination from the Middle Ages to the Seventeenth Century* (Princeton University Press, 1986); on the fusion of science and religion see also T. Hankins', *Science and the Enlightenment* (1995; 1st edn 1985). For a useful collection of articles and tracts written by scientists illustrating the integration of science and religion see D.C. Goodman (ed.) *Science and Religious Belief 1600-1900* (Open Uni. Press, 1973); see especially the extract from Robert Boyle's *The Christian Virtuoso: shewing, That by being addicted to experimental philosophy, a man is rather assisted than indisposed to be a good Christian* (1690).

[5]   On Newton's religious views see, for instance, John Brooke, 'The God of Isaac Newton', in J. Fauvel, R. Flood, M. Shortland, R. Wilson (eds), *Let Newton Be!* (New

Enlightenment can hardly be considered a simple or transparent process, one in which a new cosmological paradigm neatly replaced a traditional 'non-scientific' outlook. To hold the latter view would be tantamount to asserting that the activities of scientific minds constitute little more than the problems they study. Such a simplistic view would also tend to underestimate the potential for Christianity to adapt to and adopt new learning into its traditional cosmology.

Modern readers expecting the prodigious achievements of Newton's scientific endeavours to be parallelled in the field of hermeneutics or exegesis are likely to be a little disappointed. In his *Observations*, he certainly demonstrated his wide knowledge of the early Church. But to study Newton's considerable strivings in the field of biblical prophecy, is to encounter relatively little of anything novel or daring. Rather his endeavours should be understood as minor amendments, clarifications and elaborations of a Protestant anti-Catholic exegetical tradition already well-established before his birth. In researching his *Observations*, Newton was not, however, attempting to produce any startlingly new analysis of biblical prophecy. His over-riding aim was to give more precision to the hermeneutic of biblical exegesis, and to add, clarify and adduce appropriate, concrete historical evidence for the correlation of the prophecies with historical developments already mostly plotted by other Protestant exegetes.

Like most Dissenters (Newton was a Unitarian), whose outlook combined a virulent anti-Catholicism with anti-Anglicanism, the proof of the often complex and enigmatic prophecies of Daniel and John lay before his eyes in contemporary reality. The prophecies were widely understood by Protestants to predict a deep corruption of the Church, one which would only be erased fully by the coming of the Millennium. The baleful present - the (perceived) superstitious quasi-pagan antichristianism of Catholicism and the neopopery of Anglicanism - was

York, 1989); Scott Mandlebrote, 'A Duty of the Greatest Moment: Isaac Newton and the Writing of Biblical Criticism', in *British Journal for the History of Science*, 26 (1993); *Manuel, Religion of Isaac Newton*; Westfall, *The Life of Isaac Newton*; and understood as tangible proof of a corrupting force in historical development. The Catholic and Anglican Churches both retained the medieval episcopate, perceived by Dissenters as an historical and contemporary weapon of religious fraud and oppression; a reality which was negatively contrasted against the Presbyterian, rank-and-file Church polity advocated by most Dissenters.

Both established Churches were also Trinitarian. It is hardly surprising that some Dissenters, in their search for a simple, rational and non-oppressive Church, asked themselves if the formula of the Father, the Son and the Holy Ghost - which led to the worship of a cross on which a being half God and half human had suffered - was not also a fundamental component in the long-term venal and superstitious corruption of the Christian ministry. Comparatively little research has been devoted to the question of the relationship between the charge of priestcraft levelled at Catholicism and Anglicanism and the growth of Unitarian thought in late seventeenth-century England. Nevertheless, it can be safely argued that the increase in monotheistic thought in the second half of the seventeenth century was, at least in part, a reaction of some Dissenters against the perceived corruption of the traditional, episcopalian Christian ministry and fundamental aspects of its theological outlook. In his *Observations*, Newton's aim was to demonstrate how the corruption of the Christian ministry had been fully foreseen in biblical prophecy, proven by concrete historical development. Given that he was part of an oppressed religious minority, his deeply anti-Trinitarian and anti-episcopal stance meant that his exegesis was also profoundly polemical - even though most often partially submerged.

The success of his historico-exegetical project was, to a good degree, naturally dependent on the status of the prophecies of Daniel and John amongst Protestants. We know that Newton was aware of the need to rehabilitate or at least to reconfirm the status of the prophecies for, as he reminds his readers in Chapter 1 of his analysis of the Book of Daniel:

White's *The Last Sorcerer*.

The authority of Emperors, Kings, and Princes, is human, The authority of Councils, Synods, Bishops, and Presbyters, is human. The authority of the Prophets is divine, and comprehends the sum of religion, reckoning *Moses* and the Apostles among the Prophets; *and if an Angel from Heaven preach any other gospel*, than what they have delivered, *let him be accursed.* Their writings contain the covenant between God and his people, with instructions for keeping this covenant; instances of God's judgement upon them that break it: and predictions of things to come.[6]

Given the nature of his project, it was only to be expected that Newton would devote a large proportion of his *Observations* to detailed and complex chronologies of the historical development of kingdoms and successions of rulers correlated against the events and depictions in the prophecies. Not surprisingly, then, study of the chronology of the ancient and early medieval world occupied much of his time, of which only a fraction is evident in his *Observations*. It is possible to examine his endeavours in chronology in another of his posthumous works, the *Chronology of Ancient Kingdoms Amended* (1728). To the modern reader interested only in assimilating Newton's understanding of biblical prophecy, the detailed chronologies in his *Observations* - in which he calls upon a very wide variety of ancient and medieval sources - will not always repay the effort needed to unravel them. Those readers who wish to follow his chronologies of kingdoms, and who are not students of the ancient or medieval period will need the use of a good historical atlas. To describe the often long discourses on chronology in Newton's *Observations* as 'shambolic'[7], however, is unfair. The

---

6   The following references to Isaac Newton's *Observations upon the Prophecies of Daniel and the Apocalypse of St John. In Two Parts* (London, J. Darby and T. Browne in Bartholomew-Close, 1733), give the page reference to this edition first, followed by page references for the original 1733 edition in square brackets, i.e. in this footnote: p. 75 [14].

7   White, *The Last Sorcerer*, p. 158.

chronologies in the *Observations* admirably served Newton's purpose: to demonstrate that the complex succession of monarchs, the rise and fall of states and empires were foretold in prophecy - including the fall of Constantinople in 1453.[8]

For those readers interested in early modern historiography, Newton's chronologies also demonstrate the mode and limitations of his historical method. In an often uncritical manner, he frequently derives data for his chronologies from the non-too-reliable statements of past thinkers and historians, and at times from his own simple, often surprisingly naive, deductions. His recourse to simplistic deductive analysis is evident, for example, when he deduces the season of the year, but does not qualify or at all question the nature or usefulness of the evidence:

> soon after I find *Christ* and his Apostles on the sea of *Tiberias* in a storm so great, that the ship was covered with water and in danger of sinking, till *Christ rebuked the winds and the sea*, Matth. viii. 23. For this storm shews that winter was now come on.[9]

The often stark but nevertheless frequently symbolically rich depictions in biblical prophecy have been and are, of course, open to various interpretations depending on the political and or religious orientation of the exegete and the level of detail to which they are subjected. For the diligent and the mathematically-minded exegete such as Newton, God's message was encoded even in the fine detail of the prophecies, at times via the detail of the Creation itself. Thus, in explaining the duration of the temporal dominion of the Saracens at Damascus and Baghdad, when the Saracens are understood as the locusts which emerged from the Bottomless Pit (Rev. 9), Newton states:

> The whole time that the Caliphs of the *Saracens* reigned with a

---

[8]   Newton, *Observations*, pp. 294-5 [306-7]. For a discussion of the length of the year and its subdivisions in the ancient world see *Observations*, pp. 177-8 [137-8].

[9]   Newton, *Observations*, p. 189 [153].

temporal dominion at *Damascus* and *Bagdad* together, was 300 years, *viz.* from the year 637 to the year 936 inclusive. Now locusts live but five months; and therefore, for the decorum of the type, these locusts are said to *hurt men five months and five months*, as if they had lived about five months at *Damascus*, and again about five months at *Bagdad*; in all ten months, or 300 prophetic days, which are years.[10]

For many if not most sixteenth- and seventeenth-century Protestants, the antichristian corruption of the Church had been foretold in biblical prophecy. The bitterly hostile attitude to ancient Rome evident in Revelation (Apocalypse of St John) was considered as support for their view that the Antichrist had usurped the medieval Church. The Reformation was understood as one of the struggles in the long-term war between good and evil, and the final defeat of the Antichrist was to precede the Millennium, a thousand years of blessedness and the Second Coming of Christ. The great protagonist of the Reformation, Martin Luther, had himself identified the Papacy with the Antichrist according to the prophecy contained in the Book of Daniel.[11] Luther's work quickly influenced English Protestants, and there developed a strong English tradition of apocalyptical thought focused on the advent and future decline of the Antichrist. Paradoxically, the Catholic Queen Mary (1553-8) unwittingly helped to develop the prophetic interpretation of history in England. The consequence of her religious persecution was that many leading Protestants were forced into continental exile and into contemplation as to why God had permitted their persecution. After all, their persecution amounted to a weakening of the struggle against the Antichrist. The exiles understood that the reason for their persecution was divine punishment for the apostasy of England under Mary. In their apocalyptic scheme, Mary's England was worshipping the Beast - the Antichrist - as described in the Book of Revelation.

---

10   Newton, *Observations*, pp. 294 [304-5].

11   J. M. Headley, *Luther's view of Church History* (New Haven and London, Yale University Press, 1963), pp. 32, 195-96.

Mary's persecution was also considered by the Marian exiles to be a test of their faith, just as it had been for the many medieval Christians who had suffered for their opposition to the idolatry and corruption emanating from Rome. The Marian persecution was thus to be considered a sign of the 'true' Christian Church,[12] and as proof of God's long-term Providential plan leading to the Second Coming. But the exact nature and course of divine Providence was still a matter of some doubt, because the key biblical texts accepted by most Protestants to relate to the future unfolding of God's will - the Book of Daniel and the Book of Revelation - were shrouded in mysterious evocations and esoteric language.

Nevertheless, the Book of Revelation offered the possibility, via its developmental framework of seven seals, trumpets and vials, of constructing a chronology of the historical development of the Church, by tying recorded events of Church history to its seven stages. Bishop John Bale (1495-1563) was one of the first to pursue this chronology, but it was in the work of the martyrologist John Foxe (1516-87) that these ideas found their most influential expression in England.[13]

Just as the defeat of the Spanish Armada of 1588 was commonly considered by Protestants to be a defeat of the Antichrist and proof of God's Providence towards the 'true' Church, seventeenth-century events such as the Thirty Years War (1618-48) were interpreted as further proof of the impending defeat of the Antichrist and the imminence of the Millennium. Set against the background of unprecedented revolt and civil war across mid-seventeenth-century Europe, the English Civil War of the 1640s contributed to the production of a heightened quasi-apocalyptic atmosphere in the minds of many English Protestants. In the struggle between parliament and King Charles, the king and his

---

[12]   On the thought of the Marian exiles see J. Dawson's, `The apocalyptic thinking of the Marian exiles', in M. Wilks (ed.), *Prophecy and Eschatology, Studies in Church History*, Subsidia 10 (Oxford, Blackwell, 1994).

[13]   John Foxe, *Acts and Monuments of Matters happening in the Church* (Strasbourg, 1554, in Latin; English translation 1563).

supporters were identified by some as allies of the Antichrist.[14] There is no doubt that the unheard of events of the Civil War years served to compound the belief of many that the divine plan was drawing to a close.

In terms of war and revolt, the modern mind can easily comprehend seventeenth-century events. But for most of us it is necessary to take a leap of historical empathy to conjure up the apocalyptic outlook of its Protestant participants. One of those participants was Isaac Newton, born in the year the English Civil War commenced, 1642. For a Protestant raised in such times, to have had a cosmology entirely unaffected by the Protestant apocalyptic tradition would have been somewhat unlikely. That Newton was heir to this apocalyptic tradition is evident in his *Observations*, the only published work of Newton on prophecy, and representing just a small percentage of his overall writings on prophecy. In his *Observations* he noted the coming Millennium, the approach of which was indicated by the growing revelation of God's word by seventeenth-century exegetes. Amongst them, he opined, 'there is scarce one of note who hath not made some discovery worth knowing; and thence I seem to gather that God is about opening [revealing] these mysteries': God, in the last times, wished his divine historical scheme to be known to Christians.[15]

The interpretation of history, the present and future times via prophecy was not the preserve of tiny numbers of isolated and overly 'enthusiastic' Protestant sects, theologians or mystical thinkers. Even amongst seventeenth-century exponents of the use of reason in the investigation of religious truths, such as the Cambridge Platonist and Newton's first guide to the interpretation of biblical prophecy, Henry More (1614-87), there was a continued belief in and active investigation of biblical prophecy.[16] In the seventeenth-century, further

---

[14]   J. E. C., Hill, *Antichrist in Seventeenth Century England* (London, 1971).

[15]   Newton, *Observations*, pp. 247-8, 253.

[16]   See Henry More's *Apocalypsis apocalypseos*; or the *Revelation of St John Unveiled* (1680); and his *A Plain and Continued Exposition of the several Prophecies or Divine Visions of the Prophet Daniel* (London, 1681). On More and prophecy see also S. Hutton, `Henry

investigation of the prophecies was still considered necessary because the Marian exiles and others, it was understood, had not entirely overcome the main barrier to the comprehensive interpretation of biblical prophecy: its evidently complex and esoteric nature. The Bible was the Word of God, but He had communicated His Word, in part, via the figurative and sometimes obscure language of biblical prophecy. Thus the strange and veiled language of prophecy had to be systematically subjected to detailed and methodical analysis if divine truths were to be extracted with any definite degree of certainty as to their worldly meaning. It was thus in a 'scientific spirit that seventeenth-century Protestant scholars approached Biblical prophecy'.[17] Biblical exegesis could not, of course, be scientific. Nevertheless, biblical prophecy could be subjected to systematic analysis which attempted to harmonize its often mysterious evocations into one coherent whole. It can certainly be said that the search for - or imposition of - internal harmony within the prophecies was perhaps the foremost characteristic of Newton's exegetical approach.

Newton was the son of moderately wealthy Lincolnshire landowners and his father died before he was born. When Newton was three years old, his mother, Hannah, remarried Barnabas Smith, a rector of nearby North Witham, but Smith did not want Isaac to live with them. Consequently, Isaac was raised by his grandparents until the death of his stepfather in 1653, when he lived together with his mother and grandmother. He was, it seems, raised with a puritanical stamp;[18] and it is that experience alongside the millennial climate described above - rather than Freudian analyses of subconscious father-searching - which most fruitfully

More and the Apocalypse', in *Prophecy and Eschatology, Studies in Church History*, Subsidia 10, pp. 131-40; Mandlebrote, 'A Duty of the Greatest Moment', p. 291

[17] C. Hill, *The World Turned upside down. Radical Ideas during the English Revolution* (Harmondsworth, 1975), pp. 92-3.

[18] Westfall (*The Life of Isaac Newton*, pp. 23-4); Scott Mandlebrote ('A Duty of the Greatest Moment', pp. 285-6, 301); and White (*The Last Sorcerer*, pp. 49, 149) all agree Newton was Puritanical in outlook.

explain the origin of Newton's religious outlook. I will, therefore, not dwell on the claim that Newton's theological outlook was 'invested' with implicit comparison between true and false Gods, and 'a true father and a false father'.[19]

In 1661 Newton commenced study at Trinity College Cambridge and, it seems, he was initially preoccupied with religious studies, and his book purchases of this period reflect his outlook. We do not know of all his purchases, but we know he bought a copy of the Greek New Testament, Trelcatius's book of common places in the Holy Scriptures (1608), and John *Calvin's Institutes of the Christian Religion* (1561).[20] We also know a little more of the character of Newton's religiosity in 1662 because, in that year, he made a record of his sins. The list, mostly of petty sins, is quite unexceptional for a youth of twenty years and highlight his rather strict puritanical-sabbatarian outlook. Several sins on the list refer to his petty breaches of the Sabbath, such as indulging in the pleasantries of idle discourse.[21] We also know that Newton became a Dissenter, a Unitarian; and he was certainly not, as some have suggested, a deist.[22] Between the years 1672 and 1675 Newton listed twelve points of faith that informed his Unitarianism, including the following points:

> There is nowhere made mention of a human soul in our Saviour [the Bible] besides the word, by the meditation of which the word should become incarnate. But the word itself was made flesh and blood & took upon him the form of a servant ... It was the son of God which he sent into the world & and not a human soul that suffered for us. If there had been such a human soul in our Saviour, it would have been a

---

[19] Manuel, *Religion of Isaac Newton*, pp. 19, 103.

[20] On Newton's library see John Harrison's *The Library of Isaac Newton* (Cambridge, 1978).

[21] Hall, *Adventurer in Thought*, p. 5.

[22] For a brief but insightful discussion of Newton's Unitarianism see Hall's *Adventurer in Thought*, pp. 370-1. On the history of the deist charge, see Scott Mandlebrote, `A Duty of the Greatest Moment', pp. 281-2.

thing of too great consequence to have been wholly omitted by the Apostles.[23]

In the Autumn of 1690, Newton was occupied in preparing his first semi-public criticism of the Orthodox Trinitarian position, contained in a letter sent to John Locke in November. Newton argued that the New Testament had been falsified in Roman or early medieval times in order to promote the concept of God as a Trinity, for which St Jerome, the translator of the Vulgate, Newton held partly responsible. In his detailed and rigorous anti-Trinitarian arguments Newton invoked a considerable tally of authorities in several ancient languages, the result of nearly two decades of secret study.[24]

Like many other heterodox Protestants, however, Newton was wary of publicly exposing his dissenting beliefs. In an age when religion was still considered a public duty rather than solely a private good, and when Unitarians could still not worship freely and could be denied public offices unless they abjured their beliefs, a reluctance to advertise one's heterodoxy ought to be considered more a sign of prudence than a lack of religious conviction. But Newton was a man of principle, and rather than continue to swear insincere allegiance to the Anglican Church in order to obtain the Lucasian Professorship at Cambridge, in 1675 he sought and obtained a Royal dispensation exempting him from such vows. In the above-mentioned letter to Locke, Newton wrote that his intention was to have his attack on Trinitarianism published anonymously abroad and in French. This was not the only letter to Locke on Trinitarianism, and theological issues were frequently mentioned in his correspondence with that philosopher. Subsequently, Newton changed his mind about publication of his account of the origins of Trinitarianism, which remained unpublished until 1754.

Given his lifelong prudence on religious matters, it is no surprise that Newton's Unitarianism is relatively submerged in his *Observations*. As we shall

---

[23]   White, *The Last Sorcerer*, pp. 149-50.

[24]   For discussion of Newton's letter to Locke, see Hall, *Adventurer in Thought*, p. 237.

see, however, his animosity to Trinitarianism is evident in his depiction of the thought of Athanasius (AD *c*. 296-373), one of the most important protagonists of Trinitarian thought. Newton's anti-Trinitarianism is also implicit in various brief, but heavily loaded comments. He opines, for instance, that 'all nations' (*i.e.* including the Anglican Church) have corrupted Christianity and that the prophecies 'are not only for predicting but also for effecting a recovery and re-establishment of the long-lost truth, and setting up a kingdom wherein dwells righteousness'.[25] Newton also wrote other (unpublished) works on religious matters, including a large tract upon the language of the prophets and smaller pieces on the same theme. He also wrote a work against Roman Catholicism and another upon Solomon's Temple. He was a copious note taker and, to aid his studies, it is thought his library contained as many as thirty editions of the Bible or parts of it in a variety of modern and ancient languages.[26]

Newton has been described, with some justification, as a tortured personality, a neurotic man who was continually on the verge of nervous breakdown throughout his middle age.[27] Outstanding scientist, mathematician, historian, alchemist, and head of the Royal Mint, Isaac was a solitary, unmarried man, totally - and perhaps unhealthily - absorbed in his studies, sometimes to the exclusion of food. We know that in 1693 he suffered a type of nervous breakdown, manifested in what might be described as a neurotic concern for his future prospects.[28] Was it on account of his rather obsessive attitude to his studies, perhaps combined with an unhealthy religious 'enthusiasm', that Newton wrote a work on the seemingly obscure topic of Solomon's Temple? For religiously minded seventeenth-century scholars it was not uncommon to draw

---

[25]   Newton, *Observations*, pp. 256-7 [252].

[26]   For some comments on Newton's unpublished religious works see Hall *Adventurer in Thought*, p. 238.

[27]   Westfall, *Life of Isaac Newton*, p. 10.

[28]   For discussion on Newton's 's mental breakdown see Hall, *Adventurer in Thought*, pp. 242-6.

models of Noah's Ark, the Ark of the Covenant, and the Temple of Solomon. The aim of such men was to establish what the physical properties of such divinely inspired architecture - in relation to biblical descriptions of it and events and symbolic scenes depicted within it - might reveal about the will of God in the past, present and future, and heated debates often ensued as to the correct interpretation.[29]

The Temple of Solomon and various scenes within it appear in both the prophecy of Daniel and of John, and it was considered by Newton and others to have signified the Church Catholic[30] before its degeneration. The layout of the Temple was also very important to Newton's interpretation of biblical prophecy, and features prominently in his *Observations*. The prophetic meaning of scenes of Jewish worship and sacrifice and various vivid and symbolically rich representations that took place inside the Temple were grasped via several strategies, including identifying the exact location of an event's occurrence and its location in relation to other precise locations and events.[31] One of the main interpretative methods favoured by Newton, however, was that of simple analogy, in which, for example, the *'voices and thundrings'* around the throne of God in heaven (Rev. 4:5) relate also to 'the musick of the Temple, *and lightnings* ... [to] the sacred fire' of the Temple. When the prophecies described how the high priest of the Temple put *'all the iniquities of the children of Israel ... upon the head of the goat; and sent him away into the wilderness'*, Newton understood this also as figurative language for the very Beast that bore the Whore of Bablyon (Rome).[32]

Newton spent considerable time constructing and reconstructing the alleged form and dimensions of the Temple, and with good justification, for, in

---

[29]   On the significance of the dimensions of the Temple see, for instance, Newton's *Observations* pp. 270-1 [272-3].

[30]   Newton, *Observations*, p. 260 [255].

[31]   For an important comment on the measuring of the Temple of Solomon see Newton, *Observations* pp. 270-1 [272-3].

[32]   Newton, *Observations*, p. 298 [310-12].

the prophecies '*John* ... [was] bidden to *measure the temple and the altar*'.[33] Without a definite plan of the Temple, how could an exegete accurately interpret symbolically-loaded events described within it? The dimensions, floor plan and layout of the Temple constituted essential knowledge if God's original plan for humanity was to be extracted from the prophecies. For those readers interested in Newton's architectural vision of the Temple of Solomon, three diagrams of it were included in his *Chronology of Ancient Kingdoms Amended* (1728).

As a publishing project, Newton's *Observations*, posthumously published by his nephew Benjamin Smith, was a success. Soon after the initial publication in 1733 it was translated into Latin and German, and reprinted in English (last edition 1922);[34] various works were also published examining and discussing Newton's views on the prophecies. The analysis contained in the *Observations* was the result of half a century of study and writing from at least 1675;[35] although his interest in biblical prophecy almost certainly began earlier, perhaps in the 1660s. 'The core of everything he wrote' on religion was, as Rupert Hall has succinctly put it, 'his belief that Christianity had taken a wrong (Trinitarian) direction since the fourth century AD.'[36] Unfortunately, large sections of his religious writings have been lost, including his unpublished 'History of the Church' which disappeared in the nineteenth century.[37]

The final draft of the *Observations* was the product of much rewriting in old age, and was more restrained compared to his earlier more biting drafts.

---

[33]   Newton, *Observations*, p. 299 [313].

[34]   The last edition of Newton's *Observations* upon the Prophecies was that of Sir William Whitla (1922), but he was concerned only to defend the validity of the prophecies from a Christian perspective and did not provide any discussion of Newton and the period in which he lived.

[35]   Hall, *Adventurer in Thought*, p. 372.

[36]   Hall, *Adventurer in Thought*, p. 373.

[37]   On the fate of Newton's papers see Manuel, The *Religion of Isaac Newton*, pp. 10-13; and Hall, *Adventurer in Thought*, pp. 395-8.

Benjamin Smith decided to include part of an alternative draft of the *Observations* - the final few pages of it - as an appendage to the 1733 edition (located after the last chapter of Part Two, entitled *Advertisement*). The ultimate three pages of the *Observations* have as their finale fairly dry chronological points; whereas the version appended by Smith culminates in a reiteration of the corruption of the Church by the Whore of Babylon (Rome). Indeed, the final (half) page is vividly apocalyptic in tone, employing *Rev.* 17:15-18 to maximum anti-Catholic effect: '*the woman* [the Whore] *which thou sawest, is that great city which reigneth over the Kings of the earth* ... the great city of the *Latins* [Rome]'. At the onset of the Millennium, those European nations who - at God's will - had given homage to the Whore (Roman Catholicism, the Church of the Beast), '*shall hate the whore, and shall make her desolate and naked, and shall eat her flesh, and burn her with fire*'.

But the difference between the two endings should not be exaggerated, and the alternative ending appended by Smith cannot be said to constitute part of an earlier, much more biting draft. Any anti-Rome point made by Newton in the alternative finale is also made, often more than once, in prior chapters. In fact, Newton is most overtly anti-Trinitarian in the last chapter (preceding the appended section) where, referring to the beast or Antichrist, he notes that '[h]is mark is ✠✠✠, and his name Lateinos, and the number of his name 666'.[38] As Mary Mills notes below, the three crosses and the word Lateinos (given by Newton in Greek) are undoubtedly intended to refer to the 'Trinitarian Church, typified by the Latin (Roman) community'. Thus, while Hall and other commentators are correct to point out that, for Newton, the theological rot of Trinitarianism triumphed in the fourth century, Newton's aim was also a general attack on Roman Catholicism, viewed as the theological heir to the triumph of Trinitarianism and the transmitter of that fateful error to the Anglican Church. As to be expected from a Dissenter, his *Observations* is imbued with a thorough

---

[38]   Newton, *Observations*, p. 278 [284].

detestation of Roman Catholicism, often expressed by graphic attacks on superstition and false, idolatrous worship (albeit that the target is sometimes implied rather than overtly stated). The bald statement of Westfall, therefore, that for Newton the key enemy, apostasy, was not Rome, but Trinitarianism,[39] if left unqualified, is apt to be misleading. No seventeenth-century Protestant doubted from which direction the major long-term threat to right religion emanated: Rome.

We know that Newton and most Dissenters - despite their hatred of Anglicanism - distinguished between the perceived failure of Anglicanism to properly reform itself and the overt idolatry of Catholicism. In social religious and political terms the tyranny of Popery had to be opposed as the most dangerous enemy to Christianity. Yet this did not mean that the polemic against the quasi-popery of Anglicanism by both Unitarian and Trinitarian Dissenters was consequently subdued or silenced. Indeed, as I have illustrated in some detail elsewhere,[40] in the late-seventeenth and early-eighteenth centuries the Dissenter critique of Anglicanism reached its apogee, dismissing all traditional episcopal Church hierarchies as fraudulent and guilty of priestcraft. So profound was the Dissenting and usually pro-Presbyterian critique of Catholicism and its Anglican episcopalian progeny, that some modern historians have mistakenly identified certain Dissenters as deists: that is to say enemies of the Christian ministry in general.[41] The critique of medieval Church history contained in Newton's *Observations* is thus best understood as the Unitarian facet of the wider post-Restoration dissenting polemic against Catholicism and Anglicanism.

In this respect then, the importance of Newton's *Observations* goes beyond Newton's personal religious views. The historical schema of the *Observations* - as we shall see below - embodies the chronology of Church

---

[39] Westfall, *The Life of Isaac Newton*, p. 126.

[40] See my *Idol Temples and Crafty Priest. The Origins of Enlightenment Anticlericalism* (London, 1998).

[41] On the confusion between dissenting and deist historiography, see my *Idol Temples and Crafty Priests*, especially Chapters 6-7.

corruption held by most Dissenters, both Unitarian and Trinitarian. The *Observations* really is, therefore, a document of its time; expressing far more in historiographical terms than just a Unitarian-orientated reading of biblical prophecy, and is therefore of some importance to the study of early modern English religious thought.

As with most Dissenters, Newton's anti-Anglican outlook did not preclude giving support to Anglicanism against Catholicism. Anglicanism retained many popish features, yet it had repudiated Rome, and the Anglican Church and state was a bulwark against the threat of Catholic domination of Europe. In this period, however, anti-Catholicism encompassed far more than just religious concerns. Anti-Catholicism was equally an expression of political freedom against what were considered the benighted and despotic Catholic states of Europe, especially France. Nevertheless, Dissenters still suffered much persecution and discrimination in post-Restoration England, and four hundred Quakers are known to have died in prison in between 1660 and 1689. The Toleration Act of 1689 did not remove all the discrimination against Trinitarian Dissenters, and Unitarians did not benefit at all from the Act. Thus, even though ardent Dissenters - such as John Toland (1670-1722) - fulminated against the state-Church tyranny of Anglicanism, they also genuinely sought to defend the Protestant succession of monarchs against possible Catholic claimants. Indeed, after 1697 Toland went on to become one of the earliest English deists, yet remained solidly anti-Catholic in outlook.[42]

As Hall has illustrated, Newton defended the legitimacy of the Anglican Church inaugurated by King Henry VIII, and considered himself a part of the wider Protestant Church. But caution is always necessary when confronted with such sentiments from Dissenters. England, as most other European states, was still a confessional state, and general statements of allegiance to the state Church

---

[42]   On the defence of the Protestant succession by Toland see my *Idol Temples and Crafty Priest*, Chapter 7.

by Dissenters often amounted to little more than a principled defence of Protestantism against the political and religious threat of Catholicism - as was the case with John Toland after 1697. More significantly, therefore, we know that Newton also firmly believed that the English state and Anglican Church had no right to prescribe 'articles of communion' as necessary to salvation, and that dissent from the narrow Anglican creed could not invalidate one's membership of the whole English Protestant Church.[43] Like other Dissenters, Newton was certainly arguing for religious toleration; although virtually all Anglicans and Dissenters agreed Catholicism could not be tolerated, for Catholicism was - amongst other grave matters - understood as embodying the very epitome of religious intolerance.

In his wish for a comprehensive Anglican Church - one encompassing all the various Protestant tendencies - Newton has been described as a simplicist.[44] Given that Newton's religious views reflected the 'simple' religiosity of most Dissenters who also yearned for toleration, that implicitly pejorative description is perhaps a little unjust. In addition, and as his views indicate, it is highly unlikely that Newton intended any more than that the Anglican Church should function as a nominal Protestant figurehead rather than an ecclesiastical polity encompassing all Protestant ecclesiological outlooks. We should remember too, that Newton and his whole generation were reared in the 1640s and 1650s, a period of civil war, interregnum and of the Cromwellian Church, in which relatively broad toleration was the order of the day. From this perspective, Newton's desire for wide comprehension appears less utopian. Indeed, the common Dissenter cry for toleration during the Restoration period, and to some degree into the eighteenth century, was not understood by them as a utopian dream, but rather an urgent necessity.

For Unitarians, the Trinitarianism of the Anglican and Catholic Churches

---

[43]   Hall, *Adventurer in Thought*, pp. 374-5.

[44]   Hall, *Adventurer in Thought*, p. 375.

was a priestly corruption spawned perhaps as early as in the second century, in the work of Theophilus of Antioch (c. AD 180), but eventually triumphing in the fourth century via the Council of Nicea (AD. 325). The council was convened by Emperor *Constantine*, and the pro-Trinitarian camp was led (against the Arians) by Athanasius, who Newton vigorously pursued in his religious writings. After all, in doctrinal terms, the bishops of Rome were, for Newton, theological descendants of Athanasius. Thus, although Newton depicted 'a falling away ... soon after the days of the Apostles', the fourth century, the century of Emperor *Constantine*[45] and Athanasius, marked a significant moment in his chronology of corruption towards idolatrous saint worship.[46]

As the conclusion to his attack against early monasticism in Egypt as the purveyor of superstition to the west, and honing in on the beliefs and practices of the second-century Cataphrygians (Montanists), Newton remarks that the Cataphrygians 'brought in ... superstitions: such as were the doctrine of *Ghosts*, and of their punishment in Purgatory, with prayers and oblations for mitigating that punishment [and] ... used also the sign of the cross as a charm'.[47] Subsequently,

> [in] the fourth century ... the *Roman* Emperors then turning *Christians*, and great multitudes of heathens coming over in outward profession, these found the *Cataphrygian* Christianity more suitable to their old principles, of placing religion in outward forms and ceremonies, holy-days, and doctrines of Ghosts, than the religion of the sincere *Christians*: wherefore they readily sided with the

---

[45]   On the corruption of Christianity under Emperor Constantine, see Newton's *Observations*, pp. 220-1 [201-2].

[46]   On Athanasius and his promotion of saint worship see Newton's *Observations*, pp. 232-3 [216-7].

[47]   Newton, *Observations*, p. 220 [200].

Cataphrygian Christians, and established that Christianity before the end of the fourth century.[48]

This 'new religion' of 'sending reliques from place to place for working miracles, and thereby inflaming the devotion of the nations towards the dead Saints and their reliques, and setting up the religion of invoking their souls ... was [then also] set up by the Monks in all the *Greek* Empire' in the fourth century.[49] For Newton, of course, all this had been foreseen in prophetic scripture, and he quotes Paul's epistle to Timothy:

All these superstitions the Apostle refers to, where he saith: *Now the Spirit speaketh expressly, that in the latter times some shall depart from the faith, giving heed to seducing spirits, and doctrines of devils,* the *Dæmons and* Ghosts worshipped by the heathens, *speaking lyes in hypocrisy,* about their apparitions, the miracles done by them, their reliques, and the sign of the cross ... Tim. iv. 1, 2, 3.[50]

Newton's decision to cite the veneration of the Cross as one aspect of medieval superstition is an example of his constant but partially submerged attack on Trinitarianism. In several places, Newton linked the Trinity or facets of it to what Protestants regarded as medieval superstition. In a mischievous twist, as an example of saint worship, Newton quoted an AD 373 oration of the monk Gregory Nazianzen, to the 'newly dead' Athanasius, at the end of which Nazianzen invoked the protection of Athanasius:

Do thou look down upon us propitiously, and govern this people, as perfect adorers of the perfect Trinity, which in the Father, Son and Holy Ghost, is contemplated and worshiped: if there shall be peace, preserve me, and feed my flock with me; but if of war, bring me home,

---

48   Newton, *Observations*, p. 221 [202].

49   Newton, *Observations*, pp. 241-3 [229-30].

50   Newton, *Observations*, p. 220 [201].

place me by thyself, and by those that are like thee; however great my request. [51]

We have seen that most dissenting writers of the late- seventeenth and early-eighteenth centuries excoriated all present and past episcopal Church ministries. Their historiography was, however, hardly novel, and was based upon Puritan historical thought of a century earlier. It is true that Puritanism was, as a coherent movement, shattered by the experience of the Civil War and Interregnum years of 1642-1660, but the Puritan critique of Church history and its Presbyterian ideal continued to inform dissenting thought into the eighteenth century - the significance of which has been underestimated by some modern historians. Most Dissenters agreed with Newton that the Church had become corrupt relatively soon after the natural demise of the Apostolic Church, when a caste of venal priests arose and peddled a false superstitious religion. Prelates and theologians had created a false doctrine in order to hoodwink the masses into a tame subjection to a despotic Church hierarchy intent only on increasing its power, wealth and prestige. Most accepted that a major turning point on the road to priestcraft was the wealth and power gained as a result of the adoption of Christianity by Roman emperors in the fourth century. Yet, in many of these acerbic historical critiques, Catholicism or Anglicanism was hardly mentioned, simply because the target was to undermine the historical legitimacy of all Christian priesthoods as one of the means to bring about a rebirth of the Christian ministry based upon the Presbyterian (or apostolic) ideal in which no powerful hierarchy of priests had or could exist. [52] The notion that Newton's 'vehemence

---

[51]   Newton, *Observations*, p. 236 [220]; for other instances of linking the Trinity to superstition see Newton's *Observations*, pp. 236-7, 239-40 [220-1, 227].

[52]   See for example the Unitarian Robert Howard's *History of Religion* (London, 1694); and other Trinitarian dissenting critiques of the Church, for example John Dennis' *Priestcraft distinguished from Christianity* (London, 1715), and John Trenchard's *The Natural History of Superstition* (London, 1709).

was only equalled by the antireligious *philosophes*' of eighteenth-century France cannot, therefore, be sustained.[53]

The *Observations* was of course understood by Newton and by many of his readers not as a sectarian rant - although at some point most would have noted his hostility to Trinitarianism - but as a serious and erudite enquiry into the nature and potentially momentous significance of biblical prophecy. Above all, Newton's approach is patiently systematic. He was emphatic that a precise technique of interpretation had to be developed to decipher the prophecies. He felt that any hermeneutical system applied to prophecy should be simple and consistent: 'It is the perfection of God's works that they are all done with the greatest simplicity'[54] he asserted. He thought that ancient writers had been consistent in their use of symbolism, therefore the Jewish prophecies followed a pattern common to all ancient peoples.[55] He thus felt able to devise consistent rules (15 in number) with which to approach analysis of prophecies - elements of which will be examined below. Michael White has succinctly summarized Newton's basis for believing that the prophecies were, in principle, decipherable:

> He reasoned that because God's work and God's word came from the
> same Creator, then Nature and Scripture were also one and the same.
> Scripture was a communicable manifestation or interpretation of
> Nature, and as such could be viewed as a blueprint for life - a key to
> all meaning.[56]

Nevertheless, these divine communications were encoded. In order to decipher them, Newton stated, we have to acquaint ourselves with the 'figurative language' of the prophets. 'This language is taken from the analogy between the world natural, and an empire or kingdom considered as a world politic.' That is to say Newton equated elements of the natural world depicted in the prophecies with

---

[53]   Manuel, *Isaac Newton Historian*, p. 154.

[54]   David Brewster, *Memoirs of ... Sir Isaac Newton* (Edinburgh, 1855), vol. 2, pp. 532-4

[55]   Hall, *Adventurer in Thought*, p. 373.

earthly kingdoms and peoples. Thus, 'the heavens, and the things therein, signify thrones and dignities ... and the earth ... [the] inferior people ... Whence ascending towards heaven, and descending to the earth, are put for rising and falling in power and honour'.[57]

Newton's stress was upon accuracy and internal harmony in his interpretative system, which he considered necessary elements for providing a greater degree of precision in understanding how historical development had been predicted in scripture. His analogies between the depictions contained in the prophecies and earthly realities therefore needed to be more specific, and he went on to note that 'the Sun is put for the whole species and race of kings'. The stars signify the 'subordinate Princes and great men', whilst 'the moon [is] for the body of the common people'. For Newton, the prophecies were divine messages endowed with different levels of meaning, and as such could legitimately be read using a similar or same hermeneutical system, but employing different iconographical registers. Thus if an exegete considered the prophecies on a purely theological rather than a worldly, historical plane, then the 'Sun is Christ', and the stars the 'Bishops and Rulers of the people of God'. So, read in another context, he understood the 'inferior people' to be represented not by the Moon (as above), but rather by the planet Earth itself.

For natural events depicted in the prophecies, Newton advanced similar simple and clear equations. The 'burning anything with fire', for instance 'is put for the consuming thereof by war'. The event of 'being in a furnace for the being in slavery under another nation ... the scorching heat of the sun, for vexatious wars, persecutions and troubles inflicted by the king'. Similarly, he considered 'riding on the clouds' to be 'for reigning over much people; covering the sun with a cloud, or with smoke, for oppression of the King by the armies of an enemy'.

---

[56]   White, *The Last Sorcerer*, p. 155.

[57]   Newton, *Observations*, p. 77 [16].

Whereas the 'beginning and end of the world is signified by 'the rise and ruin of the body politic'.[58]

Newton also made use of simple opposites in his exegesis. Thus 'rain ... dew, and living water' are to be understood 'for the graces and doctrines of the Spirit; and the defect of rain, for spiritual barrenness'. Physical transformations such as 'turning things into blood', he understood as 'the mystical death of bodies politic'. Houses and ships, he took to denote 'families, assemblies, and towns, in the earth and sea politic'. Animals and vegetables 'are put for the people of several regions and conditions ... a forest for a kingdom; and a wilderness for a desolate and thin people'. Depictions of animals were considered not just for their physical form, but also their supposed qualities, thus 'several animals, as a Lion, a Bear, a Leopard, a Goat, according to their qualities, are put for several kingdoms and bodies politic'.[59]

Most importantly for the Books of Daniel and Revelation, Newton explained that when 'a Beast or Man is put for a kingdom, his parts and qualities are put for the analogous parts and qualities of the kingdom'. Thus the 'head of a Beast' denotes the 'great men who precede and govern; the tail for the inferior people, who follow and are governed'. However, if there is more than one head, they denote 'the number of capital parts, or dynasties, or dominions in the kingdom'. The horns on any head correspond 'to the number of kingdoms ... with respect to military power'. Newton also considered other qualities, for instance, 'the loudness of the voice' he equated to the 'might and power' of the beast or man. In bodily parts Newton also identified a hierarchy based partly on size of the organ, but also upon its character as derived from the nature of the bird or animal in question. Thus the 'hairs of a beast, or man, and the feathers of a bird' signify people, while the 'feet, nails, and teeth of beasts of prey', stand for 'armies and squadrons of armies; [and] the bones, for strength, and for fortified places'. The

---

[58]   . Newton, *Observations*, pp. 77-9 [17-18].

[59]   Newton, *Observations*, pp. 78-80 [19-20].

'death of a man or beast' Newton equated to the 'dissolution of a body politic or ecclesiastic', and the 'resurrection of the dead' tells the reader of the 'revival of a dissolved dominion'.[60] As Mary Mills explains below, Newton's iconography should not be dismissed as the overly-religious meanderings of an obsessive psyche. Modern scholarship too agrees that cosmic upheavals in the prophecies and the depictions of animals and many-headed beasts do indeed refer to major historical upheavals, empires and dynasties. But these depictions were intended to allude to the development of the civilizations of the ancient near east, not of Europe.

In his exegetical endeavours Newton also made use of 'mathematical' calculations standard among the techniques of the cabbalists. One such form of calculation, known as gematria, involved the translation of a name or a noun into its numerical equivalent (in the English alphabet, A being equal to 1, B to 2, and so forth) in order, for example, to prognosticate a date for the coming of the Messiah. The number of the Beast, as transmitted in Protestant folklore and forcefully stated by Newton and in Revelation itself, was of course 666: 'Here is wisdom. Let him that hath understanding count the number of the Beast: ... six hundred threescore and six' (Rev. 13:18.). This number in Revelation was possibly originally meant to indicate Emperor Nero (AD. 54-68) , who had persecuted Christians. In Hebrew letters, Nero (in the form Neron) adds up to 666.[61]

As most Protestants, Newton understood the prophecies of Daniel and John to be apocalyptic in character: they told of the fall of Christendom into corruption, and the later purification of it in the Millennium. He noted that, as

---

[60] Newton, *Observations*, pp. 79-81 [21-3].

[61] Newton, *Observations*, p. 278 [248]. Some modern theologians consider that the cryptogram 666 refers to Emperor Domitian (AD 81-96) on account of his persecution of Christians, but via the cryptogram for Nero Caesar. Nero had also persecuted Christians, and the implication of the cryptogram may have been that Domitian was to be regarded as as a return of Nero.

foretold by the Prophets and Apostles, there was 'a falling away among the Christians, soon after the days of the Apostles', and in the 'latter days God would destroy the impenitent revolters, and make a new covenant with his people'.[62] As I have illustrated elsewhere,[63] that there was an early 'falling away' was a common Dissenter opinion in the late-seventeenth and early-eighteenth centuries. The period of the pure primitive Church's decline, however, was held to represent but part of one era or empire of the four identified by Newton and like minds in the Book of Daniel and the Revelation of St John. For Newton and others, the four beasts twinned with four metals depicted in the revelation of Daniel represented the four great empires which were held to have reigned over the earth successively. It is to Daniel's vision we must now turn.

Daniel relates how the magicians, sorcerers, astrologers and Chaldean Christians had failed King Nebuchadnezzar of Babylon (605-562 BC) by their inability to describe to him and interpret a forgotten dream that had troubled his sleep. The king then turned to Daniel. Daniel was subsequently given divine aid and four empires that were to succeed each other - the depiction of which had apparently troubled the sleep of Nebuchadnezzar - were revealed to him. Later, Daniel had a another vision (Dan. 6) in which, according to Newton, the succession of empires was given its final form. Newton explains that the first empire was jointly Assyria and 'Babylonia and Media' (ancient kingdoms of the Middle East), signified by gold and a winged lion. The second (Persian) Empire was represented to Daniel by a bear and the metal silver. The third beast, the four-winged and four-headed leopard, signified an empire linked to copper, that of the Greeks. The fourth, ten-horned beast, Newton related, was 'exceeding dreadful and terrible and had great iron teeth ... such was the *Roman empire*', signified by iron.[64]

---

[62] Newton, *Observations*, p. 75 [13-14].

[63] See my *Idol Temples and Crafty Priests*.

[64] Newton, *Observations*, pp. 84, 87-89 [25, 28-30].

The ten horns of the Roman Beast were thought to represent the ten European kingdoms into which the western Roman Empire disintegrated. Two of these horns represented the two northern Italian kingdoms of Ravenna and of the Lombards, and another the Dukedom of Rome. In Daniel's vision these three were plucked out by their roots and were replaced by one little horn.[65] For Newton and others, this replacement or usurping horn, represented what would come to be St. Peter's Patrimony (the Papal States): the popes had usurped the royal prerogative of temporal dominion. The ten horns did not, however, represent a new, fifth empire, rather only the antichristian degeneration of the fourth: the earthly career of the Antichrist ensconced at Rome. The fifth kingdom (Dan. 2. 44; Rev. 20. 1-6) was understood to be the eventual Millennium.

For Newton and most Dissenters, the descent into iniquity as a consequence of the adoption of Christianity by Emperor Constantine was much deepened by the failure of the Roman Emperor at Constantinople to retain control over the western Roman Empire. That failure allowed the popes to found the basis of the Papal States, significantly augmented by the territorial Donation of the Frankish King Pepin III (714-68). In Newton's time the Papal States still existed, ruled by the priest-king at Rome. The papal usurpation of the royal prerogative to rule was considered by many to have been the point of no return in the great apostasy of Rome. Many identified this as the moment when the Antichrist began its rule, when Rome lost its remaining spiritual purity and became venal. The antichristian popes, it was said, then ruled the Church despotically, and erected a massive European ecclesiastical empire. Rome grew so powerful, rich and arrogant that it stamped on the rights of medieval kings and emperors, electing and deposing them according to its own secular needs.

---

[65] On the three kingdoms usurped by the popes see Newton, *Observations*, Pt. 1, Ch. 7, particularly pp. 133-4 [87-89].

It is from this historical vantage point that Newton (in part quoting Daniel 7) graphically described the nature of the despotic usurpations and religious frauds of the new (papal) horn that supplanted three horns: in the

> *horn were eyes like the eyes of a man ... and the same horn made war with the saints, and prevailed against them* ... By its eyes it was a Seer; and by its mouth speaking great things and changing times and laws, it was a Prophet as well as a King. And such a Seer, a Prophet and a King, is the Church of Rome. ... With his mouth he gives laws to kings and nations as an Oracle; and pretends to Infallibility, and that his dictates are binding to the whole world.[66]

Newton illustrated via a variety of sources that the beginning of the corruption of the Church into Roman idolatry, and its dominion over the western Churches was to be found in the early fourth century in the reign of Emperor Diocletian. Yet the pope had then not yet risen up 'as a horn of the Beast'. The supplanting of the other three horns was only accomplished by the acquisition of 'temporal dominion which made him one of the horns', fully achieved only 'in the latter half of the eighth century' with King Pepin's donation of 756. The final fall of the ecclesiastical and temporal kingdom of papal Rome represented by the new usurping horn would signify the 'latter days', the approach of the Millennium and the end of earthly history. Then 'God would destroy the impenitent revolters, and make a new covenant with his people', that is to say the end of earthly history and the advent of the Millennium.[67]

As a typical Protestant, Newton grew livid at the thought of what he considered to be Roman Catholic corruptions of religion. The most heinous corruption, that of idolatry, had constituted the most grave and consistent accusation laid at the door of Catholicism since the Reformation. For Newton, 'the invocation of the saints and veneration of their reliques, and such like

---

[66]   Newton, *Observations*, pp. 1213-4 [74-5].

[67]   Newton, *Observations*, pp. 75,159-60 [14, 113-4].

superstitions ... [were] introduced in the fourth and fifth centuries', as foretold in Daniel 11.[68] For many Protestants, especially Puritans and later Dissenters, the evident image and saint worship of Catholicism was considered to be but neo-paganism. Thus Oliver Ormerod's *Pagano-Papismus* (1606) was written in order to demonstrate - and stated so in its title - that *Papisme is flat Paganisme*.[69] Following in that tradition, Newton wrote

the invocation of Saints, was the attributing to their dead bodies, bones and other reliques, a power of working miracles by means of the separate souls, who were supposed to know what we do or say, and to be able to do us good or hurt, and to work those miracles. This was the very notion the heathens had of the separate souls of their antient Kings and Heroes, whom they worshiped under the names of *Saturn, Rhea, Jupiter, Juno, Mars, Venus, Bacchus, Ceres, Osiris, Isis, Apollo, Diana*, and the rest of their Gods.[70]

The degeneration of Christianity into idolatry was thought to have been predicted in prophecy. Indeed, the chronology of the four empires and the career of idolatry form the two main elements of Newton's discussion. Chapter Fourteen of Daniel in the *Observations*, entitled '*Of the* Mahuzzims', which Newton describes as 'protectors, guardians, or defenders' - that is to say saints or their equivalents - is entirely devoted to the early career of idolatry. But, as '*Daniel* in his Prophecy describes chiefly the things done amongst the nations comprehended in the body of his third Beast',[71] signifying the Greek Empire, we shall reserve some comments on the subject of idolatry until we consider Newton's treatment of the Book of Revelation and the fourth Beast.

---

68 Newton, *Observations*, p. 213 [192].

69 Oliver Ormerod, *The Picture of a Papist ... Whereunto is annexed a Certain Treatise, intituled Pagano-Papismus: wherein is proved ... that Papisme is flat Paganisme* (London, 1606).

70 Newton, *Observations*, p. 227 [209].

71 Newton, *Observations*, pp. 223, 243 [203, 230].

In deciphering the obscure formula given in Daniel for what was understood as the duration of the rule of the Antichrist at Rome (Dan. 12:6-8), Newton relied on the analysis of Joseph Mede (1586-1638) made in his *Clavis Apocalyptica* (1627), an interpretation of the Book of Revelation (1627). Along with Mede and others, Newton arrived at a figure of 1260 years, after which the Kingdom of the Antichrist would fall, by degrees, and be *'given unto the people of the Saints of the most High'*.[72] The formula for the time-span of Antichristian rule is given in the prophecy as 'for a time times and half a time':

the time of the end is said to be a *time, times, and half a time*: which is

the duration of the reign of the last horn of *Daniel's* fourth Beast, and

of the *Woman and Beast* in the *Apocalypse*.[73]

Mede had proposed that days in Daniel should be understood as years. The word 'time' was translated into a prophetic year, which equals 360 earthly years, and 'times' interpreted as signifying two prophetic years, or 720 earthly years. 'Half a time', was computed as 180 years, giving a total of 1,260 years. If many exegetes agreed on this figure, the problem remained of determining when to start counting; that is to say when did the great apostasy begin? Various dates had been proposed, including some from Newton himself. But Newton felt sure that biblical prophecy could only be properly understood after it had become historical reality, signifying that dates for the onset of the Millennium could only be speculative. In any case, to attempt to predict the date of the Millennium from biblical prophecy would have been presumptuous. As Newton reminded his readers, God had not intended to make interpreters of Prophecy into prophets.[74]

Newton was also convinced the prophecies of Daniel and St John were an integrated communication from God and thus had to be considered as a whole, for '[t]he *Apocalypse* of John is written in the same style and language with the

---

[72]   Newton, *Observations*, pp. 160 [113-4].

[73]   Newton, *Observations*, pp. 168-9 [127].

[74]   Newton, *Observations*, p. 256 [251].

prophecies of *Daniel* ... all of them together make but one complete *Prophecy*'.[75]
We too, then, are obliged to proceed to the Book of Revelation before further
developing the discussion on the coming of the Millennium. In examining the
prophecies of John, we should not, however, proceed afresh, but rather interpret
them in the light of those of Daniel because, '*Daniel's* Prophecies reach to the end
of the world'; and they 'are all of them related to one another, as if they were but
several parts of one general Prophecy, given at several times'.[76] Indeed, although

> '[t]he authority of the Prophets ... comprehends the sum of religion,
> amongst the old Prophets, *Daniel* is most distinct in order of time, and
> easiest to be understood: and therefore in those things which relate to
> the last times, he must be made the key to the rest'.[77]

In the final instance, 'to reject his [Daniel's] Prophecies, is to reject the Christian
religion, for this religion is founded upon his Prophecy concerning the *Messiah*'.[78]

Newton duly commences chapter three of his account of *Revelation* by
reminding the reader that

> The whole scene of sacred Prophecy is composed of three principal
> parts: the regions beyond *Euphrates*, represented by the two first
> Beasts of *Daniel*; the Empire of the *Greeks* on this side of *Euphrates*,
> represented by the Leopard and by the He-Goat; and the Empire of the
> *Latins* on this side of *Greece*, represented by the Beast with ten
> horns.[79]

He then outlines in what way the beasts in Daniel (and consequently the
succession of empires) relate to those in *Revelation*:

---

[75]   Newton, *Observations*, p. 259 [254].

[76]   Newton, *Observations*, pp. 83, 174 [24, 132].

[77]   Newton, *Observations*, pp. 75-6 [14-15].

[78]   Newton, *Observations*, pp. 83-4 [25]. On Christ's first and second coming predicted in
         Daniel see *Observations*, Part 1, Chapter 10, *Of the Prophecy of the Seventy Weeks*; in
         which days are also reckoned as years.

[79]   Newton, *Observations*, p. 273 [276].

The third and fourth Beasts of *Daniel* are the same with the Dragon and ten-horned Beast of *John*, but with this difference: *John* puts the Dragon for the whole *Roman* Empire while it continued entire, because it was entire when that Prophecy was given; and the Beast he considers not till the Empire became divided: and then he puts the Dragon for the Empire of the *Greeks*, and the Beast for the Empire of the *Latins*. Hence it is that the Dragon and Beast have common heads and common horns: but the Dragon hath crowns only upon his heads, and the Beast only upon his horns; because the Beast and his horns reigned not before they were divided from the Dragon: and when the Dragon gave the Beast his throne, the ten horns received powers as Kings, the same hour with the Beast.[80]

Developments in the Book of Revelation are tied to seven seals of a book - '*the scripture of truth*, which *Daniel* was commanded to *shut up and seal, till the time of the end*'[81] - which can only be opened by Jesus Christ, who is signified in the prophecy by the Lamb (Rev. 5). As the seals are progressively opened the approach of the end of human history - the Millennium, the Second Coming and the Resurrection - is revealed and the redeemed are seen in heaven. On the correlation between the seals and the decline of Church purity, Newton wrote that the apostasy of Christians

> began to work in the Apostles days, and was to continue working *till the man of sin should be revealed*. It began to work on the disciples of *Simon, Menander, Carpocrates, Cerinthus*, and such sorts of men as had imbibed the metaphysical philosophy of the *Gentiles* and *Cabalistical Jews*, and were thence called *Gnosticks*. John calls them *Antichrists*, saying that in his days there were many *Antichrists*. But

---

[80] Newton, *Observations*, pp. 273-4 [277]; the same formulation also appears on pp. 300-1 [315].

[81] Newton, *Observations*, p. 255 [249].

these being condemned by the Apostles, and their immediate disciples, put the Churches in no danger during the opening of the first four seals. The visions at the opening of these seals relate only to the civil affairs of the heathen *Roman* Empire. So long the Apostolic traditions prevailed, and preserved the Church in its purity: and therefore the affairs of the Church do not begin to be considered in this prophecy until the opening of the fifth seal. She began then to decline, and to want admonitions.[82]

The opening of the seventh seal (Rev. 8) begins a series of seven trumpet-calls. The seventh trumpet-call is followed by the proclamation of the Kingdom of God and of Christ. In terms of Newton's perception of the rise of the Antichrist and its downfall in the Millennium, however, it is the general eschatological visions described subsequent to the depiction of the last trumpet call - which for Newton 'interpret'[83] the seven seals and trumpet blasts - to which we must address ourselves. But, prior to examining those visions, we need to be aware of some more elements of Newton's iconographical scheme:

a Ruler is signified by his riding on a beast ... royal dignity, by purple or scarlet, or by a crown; ... error and misery, by drinking a cup of his or her wine that causeth it; ... worshipping or serving the false Gods of any nation, by committing adultery with their princes, or by worshipping them ... the affliction or persecution which a people suffers in labouring to bring forth a new kingdom, by the pain of a woman in labour to bring forth a manchild.[84]

In Chapter 12 of Revelations a pregnant woman, representing the pure 'primitive Church catholick', is seen in the Temple of Heaven suffering labour pains, '*she being with child* of a Christian Empire' (events corresponding to the

---

[82]   Newton, *Observations*, p. 260 [256].

[83]   For a note on the interpretative nature of the visions following the seals and trumpet calls in Revelation, see Newton's *Observations*, pp. 271-2 [274-5].

fifth seal). Her labour pains were understood to be those of the persecution of the Church by Emperor Diocletian (AD 284-305).[85] She is 'clothed with the Sun, and the moon under her feet, and upon her head a crown of twelve stars' (Rev. 12:1). Newton explains the iconography of that scene: the Church

> is represented by *a woman* in the Temple of heaven, *clothed with the sun* of righteousness, *and the moon* of *Jewish* ceremonies *under her feet, and upon her head a crown of twelve stars* relating to the twelve Apostles and to the twelve tribes of *Israel*.[86]

Also present in heaven (or the Temple) is a great red ten-horned dragon that has seven diadem crowned heads. The dragon (Satan) makes war in heaven but is defeated and 'that old serpent called the Devil and Satan, which deceiveth the whole world' was cast out of heaven. In his wrath the dragon persecutes the woman and, consequent to giving birth to a man child, the woman flees the dragon. The '*Dragon*, the Heathen *Roman* Empire, [had] *stood before her, to devour her child as soon as it was born*'. But the life of the infant was saved, signified by Emperor *Constantine*'s adoption of Christianity: '*her child*, by the victory of *Constantine* over *Licinius*, A.C. 322, *was brought up unto god and to his throne*'[87] - that is to say the True Church was protected from ultimate extinction in the subsequent papal persecutions of those Christians who resisted Roman corruption.

Pursued by the dragon, the flight of the woman '*into the wilderness*, or spiritually barren Empire of the *Latins*', was a particularly momentous event for Newton and many other Dissenting Protestants who claimed to represent the tradition of the pure primitive Church, for

---

[84]   Newton, *Observations*, p. 81 [22-3].

[85]   Newton, *Observations*, pp. 271, 300-1 [274, 314, 316].

[86]   Newton, *Observations*, p. 275 [279].

[87]   Newton, *Observations*, pp. 275-6 [280-1].

[w]hen she fled from the Temple into the wilderness, she left in the Temple *a remnant of her seed, who kept the commandments of God, and had the testimony of Jesus Christ.*[88]

Unambiguously pointing to the historical religious fraud of the Church of Rome, Newton explained that the 'glorious woman in heaven', who *'before her flight ... represented the true primitive Church of God ... afterwards ... degenerated like Ahola* and *Aholibah'*. Nevertheless, She continued to have the same 'outward form after her flight into the wilderness, whereby she quitted her former sincerity and piety, and became the great Whore. She lost her chastity, but kept her outward form and shape'. Subsequently, the dragon leaves the woman in order *'to make war with the remnant of her seed*, which she left behind her when she fled.[89]

Further on in Revelation, now bejewelled, resplendent and 'having a golden cup in her hand full of abominations and filthiness of her fornication', the woman is found sitting on a scarlet beast (rather than the dragon) 'having seven heads and ten horns' (Rev. 17:3-4). For Newton, this was a scene loaded with foreboding, 'for abomination is often put in scripture for a false God'.[90] For Protestants the mounted woman was identified with Rome, the Whore of Babylon: 'the woman which thou sawest is that great city [Rome], which reigneth over the kings of the Earth'. Thus, noted Newton, she was the Church of the Beast.[91] Roman Catholicism, therefore, gave worship to the Beast. The prophecy also predicted the creation of the Papal States:

[a]t length the woman arrived at her place of temporal as well as spiritual dominion upon the back of the Beast, where she is nourished *a time, and times, and half a time, from the face of the serpent* ... she is the eleventh horn of *Daniel's* fourth Beast ... These characters of the woman, and little horn of the Beast, agree perfectly: in respect of

---

[88]   Newton, *Observations*, p. 275 [279-80].

[89]   Newton, *Observations*, pp. 271, 275 [273, 279-281].

[90]   Newton, *Observations*, p. 176 [136].

her temporal dominion, she was a horn of the Beast; in respect of her spiritual dominion, she rode upon him in the form of a woman, and was his Church.[92]

Chapter 17 of Revelation informs us that the 'seven heads [of the scarlet beast] are seven mountains, on which the woman sitteth'. The 'ten horns are ten kings, which have received no kingdom as yet', but who will briefly share with the Beast the exercise of royal authority, before giving 'their power and strength unto the beast' (Rev. 17:9,12-13). Newton, as many other Protestants, explained that

The Angel tells him [John] further: *Here is the mind which hath wisdom: the seven heads are seven mountains, on which the woman sitteth*; Rome being built upon seven hills, and thence called the seven-hilled city.[93]

Thus the woman and Beast jointly represented the papacy, signifying that the papacy was the Antichrist. In addition, the ten horns of the Beast in Revelation represent the same ten post-Roman-Empire European kingdoms Newton identified in the ten horns of the Beast in the Book of Daniel.

For Newton, the kings of the ten European states formed from the collapse of the Roman Empire, certainly did give their kingdoms to the beast, that is to say recognized and aided the papacy in its fraudulent claim to be the legitimate and divinely ordained centre of Christianity. This portrayal formed an integral part of the common Protestant critique of the medieval and Catholic Church, which accused the Church of meddling in state affairs, of tyrannical rule inside the Church, of spiritual corruption in order to amass great wealth, and the bloody suppression of those who defended the divine truths of the Gospel. Newton (quoting Revelation), explains that the beast-mounted woman committed

---

[91]   Newton, *Observations*, p. 277 [283].

[92]   Newton, *Observations*, pp. 276-7 [282-3].

[93]   Newton, *Observations*, p. 304 [320]; for another statement on the identification of

fornication with the ten kings, and 'she was drunken with the blood of the saints'. He explained that Revelation predicted the coming of the *'false Prophets*, or *false teachers*, expressed collectively in the *Apocalypse* by the name of the false Prophet'. This false prophet would have the 'character of *Antichrist: And many*, saith he, *shall follow their lusts'*. Indeed, 'the kingdoms of the beast live deliciously with the great Whore, and the nations are made drunk with the wine of her fornication'. The beast also had the power to dictate *'that all* religious bodies of men, *who would not worship* the authority of the *Image, should be* mystically *killed*' - that is to say excommunicated. The duration of the rule of the beast-mounted woman over Church and kings Newton gave as 1260 years, the same figure he gave for the duration of the great apostasy in his analysis of the Book of Daniel.[94]

As already touched upon, the difficulty which haunted those very many English Protestants who believed in the certainty of the Millennium's arrival was the task of determining exactly when the end of human history would occur. During the momentous events of the seventeenth century (for example the Thirty Years War; and especially the super-heated atmosphere of the English Civil War, which resulted in the abolition of episcopacy and regicide) many thought the Millennium imminent. For a variety of reasons, others were more circumspect regarding predictions of its advent, but were nevertheless certain of its eventual arrival, measured either in decades or centuries to come. For some the beginning of the end (or signs of it) was expected in the late-seventeenth century: 1260 years from the decisive decline of Christianity, dated from the foundation of the orthodox Christian state under Emperor Theodosius at the end of the fourth century. In his youth, his Cambridge years, Newton had given the 1680s as one possible date for signs presaging the Millenium's arrival.[95] But the significance

---

Rome and the Beast, see Newton's *Observations* p. 275 [280]

[94]   Newton, *Observations*, pp. 249-50, 276-8 [241-2, 279-81].

[95]   Manuel, *Religion of Isaac Newton*, p. 99.

of the fourth century as a crucial period in the decline of Christianity went beyond Puritan/Dissenter ranks. Thus the Anglican Joseph Mede and the Cambridge Platonist Henry More also expected the late-seventeenth century to augur the time of the end.

Amongst Puritans and Dissenters (and some Anglicans), one common date advanced for the fully-fledged reign of the Antichrist in the Church was the year AD 607. In this year Pope Boniface III had accepted formal supremacy within the western Church by accepting the title of *episcopus universalis* (universal bishop) from the Byzantine Emperor Focas. If the span of the reign of the Beast was 1260 years, beginning from 607 for example, the resultant date for the arrival of the Millennium would have been the 1860s or thereabouts, a date not ruled out by Newton.[96] Throughout his life he contemplated other possible dates, some as late as 2370; but did not insist on the validity of any one particular date. As we have seen, Newton's religious modesty made him feel sure that the activity of studying the prophecies with the benefit of historical hindsight was very different to that of predicting the future, to which only God held the key. Thus he felt it improper and useless to continue attempts to predict a date for the Second Coming with any degree of certainty. He did, however, feel that, 'judging by the great successes of late Interpreters' of prophecy such as More and Mede, the end was 'approaching'. This was because God had intended

> that these prophecies should not be understood till the time of the end
> ... 'Tis therefore a part of this Prophecy, that it should not be understood before the last age of the world; and therefore it makes credit of the Prophecy, that it is not yet understood.[97]

Regardless of such sober considerations, the possible date for such a momentous event for the human race as the commencement of the Millennium was unlikely to be continuously ignored by interpreters of prophecy. We should

---

[96]   On the date of the 1860s see also, Westfall, *The Life of Isaac Newton*, p. 129.

[97]   Newton, *Observations*, pp. 255-6 [250-1].

therefore be surprised if Newton did not at least continue with provisional, speculative calculations. But, as we have seen, given his understanding that the prophecies had been given in a deliberately obscure form in order to conceal the date of the Millennium until 'the time of the end', he did not commit himself to any one date. This is evident when discussing Daniel's 2300 days of the 'desolation' of Christianity (Dan. 8:13-14; see also Rev. 12:6), days which 'were to last till the time of the end':

> Daniel's days are years and these years may perhaps be reckoned
> either from the destruction of the Temple by the *Romans* in the reign
> of *Vespasian*, or from the pollution of the Sanctuary by the worship of
> *Jupiter Olympius*, or from the desolation of *Judea* made in the end of
> the *Jewish* war by the banishment of all the *Jews* out of their own
> country, or from some other period which time will discover.[98]

2300 days, dated from the reign of the Emperor Vespasian (69-79 AD) results in a date of c. 2370 AD. With several possible dates for the arrival of the Millennium - and spread over centuries - it is not surprising that Newton, a man of prudence as well as deep piety, did not opt for any particular date to the exclusion of others. Rather he was patiently awaiting more evidence.

We must now turn to the very important question of Newton's self-conception, for it has been asserted that Newton considered himself a 'messenger-prophet', and our starting point is ancient knowledge, both secular and religious.

The late-seventeenth century was a period in which it was not uncommon for members of the intellectual elite still to revere the civilization of ancient Greece as a golden age of knowledge and wisdom. Newton, as many contemporary scholars, did not necessarily believe that the ancients knew more than the moderns. He felt rather that he was recovering at least the correct principles of nature via which ancient sages such as Pythagoras and Plato had

---

[98]   Newton, *Observations*, pp. 165-7 [122-4]. It seems (*Observations* p. 168 [125-6]),
         however, that Newton favoured a commencement date for the `desolation' in AD 132.

sought knowledge and wisdom. Likewise, Newton was also uncovering ancient fundamental truths from the deliberately obscure language of divine prophecy. But this did not mean he undervalued his rediscoveries: it was precisely the recovery of ancient knowledge that was a sure sign of his intellectual prowess. Newton disagreed with Henry More, who thought the ostensibly arcane language of biblical prophecy was potentially comprehensible to all. For Newton, his own ability and that of some few others to comprehend divine intentions via biblical prophecy demonstrated that they comprised a privileged group of Christians. He thought that certain religious truths were beyond the capacity of the vulgar, and that it was the duty of gifted individuals to provide guidance for the edification of the masses.[99] But, as we have already seen, he repudiated the notion that interpreters of Prophecy might second-guess God's intentions for the future. He and others were, therefore, only educated guides to the truths already present in biblical prophecy. Some modern academics, however, have ignored Newton's own views on the subject. Kochavi has argued 'that Newton's activity served as a metaphor for the construction of the Tabernacle by Moses'. Thus, as an exegete, Newton had a central role in saving true Christianity, he was as Moses, a 'messenger-prophet'.[100]

---

[99] For a discussion of the differences between More and Newton see Sarah Hutton's, `More, Newton, and the Language of Biblical Prophecy', in E. Force and R. Popkin (eds), *The Books of Nature and Scripture: Recent Essays on Natural Philosohy, Theology, and Biblical Criticism in the Netherlands of Spinoza's time and the British Isles of Newton's time* (Dordrecht, 1994).

[100] Matania Kochavi, `One Prophet Interprets Another: Sir Isaac Newton and Daniel', in Force and Popkin, *The Books of Nature and Scripture: Recent Essays*, etc., pp. 116-7, 120. This pseudo-Freudian trend was already present in Manuel, see The *Religion of Isaac Newton*, p. 23. Even the most recent work on Newton, that of White, contains (in my opinion) unsubstantiated Pseudo-psychological analyses, in which Newton's search for identity led him to identify himself with Jesus Christ (*The Last Sorcerer*, pp. 153-4). Such opinions of Newton perhaps emanate from the tradition of seeing Newton as peculiar in his religious views rather than - as was certainly the case - rather mundane.

If Kochavi is correct on this point, then the perceived success of other exegetes in the realm of biblical prophecy - which Newton also readily recognized - must surely have qualified at least some of them for the appellation of messenger-prophet. Yet there is no evidence that eminent exegetes thought of themselves, or were regarded by Newton, as latter-day Moses. Furthermore, although Newton considered he had brought some of the lost scientific principles of the ancients to light, his claims for his success as an exegete were hardly of the same magnitude. He had deciphered little of anything startlingly new in the prophecies. The general depiction of the four successive kingdoms and especially that of the degeneration of the fourth into papal inspired Beast worship - the most crucial part of the prophecies for many Protestants - was hardly original. The broad outline of the degeneration of the Church into idolatry was common to most English Protestants. Indeed John Calvin (1509-1564), whose theology had great influence in England, had also identified the papacy with the Beast in the Book of Revelation, and therefore with the Antichrist, even noting it in the marginalia to the Geneva Bible (1560). Newton's efforts were principally directed at putting the schema of historical development in the prophecies onto a more sound foundation by developing a consistent and reliable hermeneutic system to underpin it, and more precisely locating and reaffirming the chronological correlation between actual historical events and prophetic metaphor and allusion. Newton's claim to originality in the sphere of prophetic exegesis was and could only have been relatively modest.

Nevertheless, the difference between Joseph Mede's relatively egalitarian view of the abilities needed to interpret prophecy, and Newton's relatively elite stance remains. Besides his prodigious scientific achievements, what other clues are there as to why Newton might have thought of himself as a member of a privileged group of Christians? There is certainly one clue, and it is to be found in the puritanical stamp of his religious upbringing. Puritans (after the 1640s forming one subgroup under the umbrella term Dissenter or Nonconformist) were

Calvinists, and considered themselves to be either of the elect or the reprobate: the reprobate were predestined by God to go to hell and the elect to heaven. The problem was, and a genuinely vexing one for Calvinists, that only He knew if a person had been destined reprobate or elect. It was commonly accepted, however, that if one were of the elect, one would lead a godly life, and strive to excel in one's calling (natural abilities bestowed by God). We also know that Newton strayed from the Trinitarianism of Calvinism, to Unitarianism. But Unitarianism then represented but a broad collection of individuals with significant variations in belief from one Unitarian to the next. It is therefore possible that Newton never fully abandoned the Calvinist notion of predestination, and still considered himself to be one of the elect. His scientific achievements were certainly sufficiently startling to reinforce or evoke the notion that God was smiling benevolently upon Newton's life.

In attempting to understand the station Newton had assigned himself in his religious outlook, the religious climate of his youth should naturally not be overlooked. We should perhaps remind ourselves, for example, that virtually all seventeenth-century English Protestants then agreed on the importance of the Fall in the development of world history. The sin of Adam and Eve had condemned the human race to sin, because they had transmitted their sin physiologically, as proclaimed in the Westminster Confession (1643).[101] Religious affliction, therefore, could be hereditary, and the most common affliction was considered to be idolatry. Henry More, in his *Antidote Against Idolatry* (1669), noted that the souls of men 'in this lapsed state, are naturally prone to so mischievous a Disease [idolatry], as both History and daily Experience do abundantly witness'.[102] The career of this phenomenon - idolatry - was one of the major components of Newton's exegesis of biblical prophecy. It is sometimes said, however, that

---

[101]   *Westminster Confession of Faith, 1643* (Glasgow, 1985), pp. 39-40.

[102]   Henry More, *The Antidote Against Idolatry*, (1st edn 1669), in *A Brief Reply to a Late Answer to Dr. Henry More and his Antidote against Idolatry* (London, 1672), p. 48.

Unitarians rejected the determinism of original sin, believing instead in the goodness of human nature. This may be a valid statement at times and is true, for instance, of the late eighteenth-century scientist and Unitarian Joseph Priestley (1733-1804). But it cannot be said that such a positive assessment of human nature is evident in the historical development depicted in Newton's *Observations*. In the late-seventeenth and early-eighteenth centuries, Unitarian thought was perhaps more heterogeneous than some historians have hitherto realized.

There are certainly comments in Newton's writings to suggest that his distinction between elite biblical scholars and the ignorant laity may have had a theological underpinning, perhaps akin to Calvinist thought. For example, he twice cites Daniel (Dan. 12, 9-10) that 'God has so ordered the prophecies that in the latter days *the wise may understand, but the wicked shall do wickedly, and non of the wicked shall understand*.[103] If one equates the elect - or at least a loose conception of it - with the wise, and the wicked with the reprobate, one has another indication that Newton may have retained a quasi-Calvinist view of himself as one of the elect, or at least in some respects divinely favoured. But this is a very different conception to advancing the astounding assumption that Newton considered himself to be a latter day Moses; a conception such a pious man would surely have considered presumptuous or even blasphemous. Newton forthrightly upbraided those who dared to claim for themselves the role of latter-day prophets:

> The folly of Interpreters has been, to foretel times and things by this Prophecy, as if God designed to make them prophets. By this rashness they have not only exposed themselves, but brought the Prophecy also into contempt. The design of God was much otherwise. He gave this and the Prophecies of the Old Testament, not to gratify men's curiosities by enabling them to foreknow things, but that after they

---

[103]   Newton, *Observations*, p. 75 [13-14].

were fulfilled they might be interpreted by the event, and his own Providence, not to the Interpreters, be then manifested thereby to the world. For the event of things predicted many ages before, will then be a convincing argument that the world is governed by providence'.[104]

Until the time of the 'signal revolutions predicted by the holy Prophets', we can only 'content ourselves with interpreting what hath already been fulfilled.'[105]

In conclusion we can note that the seventeenth-century attempt to put the study of prophecy upon a scientific basis was doomed to failure, because, some would argue, the contents of the prophecies were themselves not amenable to scientific or quasi-scientific investigation. The fact that such an attempt today seems to some eccentric or naive, can mislead scholars in to explaining the attempt to put prophetic exegesis on a quasi-scientific footing as the product of unrestrained religious enthusiasm, or delusions of religious grandeur. Instead, we must remind ourselves that Newton lived in a period characterized by a unique combination of science and religion, a period when a new scientific outlook was being born, but when the old religious cosmology was far from moribund.

It is true that, in the eighteenth century, the study of biblical prophecy and the prophetic outlook did slowly decline. But the prophetic view was too deeply ingrained into the English Protestant psyche to be suddenly and completely snuffed out by any such short-lived phenomenon as the ultra-rationalist and anti-Church English deist Enlightenment of the years 1695-1740, as for instance Manuel has claimed.[106]

The growing secularization of society in the eighteenth and nineteenth centuries was one of the main factors in the slow decline of Protestant reliance on biblical prophecy. Many Protestants had to assimilate the fact that the Millennium

---

[104] Newton, *Observations* pp. 256-7 [251-2].

[105] Newton, *Observations*, pp. 256-7 [252-3].

[106] Manuel, The *Religion of Isaac Newton*, pp. 89-90.

had failed to arrive as soon as they might have hoped. Equally important, however, was that a fully Protestant interpretation of past and future times had already been achieved. The result of the achievements of expositors such as More, Mede and Newton was that the prophetic mine was near exhaustion. Given the nature of the subject matter, it was hardly possible to subject the *Book of Daniel and Revelation* to any greater degree of analytical precision. In any case, the historical account that such men had discerned and detected in the prophecies perfectly explained the Protestant view of Church history. The project initiated by the Marian exiles had been completed. Nevertheless, even if after Newton (some would say shortly after 1700) the practice of prophetic exposition was in slow decline, the historical and eschatological scheme of the biblical exegetes lived on in Protestant thought.

In the second half of the eighteenth century the same prophetic framework was still used by Protestants to understand the development of history and the future for Christendom and the human race.[107] By some, the name of Isaac Newton - then a byword for rational scientific study - was used to legitimate the predictive power of biblical prophecy.[108] Even amongst the scientific community of the late-eighteenth century, there were those who looked to biblical prophecy, including the discoveror of oxygen, Joseph Priestley.[109] It was perhaps more than

---

[107]   See, for example John Brown's, *A General History of the Christian Church from the Birth of our Saviour to the Present Time* (Edinburgh, 1771), vol. 1, p. 4; also Brown's *Harmony of Scripture Prophecies, and History of their Fulfilment* (Glasgow, 1784).

[108]   See for example Patrick Nisbet's *An Abridgement of Ecclesiastical History* (London, 1776), p. 104.

[109]   For Priestley's attitude towards biblical prophecy see, for example, his *General History of the Christian Church from the Fall of the Western Empire to the Present time* (Northumberland U.S.A., 1802) , vol. 1, preface pp. 28-9; also his *An Answer to Mr. Paine's Age of Reason, being a Continuation of Letters to the Philosophers and Politicians of France on the Subject of Religion, London,* 1795 (but originally Northumberland USA 1794), Letter six, `On Prophecy'; and his *The Present State of Europe compared with Antient Prophecies* (Phildelphia, 1794).

a coincidence that one of the very few influential Catholic works written on prophecy was produced by an Englishman, Charles Walmesley (1722-1797). Walmesley, Catholic priest, mathematician and astronomer, wrote *The General History of the Christian Church ... chiefly deduced from the Apocalypse of St John the Apostle* (1771). Naturally, Walmesley's pro-Catholic account of the predictions contained in the Apocalypse of St John was radically different to those of Protestants.[110]

The aim of this introduction has been neither to claim Newton as the harbinger of modern times, nor to dismiss his prophetic thought as pre-modern, but rather to locate his views in their proper context. John Maynard Keynes, on the tercentenary of Newton's birth in 1942, wrote that

> Newton was not the first of the age of reason. He was the last of the magicians, the last of the Babylonians and Sumerians ... the last great mind which looked out on the visible and intellectual world with the same eyes as those who began to build our intellectual inheritance rather less than 10,000 years ago.[111]

Keynes certainly intended his statement as a tribute to Newton, but it hardly aids us to understand Newton in the context of his own era, and could be construed by

---

[110] Walmesley's work was reprinted in Dublin 1790; London 1798; Dublin 1806, 1812 and 1815; Belfast 1816; Cork 1820 and 1821; it was also translated into French (1777 and 1790) and reprinted in English in 1846. Various extracts of Walmesley's work were also printed in England in the nineteenth century; and it was translated into German, Italian and Latin, even with five editions in the USA. Walmesley's pro-Catholic account of the Apocalypse of St John is radically different to those of Protestants. In Walmseley's account the four beasts figure relatively little, with the Seven Seals providing most of the historical framework. For Walmesley (pp. 65-6), the seven heads of the Red Dragon also signify Rome, but only ancient Rome and the emperors who persecuted Christians; and the ten horns only the barbarian nations which were employed by God to break down the heathen Roman Empire.

[111] J. M. Keynes, `Newton, the Man', in *Collected Works*, 14 vols (London, 1972), vol. 4, 363-4.

some as historically unsympathetic. If we wish to indulge in paradoxes, it would be more fitting to say that Newton's prophetic concerns help us understand the intellectual climate in which science developed and ensured a place for prophecy in the history of science.

Essential notes on Newton's approach
to biblical studies (Mary E. Mills).

The starting place for an evaluation of Newton's approach to the Bible is Newton's own purpose in commenting on the texts of Daniel and Revelation. As has already been explained above, Newton's purpose was to investigate and clarify the biblical foundations for the particular version of Christianity held by him and other dissenting contemporaries. He was not conducting a disinterested exploration of Daniel and the Apocalypse so much as drawing from them evidence to support one individual line of Christian thought and belief - one with which he was in sympathy.

The reason for Newton's exposition of the text controls, to some extent, his method and findings. He was operating from certain basic preconceptions: that the Christian Bible has a prophetic function and so is of immediate interest to a 'modern' audience: his readership could find answers to their particular questions about the purpose and destiny of human society in the biblical texts. He was also operating from a stance hostile to the Roman Catholic strand of Christianity and, indeed, to any strand where authority was vested in monarchical bishops. Thus Newton combined biblical exegesis with long accounts of the historical chronology of European society from the time of the Roman Empire onwards. It is this history which was, for him and like minds, the true meaning of the books of Daniel and Revelation.

This style of reading biblical texts is very different from that of twentieth-century interpreters of the Bible. However, there are some points in Newton's account where there is a crossing over of twentieth-century practice with Newton's own perspective. These passages are largely located in the introductory chapters to Part 1 (Daniel) and Part 2 (Revelation) of his *Observations*, in which he lays out for his readers some foundational material concerning the origin and authorship of the two texts. Newton reveals that he has carried out some considerable research - of what could be termed a 'scientific' kind. There is a basic similarity between Newton and twentieth-century exegesis here.

With regard to the origins of the texts, Newton demonstrates a concern to discover as accurately as possible when a text was written and for what purposes. In this setting, Newton is aware that Daniel originated as part of the compilation of sacred texts in ancient Judaism and that Revelation emerged as part of an early Christian resistance tradition - in response to the authority of emperors such as Nero or Domitian, whose reputation is one of persecution of Christian communities. As Newton unfolds his historico-polemical interests, weaving the work of ancient writers such as Procopius or Eusebius of Caesaria in with biblical passages, he occasionally returns to the time of the formation of the biblical texts he is exploring, as when he comments on the setting of Daniel in the Hellenistic world, using Maccabees 1/2 as parallel texts which explain some of the concerns of Daniel.

The point of contact with modern exegesis, therefore, is Newton's scholarly interest in the origins of the text and a desire to situate the text accurately in its historical context. The situating of texts helps to reveal the original purposes of the ancient writer since it is then known in what circumstances he was writing: as with Revelation's ambivalent attitude to Roman culture. The need to get back to the earliest level of writing and so find the truth about the text was a foundation stone in modern scientific biblical criticism which emerged in the nineteenth century. This style of exegesis has been entitled the 'historical-critical method', and different versions of the search for the origins of the biblical texts appeared under this heading. One version was Source Criticism, the search for the first written document lying behind the extant and expanded text. This was followed by Form Criticism, which broke the text up into many small units, each of which was an independent tradition. In a prophetic book, each oracle of a few verses in length was to be treated as a separate piece of text, passed on by word of mouth before being written down. The effect of this method was to dissect the biblical book and leave it in fragments. But each book appears as a whole text, finally. Thus attention focused on the role of the editors who collected traditional elements and brought them together into a unitary work such as the Book of Genesis, or the Pentateuch (Five Books of Moses) as a whole .

The link between this method and that of Newton is the scientific approach, seeking to locate the original work in its own age. However, Newton would be criticised by modern scholars because he takes too much for granted about the authors of biblical texts. For Newton, Samuel 1/2, for example, are written by Samuel, an opinion justified by the textual evidence of Samuel as a prophet and leader of society. But modern commentators would throw that idea out; for them all that can be said is that the content of these books may have originated in oral tales of past heroes which were written down many centuries after the event. Yet Newton's overview, that the Bible took shape eventually in the Jewish post-exilic period, and his awareness of the relevance of modern Jewish views on the origins and shape of the Hebrew Bible, are in sympathy with twentieth-century guidlelines for reading the Bible. Modern scholars have also been obliged to acknowledge how little we in fact know for certain about the biblical books and their claims. A good introductory book to read here is S. Moyise's *Introduction to Biblical Studies* (1998).

In his introduction to the *Book of Daniel* (*Observations* Pt. 1, Ch. 1), Newton assumes that the Law books of the Old Testament (OT) have some connection with the reign of Josiah, which is in keeping with the ideas of many modern scholars who have argued that the old law Book of 2 Kings is in fact some form of Deuteronomy, the fifth book of the Pentateuch. It is interesting that Newton acknowledges the connection between the biblical Pentateuch and that of the Samaritans. Modern scholars are also interested in the links between these two compilations. Although Newton is in line with modern views that the two cultures of Israel and Judah parted company as a result of conquest and colonization, his assumption that there was an absolute break in the eight to sixth centuries BC would not be acceptable to modern writers, who argue that the Samaritan religion only diverged from that of Judah at the turn of the eras (c. birth of Christ). It has already been noted that Newton is naive about the authorship of OT books, though his focus on the period of Ezra (5th-4th centuries BC) is in agreement with present thought. By some scholars, however, Ezra himself is not thought to be an historical figure, so much as a character symbolizing the lengthy scribal process of compilation of texts at that time.

In Chapter 2 Newton addresses the symbolic use of language in the Apocalypses. In general, modern scholarship is much in agreement with him. In order to understand the text it is necessary to unpack the code in use. Thus cosmic upheavals do indeed signify major historical upheavals and animals are used as symbols for human beings.[112] This is clear in 1 Enoch, another Jewish apocalypse of ancient Judaism. Newton would also be applauded for his note that features of beasts - such as several heads[113] - have the value of separate dynasties within one civilization. Where present scholarship diverges from Newton's version is in relation to his very exact scheme of equivalents and of the use he later makes of this scheme to address not the ancient near east, but the development of Europe.

For modern writers, the focus of Daniel is in the second century BC as a Jewish resistance text. It was the foreign oppressor who was being opposed, in this case the Seleucid dynasty of Syria. Commentators note the two-part nature of the book - composed of stories and visions - with Chapter 7 as the hinge of the

---

[112]   Newton, *Observations*, pp. 77-81 [16-23].

[113]   Newton, *Observations*, p. 80 [21].

work, and they speculate about possible oral sources for the stories of Daniel at the Persian court. The final date of the text must be second century, on account of its coded references to events of that time. The author, however, is unknown.

Newton begins his introduction to the *Apocalypse* (*Observations* Pt. 2, Chapter 1) with a discussion on when it was written, pointing out reasons why it could be attributed to the reigns of Domitian or Nero. Modern commentators follow the same approach and many would argue for a first edition in Nero's time, followed by a re-write in Domitian's day. Newton's attempts to fit this book as well as the Gospel of John into the life of an apostle of Jesus is also of relevance for modern scholars, some of whom have attempted a parallel account of a possible timeframe in the life of one man. However, others have become wary of this process and many would attribute Revelation to an anonymous prophet of the first century called John, since that is what the text itself claims as the name of its source.

As to the dependency of texts on one another, which Newton claims shows the Apocalypse to be the earliest texts with Gospels and Epistles coming later, modern scholars would not generally agree with this view. However, many scholars, like Newton, have noted the Jewish flavour of the work, with its many allusions to OT traditions and some, such as J.M. Ford, have argued that the first level of the book could be a pre-Christian Jewish apocalypse which was then adopted and adapted by a Christian editor.

Newton devotes Chapter 2 to the links between Revelation and the Jewish (Solomon's) Temple at Jerusalem. He points to the verbal links between Jewish accounts of the role of the high priest, of the altar and of the Ark of the Lord and the imagery of Revelation. Thus Chapter 1 of Revelation contains a vision experienced within worship which draws in angels and lampstands, as well as trumpets, which are all images derived from temple symbolism. This language turns, ultimately, on the idea that heaven and earth are parallel realms and that the

Temple is at the centre, a bridge between life in these two parts of the divine kingdom.

This part of Newton's analysis is especially interesting, since recent scholarship has turned towards a closer examination of the role of the Jewish Temple in early Jewish and Christian thought. A book by C.T.R. Hayward (*The Jewish Temple, a Non-biblical Source book*, 1996), for instance, collects Jewish texts about the Temple. Another scholar, M. Barker, has written several books on the subject of the Jewish Temple (eg. *The Gate of Heaven, History and Symbolism in the New Testament*, 1991), and on its relevance for understanding the significance of New Testament presentations of Jesus Christ. With regard to Newton's emphasis on the day of Atonement ritual, Barker has recently made an examination (*On Earth as it is in Heaven, Temple Symbolism in the New Testament*, 1995) of how such ancient ritual might have found a re-expression in the Gospel accounts of Jesus.

A further point of note is that Newton should be so interested in temple imagery and view it as so central to Christianity, when he is regarded by most as an early modern scientist. For modern readers, temple language is often obscure and irrelevant since it contains so many mythological elements, such as throne chariots. From a scientific perspective, this mythological material is to be discounted in the name of science and reason. But Newton easily unites rational-deductive thought with that of visionary perspective.

We have seen that Newton's methodology has many links with modern biblical scholarship, but he would be criticised by modern scholars for his lack of objectivity. His personal concerns interrupt his exploration of the origins of the books of Daniel and the Apocalypse and their original significance. Ironically, it has become apparent to the present century that it is impossible to arrive at the origins of biblical texts, for too much of the ancient near eastern past has been lost or destroyed. It has also emerged that historians are never wholly without subjectivity. They operate inevitably from their own time period and its intellectual and cultural assumptions. 'Postmodernity' accepts that all accounts are partial ones; with regard to biblical studies, this has meant that the search for the one truth about a text, reliant upon accurate knowledge of its sources, has been abandoned. The focus for scholars is now on the text itself and on all those who are readers of texts. Every text and every reader has an ideology, a set of preconceptions which colour the shaping of a book or the message which a reader derives from the act of reading a book. In this context Newton is of interest as an individual reader. Rather than criticising him, scholars should take an interest in examining and valuing Newton's analysis in its own right.

We know that Newton had an anti-Trinitarian agenda. Consequently, modern readers need to be aware of how he constructed his arguments. It is instructive, therefore, to examine the manner in which he utilized terms and phrases written in the ancient languages of Hebrew and Greek as supports for his commentaries.

On several occasions Newton makes use of the ancient practice of using letters of the alphabet to signify numbers. This device is utilized when he refers to texts dealing with calendar dates and the celebration of Jewish festivals. Thus, he speaks of ADU (one of the rules governing the calculation of the Jewish calendar), and points out that this can signify the numbers 1(A) 4 (D) 6(U).[114] In this instance the letters of the Hebrew alphabet are standing for numbers specified, according to their place in the Hebrew alphabet. As already noted, this form of mathematical scheme forms not only part of Newton's exegesis, but also derives from a long tradition of cabbalistic readings of biblical books.

Although Newton follows the cabbalistic tradition here, and uses the Hebrew correctly, he is not always so careful in his use of the Hebrew language. Thus he translates one phrase as meaning AFTER ... him/the king.[115] In this instance, this allows Newton to establish a temporal connection between the

---

[114] Newton, *Observations*, p. 195 [163].

[115] Newton, *Observations*, pp. 167-8 [125].

subjects of chosen passages from the Hebrew Bible. However, the normal translation would be From ... him/the king - a usage followed by the Revised Standard study Bible, and leads to a different sense than the one preferred by Newton.

Sometimes it is a Greek phrase which is not exact. Thus Newton speaks of Antiochus Epimenes,[116] seemingly to refer to a Syrian ruler of the Seleucid dynasty, reigning in the 2nd century BC. The usual title for this rule is Antiochus Epiphanes and modern commentaries on Daniel refer to the king by this title. Newton specifies that the title Epimenes alludes to his wandering around without the state proper to a king. He implies eccentricity if not madness here. In this instance, it may be that Newton is playing with the themes contained in Daniel. The Book of Daniel is concerned with the arrogance of human rulers, especially those hostile to the Jews. In the Stories section of the text, a great king goes mad and wanders around like a beast of the field, eating the grass. In the Visions material, the little horn which becomes great is understood by modern commentators to be a reference to Antiochus Epiphanes, who gained control of Palestine and tampered with worship.[117] Daniel 8 implies that this ruler will act insanely, that is, he will arrogate divine authority to himself. Within the unity of the text, the king who goes mad in the first part of the book is balanced by Antiochus who acts insanely, that is without proper regard for his human status. There is thus some foundation for Newton's reference to Antiochus as a ruler whose behaviour did not fit his position.

As has already been illustrated above, Newton adapted the theme of the arrogant little horn to convey the view that the claims to authority made by the See of Rome were offensive to the deity. The language of Daniel and the Apocalypse is already heavily symbolic, with historical issues of their day

---

[116]   Newton, *Observations*, p. 207 [183].

[117]   On Newton's refutation of the little horn's identification with Antiochus Epiphanes, see *Observations*, pp. 166-7 [123-4].

encoded in the images used. Newton takes these images and replaces the historical and religious issues of the past with those of his own time. Thus he twice refers to Episkopoi, a term found in the New Testament (NT) and usually translated as bishop. The original meaning of this term is overseer; bishop is the meaning given to the word in Christian circles. In the passage surrounding this citation Newton appears to be playing on words. Thus he begins with the Danielic vision of four great beasts which signify great world empires in ancient times. For Newton, the last beast signifies the rulers of ancient Rome, and the rulers of the ten European kingdoms into which the western Roman Empire disintegrated are imaged as horns on the beast. The little horn (that which usurps three others and held by Newton to represent the authority of papal Rome[118]) has a mouth that speaks 'great things'- a sign of arrogance and pretensions to world authority. The horn also has eyes, so could be defined as one who sees, a Seer. Newton plays on the link between Seer and Overseer in order to hint at the negative value to be placed on the rule of bishops, especially the Bishop of Rome.

When Newton deals with the Apocalypse he also takes a broad view of the text and its meaning. He refers to Adultery (*moichalidos*) and also to Lusts (*aselgeias*).[119] These terms are in line with the overall interests of the biblical writer, who labels Rome as the Great Whore and talks of the kings of the earth having sex with her, a language which symbolizes the commercial and political links between Rome and its empire. The Apocalypse attacks Rome's religious and secular control of the Mediterranean world as though this power were sexual impurity. However, the most often used term in this context is that of harlotry (*Porneia*), and the references are thus to the whore and to whoring. Although the terms adultery and lust are not unconnected with the concept of whoring, the text of the Apocalypse does not make use of them in the verse which Newton appears to be quoting. He is happy, it seems, to give a broad picture of the text without

---

[118] See Newton, *Observations*, pp. 123-4 [74-5].

[119] Newton, *Observations*, pp. 249-50 [241-2].

being too exact in his references. For Newton the harlot is the Pope in Rome, an attribution which formed part of Protestant religious imagery in the sixteenth and seventeenth centuries. Newton regarded the political themes of Revelation 17-19 as pointing to the growth of the Papal States and to the idolatrous veneration which Roman Catholics had for the Roman See.

In all these instances Newton's use of the ancient language versions of the biblical text allows his contemporary concerns to be seen. He is prepared to translate passages in a manner which is generally appropriate, but which focus more on seventeenth-century meaning than on close connection with the readers of the first century or even earlier. Thus his religious views - and those of many Protestants - are upheld as themselves 'prophetic' since they reveal that the God of the Christian Bible is alive and active in the present day. A further and more complicated version of Newton's method occurs when he links the New Testament Book of Hebrews with the Apocalypse. He gives an account which has connections with the actual text of the two works, but which mixes and weaves them together fairly freely. Melchisedek, the priest-king from Genesis 14 is a figure developed in Hebrews as a type of the priesthood of Christ, which is superior to the Jewish priesthood of the Levites (one of the twelve tribes of ancient Israel). Hebrews also refers to the two-edged sword which divides between sinew and bone. On the other hand, the Apocalypse (19) refers to a rider on a white horse who is the Word of God and whose might brings about the end of the world and prepares the way for God's kingdom. Newton freely interweaves these images to make a single message.

This process of conflation is especially clear with Newton's reference to REST. Hebrews 4:9 speaks of the Sabbatismos or Sabbath Day Rest which awaits the people of God. Revelation 20 tells of a thousand year reign when Christ and his faithful will rule the earth, prior to the final battle at the end of the world. The faithful are here those who lost their lives for loyalty to Christ and they will be resurrected to reign with him. Newton puts these two passages together so that the

Sabbath Rest turns into a millennial rest.[120] Sabbath Day observance thus gains a new significance, linked with crucial events during the last days. This was a matter of great importance for Newton, since he was a Sabbatarian: someone for whom strict observance of the Sabbath Day was an essential part of religious practice. It has already been noted that Newton recorded amongst his sins breaches of the Sabbath Day observance; and it was his concern for the Lord's Day which led him to create the composite piece of exegesis discussed above.

The same concern may explain Newton's reference to the Book of Luke as speaking of the Passover feast (a Jewish Spring festival) having two Sabbaths, which Newton then links with the two Sundays of Easter.[121] It is not clear which passage Newton is in fact using here. He has spoken of a text from Matthew 12 just before the reference to Luke. In the paragraph following, Newton refers to a Sabbath scene from the Gospel books where Jesus healed a man - the scene in Matthew 12 and Luke 6. In these two chapters there is indeed information concerning Jesus and the Sabbath Day observance required by the Pharisees (a Jewish religious party), but this is not said to be the Passover time. The stories of controversy about the use of the Sabbath in these texts do lead onto the healing of a sick man on the Sabbath; but the exact combination of ideas cited by Newton are not to be found in them. Newton appears to be constructing an over-arching argument about the Sabbath Day from a somewhat vague recollection of actual biblical material.

Newton's use of passages from ancient language versions of the Bible, then, is governed in good part by his concern to show that those texts support his own views. Sometimes a collage effect develops in which different passages are woven together to produce a Newtonian interpretation of Scripture. Newton places in his commentary indications of his views on the unitary nature of the deity and of his belief that the Christian doctrine of the Trinity is a corruption of

---

[120]   Newton, *Observations*, p. 248 [239].

[121]   Newton, *Observations*, pp. 189-191 [153-4].

religious truth promulgated by bishops - above all the Bishop of Rome - for their own glorification. In his treatment of the Beast, for instance, Newton claims that the mark of the Beast is ✠✠✠ and that the name of the Beast is Lateinos.[122] These are additions to the text, as far as current critical editions go, but they indicate to an alert reader that the Beast, the agent of the devil, is none other than the Trinitarian Church, typified by the Latin (Roman) community.

Some important methodological and technical considerations on the preparation and use of this edition of the *Observations on the Prophecies*.

The aim of this edition is to make Newton's *Observations* more digestible to non-specialists, yet provide the reader with the text, as far as possible, as it was first printed in 1733 (*Observations upon the Prophecies of Daniel and the Apocalypse of St John. In Two Parts* (London, J. Darby and T. Browne in Bartholomew-Close). I have thus preserved the 1733 edition's text format, abbreviated references, spelling variations and inconsistencies, grammar, its extensive use of italics for quotations, capital lettering and its ae – æ or in italics *æ* - ligatures (to avoid confusion I have not used 'oe' ligatures). I have inserted nothing into the main body of the text except superscript asterisks to indicate glossary references, and transliterations of the few Greek and Hebrew passages (on which see below). Where there appear to be typographical errors and omissions, I have corrected or supplied them in the footnotes inside square brackets.

I have departed from a major alteration made by William Whitla in his edition of 1922, and have retained the numerous and often lengthy Latin sections in the main body of the text; but I have also provided translations in the footnotes. This decision was based upon a fact evident to any reader of the 1733 edition,

---

[122]   Newton, *Observations*, p. 278 [284]. Lateinos originally given in Greek characters.

namely that the Latin sections, taken from a variety of historical sources, are integral to Newton's account.

Newton's use of ancient languages - Hebrew and Greek - was slight. Nevertheless, the few words and phrases in those languages often refer to biblical matters, sometimes of some importance. Hence Mary Mills (above) has provided some insightful comments on Newton's use of ancient languages and his approach to biblical studies. For most readers, however, these languages and their alphabets will be unknown, and so those words and phrases in Greek and Hebrew have been transliterated by Mary Mills in order to render them at least phonetically intelligible to most readers. In the footnotes, she has also provided translations of the transliterated passages. Where Newton himself has translated the Greek or Hebrew within the main text, I have signalled those words originally given in Greek or Hebrew characters.

Where Newton has cited authorities in the text itself, I have left them as found. His marginal notes, however, I have incorporated into the text as footnote references, as close to their original position on the page as possible (marginal notes often have the drawback of imprecision because they do not always refer the reader to any precise point in the text). Where Newton signalled notes in the text by the use of a, b, c, etc., their position remains unchanged but converted to the conventional numerical form (the original letter signals are given in the footnotes). Where his footnotes are very long and important to the comprehension of the text, I have left them in the main body of the text using a smaller font (as on *Observations* pp. 177-8 [137-8]). In the footnotes, my translations and/or comments are distinguished from those of Newton's by being contained inside square brackets (inside which I have used ordinary parentheses where necessary). Therefore anything outside of the square brackets represents the original text of the 1733 edition. But note that the square brackets in Newton's main text are all his own.

Newton's *Observations* are densely populated with references to the biblical past, the Church Fathers, various ecclesiastical figures, historians of the Church, ancient and medieval place names and several different calendar conventions. For the non-specialist, therefore, reading the *Observations* is a potential nightmare of unfamiliar terms. In order to restrict the glossary to a manageable size, for the most part I have decided not to list biblical characters, most ancient figures or geograpical locations. Some readers will, therefore, need to have recourse to an historical atlas and dictionaries of the Bible, the Church and the ancient world.

The main aim of this edition is to enable the reader to understand Newton's prophetic thought in the context of his own period. I have, therefore, provided glossary notes mainly on the many historical and contemporary sources he cited to support his views, so providing some indication of the sources drawn upon by biblical scholars of his period. The Glossary also contains references to medieval religious figures, sects and various other terms possibly new to the non-specialist. Importantly, the Glossary contains notes on the several different calendar conventions used by Newton. The existence of glossary references I have signalled by the use of a superscript asterisk (*).

Pagination throughout this edition is mine; although where I have quoted Newton in the Introduction, I have provided page references (in square brackets) to the 1733 edition of his *Observations*.

S. J. Barnett,
London, August 1998.

OBSERVATIONS UPON THE PROPHECIES OF DANIEL, AND THE APOCALYPSE OF ST. JOHN.

In Two Parts

By Sir Isaac Newton.

LONDON

Printed by J. Darby and T. Browne in Bartholomew-Close.

MDCCXXXIII

To the Right Honourable PETER Lord KING,

Baron of *Ockham*,

Lord High Chancellor of *Great Britain*.

My Lord,

I SHALL *make no Apology for addressing the following sheets to Your Lordship, who lived in a long intercourse of Friendship with the Author; and, like him, amidst occupations of a different nature, made Religion your voluntary Study; and in all your Enquiries and Actions, have shewn the same inflexible Adherence to Truth and Virtue.*

I shall always reckon it one of the Advantages of my Relation to Sir Isaac Newton, that it affords me an opportunity of making this publick acknowledgment of the unfeigned Respect of, My Lord, Your Lordship's most obedient, and most humble Servant, Benj. Smith.

Table of Contents.

Part I

OBSERVATIONS ON THE PROPHECIES OF DANIEL

66

Part II

OBSERVATIONS UPON THE APOCALYPSE OF ST. JOHN

PART I

OBSERVATIONS UPON THE PROPHECIES OF DANIEL

CHAPTER I

Introduction concerning the Compilers of the books of the Old Testament.

When *Manasses** set up a carved image in the house of the Lord, and built altars in the two courts of the house, to all the host of Heaven, and us'd inchantments and witchcraft, and familiar spirits, and for his great wickedness was invaded by the army of *Asserhadon*, king of *Assyria*, and carried captive to *Babylon*; the book of the Law* was lost until the eighteenth year of his grandson *Josiah*.[1] Then Hilkiah the High Priest, upon repairing to the Temple, found it there: and the king lamented that their fathers had not done after the words of the book, and commanded that it should be read to the people, and caused the people to renew the holy covenant with God. This is the book of the Law now extant.[2]

When *Shishak** came out of Eygpt and spoil'd the Temple, and brought *Judah* into subjection to the monarchy of *Eygpt*, (which was in the fifth year of *Rehoboam*)

---

[1]   2 Chron. xxxiii. 5-7.

[2]   2 Chron. xxiv.

the Jews continued under great troubles for about twenty years; being *without the true God, and without a teaching priest, and without Law: and in those times there was no peace to him that went out, nor to him that came in, but great vexations were upon all the inhabitants of the countries, and nation was destroyed of nation, and city of city, for God did vex them with all adversity.*[3] But when *Shishak* was dead, and *Egypt* fell into troubles, *Judah* had quiet ten years; and in that time *Asa* built fenced cities in *Judah*, and got up an army of 580000 men, with which, in the 15th year of his reign, he met and overcame *Zerah* the *Ethiopian*, who had conquered *Egypt* and *Lybia*, and *Troglodytica*, and came out with an army of 1000000 *Lybians* and *Ethiopians*, to recover the countries conquered by *Sesac*.[4] And after this victory *Asa* dethroned his mother for idolatry, and he renewed the Altar, and brought new vessels of gold and silver into the Temple; and he and the people entered into a new covenant to seek the Lord God of their fathers, upon pain of death to those who worshipped other Gods; and his son *Jehosaphat* took away the high places, and in the third year of his reign sent home some of his Princes, and of the Priests and Levites, to teach in the cities of *Judah*: and they had the book of Law with them, and went about throughout all the cities of *Judah*, and taught the people. This is the book of the Law which was afterwards lost in the reign of *Josiah*, and therefore it was written before the third year of *Jehosaphat*.[5]

The same book of the Law was preserved and handed down to posterity by the *Samaritans*, and therefore was received by the ten Tribes before their captivity. For when the ten Tribes were captivated, a Priest of the captivity was sent back to *Bethel*, by order of the King of *Assyria*, to instruct the new inhabitants of *Samaria, in the manner of the God of the land*; and the *Samaritans* had the *Pentateuch** from this

---

[3]   2 Chron. xii. 2-4, 8-9. & xv. 3, 5-6.

[4]   2 Chron. 1, 6-9, 12.

[5]   2 Chron. xv. 3, 12-13, 16, 18.

Priest, as containing the law or *Manner of the God of the land*, which he was to teach them.[6] For they persevered in the religion which he had taught them, joining with it the worship of their own Gods; and by persevering in what they had been taught, they preserved this book of their Law in the original character of the *Hebrews*, while the two Tribes, after their return from Babylon, changed the character to that of the *Chaldees*, which they had learned at *Babylon*.[7]

And since the *Pentateuch* was received as the book of the Law, both by the two Tribes and by the ten Tribes, it follows that they received it before they became divided into two Kingdoms. For after the division, they received not laws from one another, but continued at variance. *Judah* could not reclaim *Israel* from the sin of *Jeroboam*, and *Israel* could not bring *Judah* to it. The *Pentateuch* therefore was the book of the Law in the days of *David* and *Solomon*. The affairs of the Tabernacle and Temple were ordered by *David* and *Solomon*, according to the Law of this book; and *David* in the 78th Psalm, admonishing the people to give ear to the Law of God, means the Law of this book. For in describing how their forefathers kept it not, he quotes many historical things out of the books of *Exodus* and *Numbers*.

The race of the Kings of *Edom*, before there reigned any King over *Israel*, is set down in the book of *Genesis*,[8] and therefore that book was not written entirely in the form now extant, before the reign of *Saul*. The writer set down the race of those Kings till his own time, and therefore wrote before *David* conquered *Edom*. The *Pentateuch* is composed of the Law and the history of God's people together, and the history hath been collected from several books, such as were the history of the Creation composed by *Moses*, *Gen.* ii. 4. the book of the generations of *Adam, Gen.* v. i and the book of the wars of the Lord, *Num.* xxi. 14. This book of wars contained

---

[6]   2 Kings xvii. 27-8, 32-3.

[7]   2 Kings 34, 41.

[8]   Gen. xxxvi 31.

what was done at the Red-sea, and in the journeying of *Israel* thro' the Wilderness, and therefore was begun by *Moses*. And *Joshua* might carry it to the conquest of *Canaan*. For *Joshua* wrote some things in the book of the Law of God, *Josh.* xxiv. 26 and therefore might write his own wars in the book of wars, those being the principal wars of God. These were publick books, and therefore not written without the authority of *Moses* and *Joshua*. And *Samuel* had leisure in the reign of *Saul*, to put them into the form of the books of *Moses* and *Joshua* now extant, inserting into the book of *Genesis*, the race of Kings of *Edom*, until there reigned a King in *Israel*.

The book of the *Judges* is a continued history of the *Judges* down to the death of the *Sampson*, and therefore was compiled after his death, out of the Acts of the *Judges*. Several things in this book are said to be done *when there was no King in* Israel, *Judg.* xvii. 6. xviii. 1. xix. 1. xxi. 25. and therefore this book was written after the beginning of the reign of *Saul*. When it was written, the *Jebusites* dwelt in *Jerusalem*, Jud. i. 21. and therefore it was written before the eighth year of *David*, 2 *Sam.* v. 8. and 1 *Chron.* xi. 6. The books of *Moses, Joshua,* and *Judges,* contain one continued history, down from the Creation to the death of *Sampson*. Where the *Pentateuch* ends, the book of *Joshua* begins; and where the book of *Joshua* ends, the book of *Judges* begins. Therefore all these books have been composed out of the writings of *Moses, Joshua,* and other records, by one and the same hand, after the beginning of the reign of *Saul*, and before the eighth year of *David*. And *Samuel* was a sacred writer, 1 *Sam.* x. 25. acquainted with the history of *Moses* and the *Judges*, 1 *Sam.* xii. 8-12. and had the leisure in the reign of *Saul*, and suffcent authority to compose these books. He was a Prophet, and judged *Israel* all the days of his life, and was in the greatest esteem with the people; and the Law by which he was to judge the people was not to be published by less authority than his own, the Law-maker being not inferior to the judge. And the book of *Jasher*,* which is quoted in the book of *Joshua*, *Josh.* x. 13. was in being at the death of *Saul*, 2 *Sam.* i. 18.

At the dedication of the Temple of *Solomon*, when the Ark was brought into the most holy place, there was nothing in it but the two tables, 1 *Kings* viii. 9 and therefore when the *Philistines* took the Ark, they took out of it the book of the Law, and the golden pot of Manna, and *Aaron's* Rod. And this and other losses in the desolation of *Israel*, by the conquering *Philistines*, might give occasion to *Samuel*, after some respite from those enemies, to recollect the scattered writings of *Moses* and *Joshua*, and the records of the Patriarchs and Judges, and compose them in the form now extant.

The book of *Ruth* is a history of things done in the days of the *Judges*, and may be looked upon as an addition to the books of the *Judges*, written by the same author, and at the same time. For it was written after the birth of *David*, *Ruth* iv. 17, 22. and not long after, because the history of *Boaz* and *Ruth*, the great grandfather and great grandmother of *David*, and that of their contemporaries, could not well be remembered above two or three generations. And since this book derives the genealogy of *David* from *Boaz* and *Ruth*, and omits *David's* elder brothers and his sons; it was written in honour of *David*, after he was anointed King by *Samuel*, and before he had children in *Hebron*, and by consequence in the reign of *Saul*. It proceeds not to the history of *David*, and therefore seems to have been written presently after he was anointed. They judge well therefore those who ascribe to *Samuel* the books of *Joshua*, *Judges*, and *Ruth*.

Samuel is also reputed the author of the first book of *Samuel*, till the time of his death. The two books of *Samuel* cite no authors, and therefore seem to be originals. They begin with his genealogy, birth and education, and might be written partly in his life-time by himself or his disciples the prophets at *Naioth* in *Ramah*, 1 *Sam.* xix. 18-20. and partly after his death by the same disciples.

The books of the *Kings* cite other authors, as the book of the Acts of *Solomon*, the book of the *Chronicles* of the Kings of *Israel*, and the book of the *Chronicles* of the Kings of *Judah*. The books of the *Chronicles* cite the book of *Samuel* the Seer, the book of *Nathan* the Prophet, and the book of *Gad* the Seer, for the Acts of David; the book of *Nathan* the Prophet, the Prophecy of *Ahijah* the *Shilonite*, and the visions of *Iddo* the Seer, for the Acts of *Solomon*; the book of *Shemajah* the Prophet, and the book of *Iddo* the Seer concerning genealogies, for the Acts of *Rehoboam* and *Abijab*; the book of the Kings of *Judah* and *Israel* for the Acts of *Asa, Joash, Amaziah, Jotham, Ahaz, Hezekiah, Manesseh*, and *Josiah*; the book of *Hanani* the Seer, for the Acts of *Jehosophat*; and the visions of *Isaiah* for the Acts of *Uzziah* and *Hezekiah*. These books were therefore collected out of the historical writings of the antient Seers and Prophets. And because the books of the *Kings* and *Chronicles* quote one another, they were written at one and the same time. And this time was after the return from the *Babylonian* captivity, because they bring down the history of *Judah*, and the genealogies of the Kings of *Judah*, and of the High Priests, to that captivity. The book of *Ezra* was originally a part of the book of the *Chronicles*, and has been divided from it. For it begins with the last verses of the books of the *Chronicles*, and the first book of *Esdras* begins with the two last chapters thereof. *Ezra* was therefore the compiler of the books of *Kings* and *Chronicles*, and brought down the history to his own times. He was a ready scribe in the Law of God; and for assisting him in this work *Nehemias* founded a library, and *gathered together the acts of the kings and the Prophets, and of David, and the Epistles of the Kings concerning the holy gifts*, 2 *Macaab*. ii. 13. By the Acts of *David* I understand here the two books of *Samuel*, or at least the second book. Out of the Acts of the Kings, written from time to time by the Prophets, he compos'd the books of the Kings of *Judah*, and *Israel*, and the *Chronicles* of the Kings of *Israel*. And in doing thus he joined those Acts together, in due order of time, copying the very words of the authors, as is manifest from hence, that the books of the *Kings* and *Chronicles* frequently agree with one another in words for many sentences together. Where they agree in sense, there they agree in words also.

So the Prophecies of *Isaiah*, written at several times, he has collected into one body. And the like he did for those of *Jeremiah*, and the rest of the Prophets down to the days of the second Temple. The book of *Jonah* is the history of *Jonah* written by another hand. The book of *Daniel* is a collection of papers written at several times. The six last chapters contain Prophecies written at several times by *David* himself: the six first are a collection of historical papers written by others. The fourth chapter is a decree of *Nebuchadnezzar*. The first chapter was written after *Daniel's* death: for the author saith, that *Daniel* continued to the first year of *Cyrus*; that is, to his first year over the *Persians* and *Medes*, and third year over *Babylon*. And, for the same reason, the fifth and sixth chapters were also written after his death. For they end with these words: *So this* Daniel *prospered in the reign of* Darius, *and in the reign of* Cyrus *the Persian*. Yet these words might be added by the collector of the papers, whom I take to be *Ezra*.

The Psalms composed by *Moses*, *David*, and others, seem to have been also collected by *Ezra* into one volume. I reckon him to be the collector, because in this collection I meet with Psalms as late as the *Babylonian* captivity, but with none later.

After these things *Antiochus Epiphanes** spoiled the Temple, commanded the *Jews* to forsake the Law upon pain of death, and caused the sacred books to be burnt wherever they could be found: and in these troubles the book of the *Chronicles* of the Kings of *Israel* was entirely lost. But upon recovering from this oppression, *Judas Maccabaeus* gathered together all those writings that were to be met with, 2 *Maccab*. ii. 14. and in reducing them into order, part of the Prophecies of *Isaiah*, or some other Prophet, have been added to the end of the Prophecies of *Zechariah*; and the book of *Ezra* has been separated from the book of the *Chronicles*, and set together in two different orders; in one order in the book of *Ezra*, received into the Canon, and in another order into the first book of *Esdras*.

After the *Roman* captivity, the *Jews* for preserving their traditions, put them in writing in their *Talmud*; and for preserving their scriptures, agreed upon an Edition, and pointed it, and counted the letters of every sort in every book: and by preserving only this Edition, the antienter various lections, except what can be discovered by means of the *Septuagint* Version, are now lost; and such marginal notes, or other corruptions, as by the errors of the transcribers, before this Edition was made, had crept into the text, are now scarce to be corrected.

The *Jews* before the *Roman* captivity, distinguished the sacred books into the Law, the Prophets, and the *Hagiographa*, or holy writings; and read only the Law and the Prophets in their Synagogues. And Christ and his Apostles laid the stress of religion upon the Law and the Prophets, *Matt.* vii. 12. xxii. 4. Luke xvi. 16, 29 31. xxiv. 44. *Acts* xxiv. 14. xxvi. 22. *Rom.* iii. 21. By the *hagiographa* they meant the historical books called *Joshua, Judges, Ruth, Samuel, Kings, Chronicles, Ezra, Nehemiah*, and *Esther*, the book of *Job*, the *Psalms*, the books of *Solomon*, and the *Lamentations*. The *Samaritans* read only the *Pentateuch*: and when *Jehosaphat* sent men to teach in the cities, they had with them only the book of the Law; for the Prophecies now extant were not then written. And upon the return from the *Babylonian* captivity, *Ezra* read only the book of the Law to the people, from morning to noon, on the first day of the seventh month; and from day to day in the feast of the Tabernacles: for he had not yet collected the writings of the Prophets into the volume now extant; but instituted the reading of them after the collection was made. By reading the Law and the Prophets in the Synagogues, those books have been kept freer from corruption than the *Hagiographa*.

In the infancy of the nation of Israel, when God had given them a Law, and made a covenant with them to be their God if they would keep his commandments, he sent Prophets to reclaim them, as often as they revolted to the worship of other Gods: and upon their returning to him, they sometimes renewed the covenant which they had broken. These Prophets he continued to send till the days of *Ezra*: but after their Prophecies were read in the Synagogues, those Prophecies were thought sufficient. For if the people would not hear *Moses* and the old Prophets, they would hear no new ones, *no not tho they should rise from the dead.* At length when a new truth was to be preached to the *Gentiles*, namely, *that Jesus was the Christ*, God sent new Prophets and Teachers: but after their writings were also received and read in the Synagogues of the Christians, Prophecy ceased a second time. We have *Moses*, the Prophets, and Apostles, and the words of Christ himself; and if we will not hear them, we shall be more inexcusable than the *Jews*. For the prophets and Apostles have foretold, that as *Israel* often revolted and brake the covenant, and upon repentance renewed it; so there should be a falling away among the Christians, soon after the days of the Apostles; and that in the latter days God would destroy the impenitent revolters, and make a new covenant with his people. And the giving ear to the Prophets is a fundamental character of the true Church. For God has so ordered the Prophecies, that in the latter days *the wise may understand, but the wicked shall do wickedly, and none of the wicked shall understand, Dan.* xii. 9-10. The authority of Emperors, Kings, and Princes, is human, The authority of Councils, Synods, Bishops, and Presbyters, is human. The authority of the Prophets is divine, and comprehends the sum of religion, reckoning *Moses* and the Apostles among the Prophets; and *if an Angel from Heaven preach any other gospel*, than what they have delivered, *let him be accursed.* Their writings contain the covenant between God and his people, with instructions for keeping this covenant; instances of God's judgement upon them that break it: and predictions of things to come. While the people of God keep the covenant, they continue to be his people: when they break it they cease to be his people or church, and become *the Synagogue of Satan, who say they are* Jews *and are not*. And no power on earth is authorized to alter this covenant.

The predictions of things to come relate to the state of the Church in all ages: and amongst the old Prophets, *Daniel* is most distinct in order of time, and easiest to be understood: and therefore in those things which relate to the last times, he must be made the key to the rest.

CHAPTER II

Of the Prophetic Language.

For understanding the Prophecies, we are, in the first place, to acquaint our-selves with the figurative language of the Prophets, This language is taken from the analogy between the world natural, and an empire or kingdom considered as a world politic.

Accordingly, the whole world natural consisting of heaven and earth, signifies the whole world politic, consisting of thrones and people, or so much of it as is considered in the Pophecy: and the things in that world signify the analogous things in this. For the heavens, and the things therein, signify thrones and dignities, and those who enjoy them; and the earth, with the things thereon, the inferior people; and the lowest parts of the earth, called *Hades* or Hell, the lowest or most miserable part of them. Whence ascending towards heaven, and descending to the earth, are put for rising and falling in power and honour: rising out of the earth, or waters, and falling into them, for the rising up to any dignity or dominion, out of the inferior state of the people, or falling down from the same into that inferior state; descending into the lower parts of the earth, for descending to a very low and unhappy estate; speaking with a faint voice out of a dust, for being in a weak and low condition; moving from one place to another, for translation from one office, dignity, or dominion, to another; great earthquakes, and the shaking of heaven and earth, for the shaking of kingdoms, so as to distract or overthrow them; the creating of a new heaven and earth, and the passing away of an old one, or the beginning and end of the world, for the rise and ruin of the body politic signified thereby.

In the heavens, the Sun and Moon are, by interpreters of dreams, put for the persons of Kings and Queens; but in sacred Prophecy, which regards not single persons, the Sun is put for the whole species and race of Kings, in the kingdom or kingdoms of the world politic, shining with regal power and glory; the Moon for the body of the common people, considered as the King's wife; the Stars for for the subordinate Princes and great men, or for Bishops and Rulers of the people of God, when the Sun is Christ; light for the glory, truth, and knowledge, wherewith great and good men shine and illuminate others; darkness for obscurity of condition, and for error, blindness and ignorance; darkning, smiting, or setting of the Sun, Moon, and Stars, for the ceasing of a kingdom, or for the desolation thereof, proportional to the darkness; darkning the Sun, turning the Moon into blood, and falling of the Stars, for the same; new Moons for the return of a dispersed people into a body politic or ecclesiastic.

Fire and meteors refer to both heaven and earth, and signify as follows; burning anything with fire, is put for the consuming thereof by war; a conflagration of the earth, or turning a country into a lake of fire, for the consumption of a kingdom by war; the being in a furnace, for the being in slavery under another nation; the ascending up of the smoke of any burning thing for ever and ever, for the continuation of conquered people under the misery of perpetual subjection and slavery; the scorching heat of the sun, for vexatious wars, persecutions and troubles inflicted by the King; riding on the clouds, for reigning over much people; covering the sun with a cloud, or with smoke, for the oppression of the King by the armies of an enemy; tempestuous winds, or the motion of the clouds, for wars; thunder, or the voice of a cloud, for the voice of a multitude; a storm of thunder, lightning, hail, and overflowing rain, for a tempest of war descending from the heavens and clouds politic on the heads of their enemies; rain, if not immoderate, and dew and living water, for the graces and doctrines of the Spirit; and the defect of rain, for spiritual barrenness.

In the earth, the dry land and congregated waters, as a sea, a river, a flood, are put for the people of several regions, nations, and dominions; embittering of waters, for great affliction of the people by war and persecution; turing things into blood, for the mystical death of the bodies politic, that is for their dissolution; the overflowing of a sea or river, for the invasion of the earth politic, by the people of the waters; drying up of waters, for the conquest of their regions by the earth, fountains of water for cities, the permanent heads of rivers politic; mountains and islands, for the cities of the earth and sea politic, with the territories and dominions belonging to those cities; dens and rocks of mountains, for the temples of cities; the hiding of men in those dens and rocks, for the shutting up of idols in their temples; houses and ships, for families, assemblies, and towns, in the earth and sea politic; and a navy of ships of war, for an army of that kingdom that is signified by the sea.

Animals also and vegetables are put for the people of several regions and conditions; and particularly, trees, herbs, and land animals, for the people of the earth politic: flags, reeds, and fishes, for those of the waters politic; birds and insects, for those of the politic heaven and earth; a forest for a kingdom; and wilderness for a desolate and thin people.

If the world politic, considered in prophecy, consists of many kingdoms, they are represented by as many parts of the world natural; as the noblest by the celestial frame, and then the Moon and Clouds are put for the common people; the less noble, by the earth, sea, and rivers, and by the animals or vegetables, or buildings therein; and then the greater and more powerful animals and taller trees, are put for Kings, Princes, and Nobles. And because the whole kingdom is the body politic of the King, therefore the Sun, or a Tree, or a Beast, or Bird, or a Man, whereby the King is represented, is put in a large signification for the whole kingdom; and several animals, as a Lion, a Bear, a Leopard, a Goat, according to their qualities, are put for several kingdoms and bodies politic; and sacrificing of beasts, for slaughtering and conquering of kingdoms; and friendship between beasts, for peace between kingdoms. Yet sometimes vegetable and animals are by certain epithets or circumstances, extended to other significations; as a Tree, when called the *tree of life* or *of knowledge*; and a Beast, when called *the old serpent*, or worshipped.

When a Beast or man is put for a kingdom, his parts and qualities are put for the analogous parts and qualities of the kingdom; as the head of a Beast, for the great men who precede and govern; the tail for the inferior people, who follow and are governed; the heads, if more than one, for the number of capital parts, or dynasties, or dominions in the kingdom, whether collateral or successive, with respect to the civil government; the horns on any head, for the number of kingdoms in that head, with respect to military power, seeing for understanding, and the eyes of men of understanding and policy, and in matters of religion for Episkopoi,[1] Bishops; speaking, for making laws; the mouth, for a law-giver, whether civil or sacred; the loudness of the voice, for might and power; the faintness thereof, for weakness; eating and drinking, for acquiring what is signified by the things eaten and drank; the hairs of a beast, or man, and the feathers of a bird, for people; the wings for the number of kingdoms represented by the beast; the arm of a man, for his power, or for any people wherein his strength and power consists; his feet, for the lowest of the people, or for the latter end of the kingdom; the feet, nails, and teeth of beasts of prey, for armies and squadrons of armies; the bones, for strength, and for fortified places; the flesh, for riches and possessions; and the days of their acting, for years; and when a tree is put for a kingdom, its branches, leaves and fruit, signify as do the wings, feathers, and food or a bird or beast.

---

[1]   [Episkopoi originally given in Greek characters.]

When a man is taken in a mystical sense, his qualities are often signified by his actions, and by the circumstances of things about him. So a Ruler is signified by his riding on a beast; a Warrior and Conqueror, by his having a sword and bow; a potent man, by his gigantic stature; a Judge, by weights and measures; a sentence of absolution, or condemnation, by a white or a black stone; a new dignity, by a new name; moral or civil qualifications, by garments; honour and glory, by splendid apparel; royal dignity, by purple or scarlet, or by a crown; righteousness, by white and clean robes; wickedness, by spotted and filthy garments; affliction, mourning, and humiliation, by clothing in sackcloth; dishonour, shame, and want of good works, by nakedness; error and misery, by drinking a cup of his or her wine that causeth it; propagating any religion for gain, by exercising traffick and merchandize with that people whose religion it is; worshipping or serving the false Gods of any nation, by committing adultery with their princes, or by worshipping them; a Council of a Kingdom, by its image; idolatry, by blasphemy; overthrow in war, by a wound of a man or beast; a durable plague of war, by a sore or pain; the affliction or persecution which a people suffers in labouring to bring forth a new kingdom, by the pain of a woman in labour to bring forth a manchild; the dissolution of a body politic or ecclesiastic, by the death of a man or beast; and the revival of a dissolved dominion, by the resurrection of the dead.

CHAPTER III

Of the vision of the Image composed of four Metals.

The Prophecies of *Daniel* are all of them related to one another, as if they were but several parts of one general Prophecy, given at several times. The first is the easiest to be understood, and every following Prophecy adds something new to the former. The first was given in a dream to *Nebuchadnezzar*, King of *Babylon*, in the second year of this reign; but the King forgetting his dream, it was given again to *Daniel* in a dream, and by him revealed to the King. And thereby, *Daniel* presently became famous for wisdom, and revealing of secrets: insomuch that *Ezekiel* his contemporary, in the nineteenth year of *Nebuchadnezzar, spake thus of him to the King of Tyre: Behold*, saith he, *thou art wiser than* Daniel, *there is no secret that they can hide from thee*, Ezek. xxviii. 3. And the same *Ezekiel*, in another place, joins *Daniel* with *Noah* and *Job*, as most high in the favour of God, *Ezek.* xiiv. 14, 16, 18, 20. And in the last year of *Belshazzar*, the queen mother said of him to the King: *Behold there is a man in thy kingdom, in whom is the spirit of the holy gods; and in the days of thy father, light and understanding and wisdom, like the wisdom of the gods, was found in him; whom the king* Nebuchadnezzar *thy father, the king, I say, thy father made master of the magicians, astrologers,* Chaldeans *and soothayers: forasmuch as an excellent spirit, and knowledge, and understanding, interpreting of dreams, and shewing of hard sentences, and dissolving of doubts, were found in the same* Daniel, *whom the king named* Belteshazzar, Dan. v. 11-12. *Daniel* was in the greatest credit amongst the *Jews*, till the reign of the *Roman* Emperor *Hadrian*: and to reject his Prophecies, is to reject the Christian religion, for this religion is founded upon his Prophecy concerning the *Messiah*.

Now in this vision of the Image composed of four metals, the foundation of all *Daniels's* Prophecies is laid. It represents a body of four great nations, which should reign over the earth successively, *viz.* the people of *Babylonia*, the *Persians*, the *Greeks*, and the *Romans*. And by a stone cut out without hands, which fell upon the feet of the Image, and brake all the four Metals to pieces, *and became a great mountain, and filled the whole earth*; it further represents that a new kingdom should arise, after the four, and conquer all those nations, and grow very great, and last to the end of all ages.

The head of the Image was of gold, and signifies the nations of *Babylonia*, who reigned first, as *Daniel* himself interprets. *Thou art this head of gold*, saith he to *Nebuchadnezzar*. These nations reigned till *Cyrus* conquered *Babylon*, and within a few months after that conquest revolted to the *Persians*, and set them up above the *Medes*. The breast and arms of the Image were of silver, and represent the *Persians* who reigned next. The belly and thighs of the Image were of brass, and represent *Greeks*, who, under the dominion of *Alexander* the great, conquered the *Persians*, and reigned next after them. The legs were of iron, and represent the *Romans* who reigned next after the Greeks, and began to conquer them in the eighth year of Antiochus *Epiphanes*.* For in that year they conquered *Perseus* King of *Macedon*, the fundamental kingdom of the *Greeks*; and from thence forward grew into a mighty empire, and reigned with great power till the days of *Theodosius* the great. Then by the incursion of many northern nations, they brake into many smaller kingdoms, which are represented by the feet and toes of the Image, composed part of iron, and part of clay. For then, saith *Daniel, the kingdom shall be divided and there shall be in it of the strength of iron, but they shall not cleave one to another.*

And in the days of these Kings, saith *Daniel, shall the God of heaven set up a kingdom which shall never be destroyed: and the kingdom shall not be left to other people; but it shall break in pieces, and consume all these kingdoms, and it shall stand for ever. Forasmuch as thou sawest that the stone was cut out of the mountains without hands, and that it brake in pieces the iron, the brass, the clay, the silver and the gold.*[1]

---

[1]   Chap. ii. 41, &c.

CHAPTER IV

Of the vision of the four Beasts.

In the next vision, which is of the four Beasts, the Prophecy of the four Empires is repeated, with several new additions; such as are the two wings of the Lion, the three ribs in the mouth of the Bear, the four wings and four heads of the Leopard, the eleven[1] horns of the fourth Beast, the son of man coming in the clouds of Heaven, to the Antient of Days sitting in judgment.

The first Beast was like a lion, and had eagle's wings to denote the kingdoms of *Babylonia* and *Media*, which overthrew the *Assyrian* Empire, and divided it between them, and thereby became considerable, and grew into great Empires. In the former Prophecy, the Empire of *Babylonia* was represented by the head of gold; in this both Empires are represented together by the two wings of the lion. *And I beheld,* saith *Daniel, till the wings thereof were pluckt, and it was lifted up from the earth, and made to stand upon the feet as a man, and a man's heart* was given to it, that is, till it was humbled and subdued, and made to know its human state.[2]

The Second Beast was like a bear, and represents the Empire, which reigned next after the *Babylonians*, that is, the Empire of the *Persians*. Thy kingdom is divided, or broken, saith *Daniel* to the last king of *Babylon, and given to the* Medes *and* Persians, *Dan.* v. 28. This Beast *raised itself up on one side*; the *Persians* being

---

[1]   [In Daniel, the fourth beast has ten horns (Dan. 7:7), but three are uprooted and replaced by a little horn (Dan. 7:8), thus Newton can speak of a total of eleven horns.]

[2]   Chap. vii. 4.

88

under the *Medes* at the fall of *Babylon*, but presently rising up above them. *And it had three ribs in the mouth of it, between the teeth of it,* to signify the kingdoms of *Sardes, Babylon,* and *Egypt,* which were conquered by it, but did not belong to its proper body. And it devoured much flesh, the riches of those three kingdoms.[3]

The third Beast was the kingdom which succeeded the *Persian*; and this was the empire of the *Greeks, Dan.* viii. 6-7, 20-21. It was *like a Leopard,* to signify its fierceness; and had four heads and four wings, to signify that it should become divided into four kingdoms, *Dan.* viii, 22. for it continued in a monarchical form during the reign of *Alexander* the great, and his brother *Aridæus,* and young sons *Alexander* and *Hercules*; and then brake into four kingdoms by the governors of provinces putting crowns on their own heads, and by mutual consent reigning over their provinces. *Cassander* reigned over *Macedon, Greece,* and *Epirus*; *Lysimachus* over *Thrace* and *Bythnia*; *Ptolemy* over *Egypt, Lybia, Arabia, Coelosyria,* and *Palestine*; and *Seleucus* over *Syria.*

The fourth Beast was the empire which succeeded that of the *Greeks,* and this was the *Roman.* This beast was exceeding dreadful and terrible, and had great iron teeth, and devoured and brake in pieces and stamped the residue with its feet; and such was the *Roman* empire. It was larger, stronger, and more formidable and lasting than any of the former. It conquered the kingdom of *Macedon,* with *Illyricum* and *Epirus,* in the eighth year of *Antiochus Epiphanes,** *Anno Nabonass.** 580; and inherited that of *Pergamus, Anno Nabonass.* 615; and conquered that of *Syria, Anno Nabonass.* 679, and that of *Egypt, Anno Nabonass.* 718. And by these and other conquests it became greater and more terrible than any of the three former Beasts. This Empire continued in its greatness till the reign of *Theodosius* the great; and then brake into ten kingdoms, represented by the ten horns of this beast; and continued in a broken form, till the Antient of days sat in a throne like firery flame, and *the*

---

[3]   Chap. vii. 5.

judgement was set, and the books were opened, and the Beast was slain and his body destroyed, and given to the burning flames; and one like the son of man came with the clouds of heaven, and came to the antient of days,[4] and received dominion over all nations, and judgment was given to the saints of the most high, and the time came that they possessed the kingdom.

I beheld, saith *Daniel, till the Beast was slain, and his body destroyed, and given to the burning flames. As concerning the rest of the Beasts, they had their dominion taken away: yet their lives were prolonged for a season and a time.*[5] And therefore all the four Beasts are still alive, tho the dominion of the three first be taken away. The nations of *Chaldea* and *Assyria* are still the first Beast. Those of *Media* and *Persia* are still the second Beast. Those of *Macedon, Greece* and *Thrace, Asia minor, Syria* and *Egypt,* are still the third. And those of *Europe,* on this side of *Greece,* are still the fourth. Seeing therefore the body of the third Beast is confined to the nations on this side [of] the river *Euphrates,* and the body of the fourth Beast is confined to the nations on this side *Greece;* we are to look for all the four heads of the third Beast, among the nations on this side of the river *Euphrates;* and for all the eleven horns of the fourth Beast, among the nations on this side of *Greece.* And therefore, at the breaking of the *Greek* empire into four kingdoms of the *Greeks,* we include no part of the *Chaldeans, Medes* and *Persians* in those kingdoms, because they belonged to the bodies of the two first Beasts. Nor do we reckon the *Greek* empire seated at Constantinople, among the horns of the fourth Beast, because it belonged to the body of the third.

---

[4]   Chap. vii, 13.

[5]   Chap. vii. 11-12.

CHAPTER V

Of the Kingdoms represented by the feet of the Image composed of iron and clay.

Dacia was a large country bounded on the south by the *Danube*, on the east by the *Euxime* sea, on the north by the river *Neister* and the mountain *Crapac*, and on the west by the river *Tibesis*, or *Teys*, which runs southward into the *Danube* a little above *Belgrade*. It comprehended the countries now called *Transylvania*, *Moldavia*, and *Wallachia*, and the eastern part of the upper Hungary. Its antient inhabitants were called *Getæ* by the *Greeks*, *Daci* by the *Latins*, and *Goths* by themselves. *Alexander* the great attacked them, and *Trajan* conquered them, and reduced their country into a Province of the *Roman* empire: and thereby the propagation of the Gospel among them was much promoted. They were composed of several *Gothic* nations, called *Ostrogoths, Visigoths, Vandals, Gepides, Lombards, Burgundians, Alans*, etc. who all agreed in their manners, and spake the same language, as *Procopius** represents. While they lived under the *Romans*, the *Goths* or *Ostrogoths* were seated in the easter parts of *Dacia*, the *Vandals* in the western part upon the river *Teys*, where the rivers *Maresh* and *Keresh* run into it. The *Visigoths* were between them. The *Gepides*, according to *Jornandes,** were upon the *Vistula*. The *Burgundians*, a *Vandalic* nation, were between the *Vistula* and the southern fountain of the *Boristhenes*, at some distance from the mountain *Crapac* northwards, where *Ptolemy* places them, by the names of *Phrugundiones* and *Burgiones*. The *Alans*, another *Gothic* nation, were between the northern fountain of the *Boristhenes* and the mouth of the river *Tanais*, where *Ptolemy* placeth the mountain *Alanus*, and western side of the *Palus Mæotis*.[1]

These nations continued under the dominion of the *Romans* till the second year of the emperor *Philip*, and then for want of their military pay began to revolt; the *Ostrogoths* setting up a kingdom, which, under their Kings *Ostrogotha, Cniva, Araric, Geperic*, and *Hermanaric*, increased till the year of Christ 376; and then by an incursion of the *Huns* from beyond the *Tanais*, and the death of *Hermanaric*, brake into several smaller kingdoms. *Hunnimund*, the son of *Hermanaric*, became King over the *Ostrogoths*; *Fridigern* over the *Visigoths*; *Winithar*, or *Vinithar*, over a part of the *Goths* called *Gruthungi* by *Ammian*,[2] *Gothunni* by *Claudian*, and *Sarmatæ* and *Scythians* by others: *Athanaric* reign'd over another part of the *Goths* in *Dacia*, called *Thervingi*; *Box* over the *Antes* in *Sarmatia*; and the *Gepides* had also their King. The *Vandals* fled over the *Danube* from *Geberic* in the latter end of the reign of *Constantine* the great, and had seats granted them in *Pannonia* by the emperor, where they lived quietly forty years, *viz.* till the year 377, when several *Gothic* nations flying from the *Hunns* came over the *Danube*, and had seats granted them in *Mæsia* and *Thrace* by the *Greek* emperor *Valens*. But the next year they revolted, called in some *Goths, Alans* and *Hunns*, from beyond the *Danube*, and routed the *Roman* army, slew the emperor *Valens*, and spread themselves into *Greece* and *Pannonia* as far as the *Alps*. In the years 379 and 380 they were checkt by the arms of the Emperors *Gratian* and *Theodosius*, and made a submissive peace; the *Visigoths* and *Thervingi* returned to their seats in *Mæsia* and *Thrace*, the *Hunns* retired over the *Danube*, and the *Alans* and *Gruthingi* obtained seats in *Pannonia*.

About the year 373, or 374, the *Burgundians* rose from their seats upon the *Vistula*, with an army of eighty thousand men to invade *Gallia*; and being opposed,

---

[1]   Procop. 1. i. de Bello Vandalico.

[2]   [Newton meant Ammianus?*]

seated themselves upon the northern side of the *Rhine* over against *Mentz*. In the year 358, a body of the *Salian Franks*, with their King, coming from the river *Sala*, were received into the Empire by the Emperor *Julian*, and seated in *Gallia* between *Brabant* and the *Rhine*: and their *King Mellobaudes* was made *Comes domesticorum*, by the Emperor *Gratian*. *Richomer*, another noble *Salian Frank*, was made *Magister utriusque Militiae*, by *Theodosius*; and A.C. 384, was consul with *Clearchus*. He was a great favourite of *Theodosius*, and accompanied him in his wars against *Eugenius*, but died in the expedition, and left a son called *Theudomir*, who afterwards became King of the *Salian Franks* in *Brabant*. In the time of this war some *Franks* from beyond the *Rhine* invaded *Gallia* under the conduct of *Genobald*, *Marcomir* and *Suno*, but were repulsed by *Stilico*; and *Marcomir* being slain, was succeeded in *Germany* by his son *Pharamond*.

While these nations remained quiet within the *Empire*, subject to the *Romans*, many others continued so beyond the *Danube* till the death of the Emperor *Theodosius*, and then rose up in arms. For *Paulus Diaconus** in his *Historia Miscell. lib.* xiv. speaking of the times next after the death of this emperor, tells us: '*Eodem tempore erant Gothi & aliæ gentes maximae trans Danubium habitantes: ex quibus rationabiliores quatuor sunt, Gothi scilicet, Huisgothi, Gepides & Vandali; & nomen tantum & nihil aliud mutantes. Isti sub Arcadio & Honorio Danubium transeuntes, locati sunt in terra Romanorum: & Gepides quidem, ex postea divisi sunt Longobardi & Avares, villas, quae sunt circa Singidonum & Sirmium, habitavere*':[3] and

---

[3]   [Trans.: 'At that time there were Goths and other powerful tribes dwelling beyond the Danube; of these the more important were four, namely the Goths, Huisogoths, Gepides and the Vandals. The only difference between them being one of name. In the time of Arcadius and Honorius they crossed the Danube and settled in Roman territory, and the Gepides, from whom afterwards the Longobards sprang as distinct peoples, inhabited the districts surrounding Singido and Sermium.']

Procopius* in the beginning of his *Historia Vandalica* writes to the same purpose. Hitherto the Western Empire continued entire, but now brake into many kingdoms.

Theodosius died A.C. 395; and then the *Visigoths*, under the conduct of *Alaric* the successor of *Frigidern*, rose from their seats in *Thrace*, and wasted *Macedon*, *Thessaly*, *Achaia*, *Peloponnesus*, and *Epirus* with fire and sword for five years together; when turning westward, they invaded *Dalmatia*, *Illyricum* and *Pannonia*; and from thence went into *Italy* A.C. 402; and the next year were so beaten at *Pollentia* and *Verona*, by *Stilico* the commander of the forces of the *Western Empire*, that *Claudian* calls the remainder of the forces of *Alaric*, *tanta ex gentes reliquis breves, and Prudentius, Gentem deletam.*[4] Thereupon *Alaric* made peace with the Emperor, being so far humbled, that *Orosius* saith, he did, *pro pace optima & quibuscunque sedibus suppliciter & simpliciter orare.*[5] This peace was ratified by mutual hostages; *Ætius* was sent hostage to *Alaric*; and *Alaric* continued a free Prince in the seats now granted to him.

When *Alaric* took up arms, the nations beyond the *Danube* began to be in motion; and the next winter, between A.C. 395 and 396, a great body of *Hunns*, *Alans*, *Ostrogoths*, *Gepides*, and other northern nations, come over the frozen *Danube*, being invited by *Rufinus*: when their brethren, who had obtained seats within the Empire, took up arms also. *Jerome** calls this great multitude *Hunns*, *Alans*, *Vandals*, *Goths*, *Samaritians*, *Quades*, and *Marcomans*; and saith, that they invaded all places between *Constantinople* and the *Julian Alps*, wasting *Scythia*, *Thrace*, *Macedon*, *Dardania*, *Dacia*, *Thessaly*, *Achaia*, *Epirus*, *Dalmatia*, and all

---

[4]   [Trans.: `the scanty remnants of a mighty nation, and Prudentius calls them an annihilated nation.']

[5]   [Trans.: `humbly and sincerely entreat him for the blessings of peace, and whatever dwelling places seemed good to him.']

Panonnia. The *Suevians* also invaded *Rhætia*; which gave *Alaric* an opportunity of invading *Italy*, as *Claudian* thus mentions.

Non nisi perfidiâ nacti penetrabile tempus,
Irrupere Getæ, nostras dum Rhætia vires
Occupat, atque alio desudant Marte cohortes.[6]

And when *Alaric* went from those parts into *Italy*, some other barbarous nations invaded *Noricum* and *Vindelicia*, as the same Poet *Claudian* writes:

Jam foedera gentes
Exueurunt, Latiique auditâ clade feroces
Vendelicos saltus & Norica rura tenebant.[7]

This was in the years 402 and 403. And among these nations I reckon the *Suevians*, *Quades* and *Marcomans*; for they were all in arms at this time. The *Quades* and *Marcomans* were *Suevian* nations; and they and the *Suevians* came originally from *Bohemia*, and the river *Suevus* or *Sprake* in *Lusatia*; and were now united under one common King called *Ermeric*, who soon after led them into *Gallia*. The *Vandals* and *Alans* might also about this time extend themselves into *Noricum*. *Uldin* also with a great body of *Hunns* passed the *Danube* about the time of *Chrysostom's** banishment, that is A.C. 404, and wasted *Thrace* and *Mæsia*. *Radagaisus*, King of the

---

6 [Trans.: `Only by treachery did the Getae find the opportunity for invasion and burst in upon us, while our men were occupied in Rhætia, and our cohorts struggling in a distant field.']

7 [Trans.: `Already the tribes had discarded their pact, and the Latins, fierce at the noise of that misfortune, were defending the passes of Vindelicia and the fields of Noricum.']

Gruthunni and successor of *Winithar*, inviting over more barbarians from beyond the Danube, invaded *Italy* with an army of above two hundred thousand *Goths*; and within a year or two, A.C. 405 or 406, was overcome by *Stilico* and perished with his army. In this war *Stilico* was assisted with a great body of *Hunns* and *Ostrogoths*, under the conduct of *Uldin* and *Sarus*, who were hired by the Emperor *Honorius*. In all this confusion it was necessary for the *Lombards* in *Pannonia* to arm themselves in their own defence, and assert their liberty, the *Romans* being no longer able to protect them.

And now *Stilico* purposing to make himself Emperor, procured a military prefecture for *Alaric*, and sent him into the East in the service of *Honorius* the *Western* Emperor, committing some *Roman* troops to his conduct to strengthen his army of *Goths*, and promising to follow soon with his own army. His pretence was to recover some regions of *Illyricum*, which the *Eastern* Emperor was accused to detain injuriously from the *Western*; but his secret design was to make himself Emperor, by the assistance of the *Vandals* and their allies: for he himself was a *Vandal*. For facilitating this design, he invited a great body of the barabrous nations to invade the *Western Empire*, while he and *Alaric* invaded the *Eastern*. And these nations under their several Kings, the *Vandals* under *Godegisilus*, the *Alans* in two bodies, the one under *Goar*, the other under *Resplendial*, and the *Suevians*, *Quades*, and the *Marcomans*, under *Ermeric*, marched thro' *Rhœtia* to the side of the Rhine, leaving their seats in *Pannonia* to the *Hunns* and *Ostrogoths*, and joined the *Burgundians* under *Gundicar*, and ruffled the *Franks* in their further march. On the last of December A.C. 406, they passed the *Rhine* at *Ments*, and spread themselves into *Germania* prima and the adjacent regions; and amongst other actions the *Vandals* took *Triers*. Then they advanced into Belgium, and began to waste that country. Whereupon the *Salian Franks* in *Brabant* took up arms, and under the conduct of *Theudomir*, the son of *Ricimer*, or *Richomer*, abovementioned, made so stout a resistance, that they slew almost twenty thousand of the *Vandals*, with their King *Godegesilus*, in battle; the rest escaping only by a party of *Respendial's Alans* which came timely to their assistance.

The *British* soldiers, alarm'd by the rumour of these things, revolted, and set up Tyrants there; first *Marcus*, whom they slew presently; then *Gratian*, whom they slew within four months; and lastly *Constantine*, under whom they invaded *Gallia* A.C. 408, being favoured by *Goar* and *Gundicar*. And *Constantine* having possessed a good part of *Gallia*, created his son *Constans Caesar*, and sent him into *Spain* to order his affairs there, A.C. 409.

In the mean time *Resplendial*, seeing the aforesaid disaster of the *Vandals*, and that *Goar* was gone over to the *Romans*, led his army from the *Rhine*; and together with the *Suevians* and residue of the *Vandals*, went towards *Spain*; the *Franks* in the mean time prosecuting their victory so far as to retake *Triers*, which after they had plundered they left to the *Romans*. The *Barbarians* were at first stopt by the *Pyrenean* mountains, which made them spread themselves into *Aquitain*: but the next year they had the passage betrayed by some soldiers of *Constans*; and entering *Spain* 4 Kal. *Octob.* A.C. 409, they conquered everyone what he could; and at length, A.C. 411, divided their conquests by lot; the *Vandals* obtained *Boetica*, and part of *Gallæcia*; and the *Alans Lusitania* and the *Carthaginian* Province: the Emperor for the sake of peace confirming them in those seats by grant A.C. 413.

The *Roman Franks* obovementioned, having made *Theudomir* their King, began strait after conquest of the *Vandals* to invade their neighbours also. The first they set upon were the *Gauls* of *Brabant*[8]: but meeting with notable resistance, they desired their alliance: and so those *Gauls* fell off from the *Romans*, and made an intimate league with the *Franks* to be as one people, marrying with one another, and conforming to one another's manners, till they became one without distinction. Thus

---

[8] Galli Arborici: *whence the region was named* Arboricbant, *and by contraction Brabant.*

by the access of these *Gauls*, and of the foreign *Franks* also, who afterwards came over the *Rhine*, the *Salian* kingdom soon grew very great and powerful.

Stilico's expedition against the *Greek* Emperor was stopt by the order of *Honorius*; and then *Alaric* come out of *Epirus* into *Noricum*, and requested a sum of money for his service. The senate was inclined to deny him, but by *Stilico's* mediation granted it. But after some time *Stilico* being accused of a traitorous conspiracy with *Alaric*, and slain 10 Kal. *Sept.* A.C. 408; *Alaric* was thereby disappointed of his money, and reputed an enemy to the Empire; he then broke strait into *Italy* with the army he brought out of *Epirus*, and sent to his brother *Adolphus* to follow him with what forces he had in *Pannonia*, which were not great, but yet not to be despised. Thereupon *Honorius* fearing to be shut up in *Rome*, retired to *Ravenna* in October A.C. 408. And from that time *Ravenna* continued to be the seat of the *Western* Emperors. In those days the *Hunns* also invaded *Pannonia*; and seizing the deserted seats of the *Vandals*, *Alans*, and *Goths*, founded a new kingdom there. *Alaric* advancing to *Rome* beseiged it, and 9 Kal. *Sept.* A.C. 410 took it: and afterwards attempting to pass into *Africa*, was shipwrackt. After which *Honorius* made peace with him, and got up an army to send against the Tyrant *Constantine*.

At the same time *Gerontius*, one of *Constantine's captains*, revolted from him, and set up *Maximus* Emperor in *Spain*. Whereupon *Constantine* sent *Edobec*, another of his captains, to draw to his assistance, the *Barbarians* under *Goar* and *Gundicar* in *Gallia*, and supplies of *Franks* and *Alemans* from beyond the *Rhine*; and committed the custody of *Vienne* in *Gallia Narbonensis* to his son *Constans*. *Gerontius* advancing, first slew *Constans* at Vienne, and then began to besiege *Constantine* at *Arles*. But *Honorius* at the same time sending *Constantius* with an army on the same errand, *Gerontius* fled, and *Constantius* continued the siege, strengthened by the access of the greatest part of the soldiers of *Gerontius*. After four months siege, *Edobec* having procured succours, the *Barbarian* Kings at *Ments*, *Goar* and *Gundicar*, constitute *Jovinus* Emperor, and together with him set forward to relieve *Arles*. At their approach *Constantius* retired. They pursued, and he beat them by surprize; but not procuring his victory, the *Barbarians* soon recovered themselves; yet not so as to hinder the fall of the tyrants *Constantine, Jovinus* and *Maximus*. Britain could not be recovered to the Empire, but remained ever after a distinct kingdom.

The next year, A.C. 412, the *Visigoths* being beaten in *Italy*, had *Aquitain* granted them to retire into: and they invaded it with much violence, causing the *Alans* and *Burgundians* to retreat, who were then depopulating of it. At the same time the *Burgundians* were brought to peace; and the Emperor granted them for inheritance a region upon the *Rhine* which they had invaded: and the same, I presume, he did with the *Alans*. But the *Franks* not long after retaking and burning *Triers, Castinus*, A.C. 415, was sent against them with an army, who routed them and slew *Theudomir* their King. This was the second taking of *Triers* by the *Franks*. It was therefore taken four times, once by the *Vandals* and thrice by the *Franks*. *Theudomir* was succeeded by *Pharamond*, the Prince or King of the *Salian Franks* in *Germany*. From thence he brought new forces, reigned over the whole, and had seats granted to his people within the Empire near the *Rhine*.

And now the *Barbarians* were all quieted, and settled in several kingdoms within the Empire, not only by conquest, but also by the grants of the Emperor *Honorius*. For *Rutilius** in his *Itinerary*, written in Autumn, *Anno Urbis** 1169, that is, according to *Varro's* computation then in use, A.C. 416, thus laments the wasted fields:

100

Illa quidem longis nimium deformia bellis;[9]

And then adds,

Jam tempus laveris post longa incendia fundis
Vel pastorales ædificare casas.[10]

And a little after,

Æternum tibi Rhenus aret.[11]

And *Orosius* in the end of his history, which was finished A.C. 417, represents now a general pacification of the barbarous nations by the words *comprimere, coangustare, addicere gentes immanissimas*; terming them *imperio addictas*, because they had obtained seats in the Empire by league and compact; and *coangustatas*, because they did no longer invade all regions at pleasure, but by the compact remained quiet in the seats then granted them. And these are the kingdoms, of which the feet of the Image were henceforward composed, and which are represented by iron and clay intermixed, which did not stick to one another, and were of different strength.

---

[9] [Trans.: `Yonder fields all too deformed with war's long stay.']

[10] [Trans.: `Now it is time, after war's long conflagrations, to build huts for shepherds on the devastated farms.']

[11] [Trans.: `May Rhinelanders eternally plough their fields.']

CHAPTER VI

Of the Kingdoms represented by the ten horns of the fourth Beast.

Now by the wars above described the *Western* Empire of the Romans, about the time that *Rome* was besieged and taken by the *Goths*, became broken into the following ten kingdoms.

1. The kingdom of the *Vandals* and *Alans* in *Spain* and *Africa*.
2. The kingdom of the *Suevians* in *Spain*.
3. The kingdom of the *Visigoths*.
4. The kingdom of the *Alans* in *Gallia*.
5. The kingdom of the *Burgundians*.
6. The kingdom of the *Franks*.
7. The kingdom of the *Britains*.
8. The kingdom of the *Hunns*.
9. The kingdom of the *Lombards*.
10. The kingdom of *Ravenna*.

Seven of these kingdoms are thus mentioned by *Sigonius*.* *Honorio regnante, in Pannoniam Hunni, in Hispaniam Vandali, Alani, Suevi & Gothi, in Galliam Alani*

Burgundiones & Gothi, certis sedibus permissis, accepti.[1] Add the *Franks, Britains,* and *Lombards,* and you have the ten: for these arose about the same time with the seven. But then let us view them severally.

1. The Kings of the *Vandals* were, A.C. 407 *Godegefilus,* 407 *Gunderic,* 426 *Geiseric,* 477 *Hunneric,* 484 *Gundemund,* 496 *Thrasamund,* 523 *Geiseric,* 530 *Gelimer. Godegefilus* led them into *Gallia* A.C. 406, *Gunderic* into *Spain* A.C. 409, *Geiseric* into *Africa* A.C. 427; and *Gelimer* was conquered by *Belisarius* A.C. 533. Their kingdom lasted in *Gallia, Spain* and *Africa* together 126 years; and in *Africa* they were very potent. The *Alans* had only two Kings of their own in *Spain, Resplendial,* and *Ataces, Utacus* or *Othacar.* Under *Resplendial* they went into *France* A.C. 407, and into *Spain* A.C. 409. *Ataces* was slain with almost all his army by *Vallia* King of the *Visigoths* A.C. 419. And then the remainder of these *Alans* subjected themselves to *Gunderic* King of the *Vandals* in *Boetica,* and went afterwards with them into *Africa,* as I learnt out of *Procopius.** Whence the Kings of the *Vandals* styled themselves Kings of the *Vandals* and *Alans;* as may be seen in the Edict of *Hunneric* recited by *Victor in his Vandalic* persecution. In conjunction with the *Chatti,* these *Alans* gave the name of *Cathalaunia,* or *Catth-Alania,* to the Province which is still so called. These *Alans* had also *Gepides* among them; and therefore the *Gepides* came into *Pannonia* before the *Alans* left it. There they became subject to the *Hunns* till the death of *Attila* A.C. 454, and at length were conquered by the *Ostrogoths.*

2. The Kings of the *Suevians* were, A.C. 407 *Ermeric,* 438 *Rechila,* 448 *Rechiarius,* 458 *Maldra,* 460 *Frumarius,* 463 *Regismund.* And after some other kings who are unknown, reigned A.C. 558 *Theudomir,* 568 *Miro,* 582 *Euboricus,* and 583

---

[1] [Trans.:'In the reign of Honorius, the Hunns were granted certain lands and admitted into Pannonia, the Vandals, Alans, Suevi and the Goths into Spain, and the Alans, Burgundians and Goths into Gaul.']

Andeca. This Kingdom, after it had been once seated in Spain, remained always in *Gallæcia* and *Lusitania. Ermeric* after the fall of the *Alan* Kingdom, enlarged it into all *Gallæcia,* forcing the *Vandals* to retire into *Boetica* and the *Carthaginian* Province, This kingdom lasted 177 years according to *Isidorus,** and then was subdued by *Leovigildus* King of the *Visigoths,* and made a Province of his kingdom A.C. 585.

3. The Kings of the *Visigoths* were, A.C. 400 *Alaric,* 410 *Athaulphus,* 415 *Sergeric* and *Vallia,* 419 *Theoderic,* 451 *Thorismund,* 452 *Theoderic,* 465 *Euric,* 482 *Alaric,* 505 *Gensalaric,* 526 *Amalaric,* 531 *Theudius,* 548 *Theudisclus,* &c. I date this kingdom from the time that *Alaric* left *Thrace* and *Greece* to invade the *Western Empire.* In the end of the reign of *Athaulphus* the *Goths* were humbled by the *Romans,* and attempted to pass out of *France* into *Spain. Sergeric* reigned but a few days. In the beginning of *Vallia's* reign they assaulted the *Romans* afresh, but were again repulsed, and then made peace on this condition, that they should on behalf of the Empire invade the *Barbarian* Kingdoms in *Spain:* and this they did, together with the *Romans* in the years 417 and 418, overthrowing the *Alans* and part of the *Vandals.* Then they received *Aquitain* of the Emperor by a full donation, leaving their conquests in *Spain* to the Emperor: and thereby the seats of the conquered *Alans* came into the hands of the *Romans.* In the year 455, *Theoderic,* assisted by the *Burgundians,* invaded Spain, which was then almost all subject to the *Suevians,* and took a part of it from them. A.C. 506, the *Goths* were driven out of *Gallia* by the *Franks.* A.C. 585, they conquered the *Suevian* kingdom, and became Lords of all *Spain.* A.C. 713, the *Saracens* invaded them, but in time they have recovered their dominions, and have reigned in *Spain* ever since.

4. The kings of the *Alans* in *Gallia* were *Goar, Sambida, Eocharic, Sangibanus, Beurgus,* &c. Under *Goar* they invaded *Gallia* A.C.407, and had seats given them

near the *Rhine*, A.C. 412. Under *Sambida*, whom *Bucher** makes the successor, if not the son of *Goar*, they had the territories of *Valence* given them by *Ætius* the Emperor's General, A.C. 440. Under *Eocharic* they conquered a region of the rebelling *Galli Arborici*, given them also by *Ætius*. This region was from them named *Alenconium, quasi Alanorum conventus*. Under *Sangibanus* they were invaded, and their regal city *Orleans* was besieged by *Attila* King of the *Hunns*, with a vast army of 500000 men. *Ætius* and the *Barbarian* Kings of *Gallia* came to raise the siege, and beat the *Hunns* in a very memorable battle, A.C. 451, *in campis Catalaunicis*, so called from these *Alans* mixed with the *Chatti*. The region is now called *Campania* or *Champagne*. In that battle were slain on both sides 162000 men. A year or two after, Attila returned with an immense army to conquer this region, but was again beaten by them and the *Visigoths* together in a battle of three days continuance, with a slaughter almost as great as the former. Under *Beurgus*, or *Biorgor*, they infested *Gallia* round about, till the reign of *Maximus* the Emperor; and then they passed the *Alps* in winter, and came into *Liguria*, but were there beaten, and *Beurgus* slain, by *Ricimer* commander of the Emperor's forces, A.C. 464. Afterwards they were again beaten, by the joint force of *Odoacer* King of Italy and *Childeric* King of the Franks, about the year 480, and again by *Theudobert* King of the *Austrian Franks* about the year 511.

5. The Kings of the *Burgundians* were, A.C. 407 *Gundicar*, 436 *Gundioc*, 467 *Bilimer*, 473 *Gundobaldus* with his brothers, 510 *Sigismund*, 517 *Godomarus*. Under *Gundicar* they invaded *Gallia* A.C. 407, and had seats given them by the Emperor near the *Rhine* in *Gallia Belgica*, A.C. 412. They had *Saxons* among them and were now so potent, that *Orosius** A.C. 417 wrote of them: *Burgundionum esse prævalidam manum Galliæ hodieque testes sunt, in quibus præsumpta possessione consistunt.*[2] About the year 435 they received great

---

[2]   [Trans.: `The exceptional strength of the Burgundians is today witnessed by the provinces

overthrows by *Ætius*, and soon after by the *Hunns*: but five years after had *Savoy* granted to them to be shared with the inhabitants; and from that time became again a potent kingdom, being bounded by the river *Rhodanus*, but afterwards extending much further into the heart of *Gallia*. *Gundobald* conquered the regions about the rivers *Araris* and *Rhodanus*, with the territories of *Marseilles*; and invading *Italy* in the time of the Emperor *Glycerius*, conquered all his brethren. *Godomarus* made *Orleans* his royal seat: whence the kingdom was called *Regnum Aurelianorum*. He was conquered by *Clotharius* and *Childebert*, Kings of the *Franks*, A.C. 526. From thence forward this kingdom was sometimes united to the kingdom of the *Franks*, and sometimes divided from it, till the reign of *Charles* the great, who made his son *Carlottus* King of *Burgundy*. From that time, for about 300 years together, it enjoyed its proper kings; and was then broken into the Dukedom of *Burgundy*, County of *Burgundy*, and County of *Savoy*; and afterwards those were broken into other lesser Counties.

6. The Kings of the *Franks* were A.C. 407 *Theudomir*, 417 *Pharamond*, 428 *Clodio*, 448 *Merovæus*, 456 *Childeric*, 482 *Clodovæus*, &c. *Windeline* and *Bucher*,* two of the most diligent searchers into the originals of this kingdom, make it begin the same year with the *Barbarian* invasions of *Gallia*, that is, A.C. 407. Of the first Kings there is in *Labbe's* * *Bibliotheca M.S.* this record.

Historica quaedam excerpta ex veteri stemmate
genealogico Regum Franciæ.

Genobaldus, Marcomerus, Suno, Theodemeris. Isti duces vel reguli extiterunt à principio gentis Francorum diversis temporibus. Sed incertum relinquunt historici quali sibi procreations lineâ successerunt.

Pharamundus: sub hoc rege suo primo Franci legibus se subdunt,

of Gaul, the possession of which they seized and in which they are now established.']

quas primores eorum tulerunt Wisogastus, Atrogastus, Salegastus.

Chlochilo. Iste, transito Rheno, Romanos in Carbonaria, sylva devicit, Camaracum cepit & obtinuit, annis 20 regnavit. Sub hoc rege Franci usque Summam progressi sunt.

Merovechus. Sub hoc rege Franci Trevirum destruunt, Metim succendunt, usque Aurelianum perveniunt[3].

Now for *Genobaldus, Marcomer* and *Suno*, they were captains of the *Transrhenane Franks* in the reign of *Theodosius*, and concern us not. We are to begin with *Theudomir* the first *King* of the rebelling *Salii*, Called *Didio* by *Ivo Cartonensis*,* and *Thiedo* and *Theudomerus* by *Rhenanus*.* His face is extant in a coin of gold found with this insription, THEUDEMIR REX, published by *Petavius*,* and still or lately extant, as *Windeline* testifies: which shews that he was a King, and that in *Gallia*; seeing that rude *Germany* understood not then the coining of money, nor used either *Latin* words or letters. He was the son of *Ricimer*, or *Richomer*, the favourite of the Emperor *Theodosius*; and so being a *Roman Frank*, and of the *Salian* royal blood, they

---

[3] [Trans.: `Certain historical extracts from the ancient genealogical stems of the kings of France.

Genobaldus, Marcomerus, Suno, Theodemeris: These were petty kings at different periods in the early history of the nation of the Franks. Historical writers, however, leave us in doubt as to what order or by what title they succeeded one another.

Pharamundus: Under him, their first king, the Franks submitted to those laws previously enacted by their chieftains Wisogastus, Atrogastus and Salegastus.

Chlochilo: This king crossed the Rhine, decisively defeated the Romans in the Carbonarian forest, and captured and held Camaracum. During his reign of twenty years, the Franks advanced as far as the Somme.

Merovechus: In this reign the Franks destroyed Treves, burned Metz and penetrated as far as Orleans.']

therefore upon the rebellion made him king. The whole time of his reign you have stated in *Excerptis Gregorii Turonensis* è Fredigario,* cap.* 5-8. where the making him King, the tyranny of *Jovinus*, the slaughter of the associates of *Jovinus*, the second taking of *Triers* by the *Franks*, and their war with *Castinus*, in which this King was slain, are as a series of successive things thus set down in order. *Extinctus Ducibus in Francis, denuo Reges creantur ex eadem stirpe qua prius fuerant. Eodem tempore Jovinus ornatus regios assumpsit. Constantinus fugam versus Italiam dirigit; missis a Jovino Principe percussoribus super Mentio flumine, capite truncatur. Multi nobilium jussu Jovini apud Avernis capti, et a ducibus Honorii crudeliter interempti sunt. Trevirorum civitas, factione unius ex senatoribus nomine Lucii, à Francis captà et incensa est. — Castinus Domesticorum Comes expeditionem accipit contra Francos,[4] &c.* Then returning to speak of Theudomir, he adds: *Franci electum à se regem, sicut prius fuerat, crinitum inquirentes diligenter ex genere Priami, Frigi et Francionis, super se crearunt nomine Theudemerum filium Richemeris, qui in hoc prælio quod supra memini, à Romanis interfectus est;[5]* that is, in the battle with Castinus's

---

[4] [Trans.: `After the extinction of the dukes amongst the Franks, kings were again elected from the same stock as in former times. At that same time Jovinus assumed for himself the position and honour of monarch. Constantine chose to flee towards Italy, but was beheaded at the river Mentius by assassins in the service of Jovinus. Many of the nobility were on the orders of Jovinus captured at Averni and cruelly murdered by the dukes of Honorius. The city of Treves, via the connivance of one of the senators called Lucius, was captured and burned by the Franks. Castinus, a comptroller of the household, undertook an expedition against the Franks', etc.]

[5] [Trans.: `In making a diligent search for a king from amongst themselves and, according to ancient custom, one with long hair, the Franks chose from among the family of Priamus, Frigius, Francio, one Theudemer, the son of Richemer. Theudemer was killed by the

army. Of his death *Gregory Turonensis** makes this further mention: *In consularibus legimus Theodemerum regem Francorum filium Ricimeris quondam, et Ascilam matrem ejus, gladio interfectos.*[6]

Upon this victory of the *Romans*, the *Franks* and rebelling *Gauls*, who in the time of *Theudomir* were at war with one another, united to strengthen themselves, as *Ordericus Vitalis** thus mentions. *Cum Galli prius contra Romanos rebellâssent, Franci iis sociati sunt, et pariter juncti, Ferramundum Sunonis ducis filium, sibi regem praefecerunt.*[7] *Prosper** sets down the time: *Anno 25, Honorii, Pharamundus, sibi regem præfecerunt.*[8] This, *Bucher,** well observes, refers to the end of the year 416, or the beginning of the next year, dating the years of *Honorius* from the death of *Valentinian*; and argues well, that at this time *Pharamond* was not only King by the constitution of the *Franks*, but crowned also by the consent of *Honorius*, and had a part of *Gallia* assigned him by covenant. And this might be the cause that *Roman* writers reckoned him the first King: which some not understanding, have reputed him the founder of this kingdom by an army of the *Transrhenane Franks*. He might come with such an army, but he succeeded *Theodomir* by right of blood and consent of the people. For the above cited passage of *Fredigarius,** *Extinctis Ducibus in Francis denuo Reges creantur ex eadem stirpe quâ prius fuerant,*[9] implies that the kingdom continued to this new elected family during

---

Romans in the battle mentioned above.']

[6] [Trans.: `In the consular records we read that Theudemer King of the Franks and son of Richemer was, along with his mother Ascila, killed by the sword'.]

[7] Apud Bucherum, 1. 14. c9. n. 8. [Trans.: `When the Gauls had taken the first steps to rebel against the Romans the Franks united with them, and as a united people elected as their king Ferramundus, the son of Duke Suno.']

[8] [Trans.: `In the twenty fifth year of Honorius, Pharamundus became King of France'.]

[9] [Trans.: `After the extnction of the dukes amongst the Franks, kings were again elected

the reign of more kings than one. If you date the years of *Honorius* from the death of his father, the reign of *Pharamond* might begin two years later than is assigned by *Bucher*. The *Salique* laws made in his reign, which are yet extant, shew by their name that it was the kingdom of the *Salii* over which he reigned; and, by the pecunary mulcts* in them, that the place where he reigned abounded with much money, and consequently was within the Empire; rude *Germany* knowing not the use of money, till they mixed with the *Romans*. In the Preface also to the *Salique* laws, written and prefixed to them soon after the conversion of the *Franks* to the Christian religion, that is in the reign of *Merovæus*, or soon after, the original of this kingdom is thus described: *Hæc enim gens, quæ fortis dum esset et robore valida, Romanorum jugum durissimum de suis cervicibus excussit pugnando,*[10] &c. This kingdom therefore was erected, not by invasion but by rebellion, as was described above. *Prosper** in registering their Kings in order, tells us: *Pharamundus regnat in Francia; Clodio regnat in Francia, Merovæus regnat in Francia:*[11] and who can imagine but that in all these places he meant one and same *Francia*? And yet 'tis certain that the *Francia* of *Merovæus* was in *Gallia*.

Yet the father of *Pharamond*, being king of a body of *Franks* in *Germany* in the reign of the Emperor *Theodosius*, as above, *Pharamond* might reign over the same *Franks* in *Germany* before he succeeded *Theudomir* in the kingdom of the *Salians* within the Empire, and even before *Theudomir* began his reign; suppose in the first year of *Honorius*, or when

---

from the same stock as in former times.']

[10]   [Trans.: `This nation, while it was strong and vigorous in its might, by war struck from its neck the oppressive Roman yoke.']

[11]   [Trans.: `Pharamundus reigned in France; Clodio reigned in France; Merovæus reigned in France'.]

those *Franks* begin repulsed by *Stilico*, lost their Kings *Marcomir* and *Suno*, one of which was the father of *Pharamond*: and the *Roman Franks*, after the death of *Theudomir*, might invite *Pharamond* with his people from beyond the *Rhine*. But we are not to regard the reign of *Pharamond* in *Germany*: we are to date this kingdom from its rise within the Empire, and to look upon it as strengthened by the access of other *Franks* coming from beyond the Rhine, whether in the reign of this King or in that of his successor *Clodio*. For in the last year of *Pharamond*'s reign, *Ætius* took from him a part of his possession in *Gallia*: but his successor *Clodio*, whom *Fredigarius** represents as the son of *Theudomir*, and some call *Clogio*, *Cloio*, and *Claudius*, inviting from beyond the *Rhine* a great body of *Franks*, recovered all, and carried on their conquests as far as the river *Soame*. Then those *Franks* dividing conquests with him, erected certain new kingdoms at *Cologn* and *Cambray*, and some other cities: all which were afterwards conquered by *Clodovæus*, who also drove the *Goths* out of *Gallia*, and fix'd his seat at *Paris*, where it has continued ever since. And this was the original of the present kingdom of *France*.

7. The Kings of *Britain* were, A.C. 407 or 408, *Marcus*, *Gratian*, and *Constantine* successively; A.C. 425 *Vortigern*, 466 *Aurelius Ambrosius*, 498 *Uther Pendraco*, 508 *Arthur*, 542 *Constantinus*, 545 *Aurelius Cunanus*, 578 *Vortiporeus*, 581 *malgo*, 586 *Careticus*, 613 *Cadwan*, 635 *Cadwalin*, 676 *Cadwallader*. The three first were *Roman* Tyrants, who revolted from the empire. *Orosius,** *Prosper** and *Zosimus** connect their revolt with the irruptions of the Barbarians into *Gallia*, as consequent thereunto. *Prosper*, with whom *Zosimus* agrees, puts it in the year which began the day after that irruption. The just time I thus collect: *Marcus* reigned not many days, *Gratian* four months, and *Constantine* three years. He was slain the year after the taking of *Rome*, that is A.C. 411, 14 *Kal. Octob.*

Whence the revolt was in Spring A.C. 408. *Sozomen** joins *Constantine*'s expedition into *Gallia* with *Arcadius's* death, or the times a little after; and *Arcadius* died A.C. 408 May the 1st. Now tho the reign of these Tyrants was but short, yet they gave a beginning to the kingdom of *Britain*, and so may be reckoned the first three Kings, especially since the posterity of *Constantine, viz.* his sons *Aurelius Ambrosius,* and *Uther Pendraco,* and his grandson *Arthur,* reigned afterwards. For from the time of the revolt of these Tyrants *Britain,* continued a distinct kingdom absolved from subjection to the Empire, the Emperor not being able to spare soldiers to be sent thither to receive and keep the Island, and therefore neglecting it; as we learn by the unquestionable records. For *Prosper* tells us; A.C. 410, *Variane Cos. Hac tempestate præ valetudine Romanorum, vires funditùs attenuatæ Britanniæ.*[12] And *Sigebert,** conjoining this with the siege of *Rome,* saith: *Britannorum vires attenuatæ, et substrahunt se à Romanorum dominatione.*[13] And *Zosimus** *lib.* 6. *The* Transrhenane Barbarians *invading all places, reduced the inhabitants of the island of* Britain, *and also certain Celtic nations to that pass, that they fell off from the Roman Empire; and being no longer obedient to the* Roman laws, *kata heauton, bioteuein,*[14] *they lived in separate bodies after their own pleasure. The* Britons *therefore taking up arms, and hazarding themselves for their own safety, freed their cities from the imminent* Barbarians. *In like manner all* Brabant *and some other Provinces of the* Gauls *imitating the* Britons, *freed themselves also, ejecting the* Roman *Presidents, and forming themselves into a sort of commonwealth according to*

---

12   [Trans.: 'A.C. 410, in the consulship of Varianus. At this time, owing to the weakness of the Romans, the military forces in Britain were reduced to a minimum.']

13   [Trans.: 'The military forces among the Britons were reduced: and the Britons freed themselves from Roman overlordship.']

14   [Trans.: 'Living according to their own ways' ; originally given in Greek characters.]

their own pleasure. This rebellion of Britain *and the* Celtic *nations happened when* Constantine *usurped the kingdom.* So also *Procopius* lib.* 1. *Vandal.* speaking of the same *Constantine,* saith: Constantine *being overcome in battle, was slain with his children: Bretannian mentoi Romaioi anasosasthai ouketi eschon, all'ousa hupo turannois ap'autou emeine.*[15] *Yet the* Romans *could not recover* Britain *any more, but from that time it remained under Tyrants.* And *Beda,** l. 1. c. 11. *Fracta est Roma à Gothis anno 1164 suæ conditionis; ex quo tempore Romani in Britannia regnare cessaverunt.*[16] And *Ethelwaldus: A tempore Romæ à Gothis expugnatæ, cessavit imperium Romanorum à Britannia insula, et ab aliis, quas sub jugo servitutis tenebant, multi terris.*[17] And *Theodoret,* serm.* 9. *de curand. Græc. affect.* about the year 424, reckons the Britons among the nations which were not then in subjection to the *Roman* Empire. Thus *Sigonius*: ad annum 411, Imperium Romanorum post excessum Constantini in Brittani nullum fuit.*[18]

Between the death of *Constantine* and the reign of *Vortigern* was an interregnum of about 14 years, in which the *Britons* had wars with the *Picts* and *Scots,* and twice obtained the assistance of a *Roman* legion, who drove out the enemy, but told them positively at their departure that they would come no more. Of *Vortigern's* beginning to reign there is this record in an old Chronicle in *Nennius,** quoted by *Camden** and others: *Guortigernus tenuit imperium in*

---

[15]   [Trans.: `The Romans, however, were no longer able to recover Britain, but it remained under tyrants from that time'; originally given in Greek characters.]

[16]   [Trans.: `The power of Rome was broken by the Goths in the 1164th year after the foundation of Rome, and from that date the Romans ceased to rule in Britain.']

[17]   [Trans: `From the storming of Rome by the Goths, Roman rule in the island of Britain ceased, and likewise in many other countries which they had held in servile bondage.']

[18]   [Trans.: `About the year 411, after the withdrawal of Constantine, Roman rule in Britain ceased.']

Brittania, Theodosio et Valentiniano Coss. [viz. A.C. *425.] et in quarto anno regni sui Saxones ad Brittaniam venerunt, Felice et Tauro Coss. [viz.* A.C. *428].*[19] This coming of the *Saxons, Sigebert* refers to the 4th year of *Valentinian,* which falls in with the year 428, assigned by this Chronicle: and two years after, the *Saxons* together with the *Picts* were beaten by the *Britains.* Afterwards in the reign of *Martian* the Emperor, that is, between the years 450 and 456, the *Saxons* under *Hengist* were called in by the *Britons,* but six years after revolted from them, made war upon them with various success, and by degrees succeeded them. Yet the *Britons* continued a flourishing kingdom till the reign of *Careticus*; and the war between the two nations continued til the pontificate of *Sergius* A.C. 688.[20]

8. The Kings of the *Hunns* were, A.C. 406 *Octar* and *Rugila,* 433 *Bleda* and *Attila. Octar* and *Rugila* were the brothers of *Munzuc* King of the *Hunns* in *Gothia* beyond the *Danube*; and *Bleda* and *Attila* were his sons, and *Munzuc* was the son of *Balamir.* The two first, as *Jornandes** tells us, were Kings of the *Hunns,* but not of them all; and had the two last for their successors. I date the reign of the *Hunns* in *Pannonia* to them, A.C. 407. *Sigonius** from the time that the *Visigoths* relinquished *Pannonia* A.C 408. *Constat.* saith he, *quod Gothis ex Illyrico profectis, Hunni successerunt, atque imprimis Pannoniam tenuerunt. Neque enim Honorius viribus ad resistendum in tantis difficultatibus destitutus, prorsus eos prohibere potuit, sed meliore consilio, animo ad pacem converso, foedus cum eis, datis aceptisque obsidibus fecit; ex quibus qui dati sunt, Ætius, qui etiam Alarico*

---

[19]   [Trans.: `Guortigernus gained control in Britain in the consulship of Theodosius and Valentinianus and, in the fourth year of his reign, in the consulship of Felix and Taurus, the Saxons invaded Britain.']

[20]   Rolevinc's* Antiqua Saxon, l. 1. c. 6.

tributus fuerat, præcipue memoratur.[21] How *Ætius* was hostage to the *Goths* and *Hunns* is related by *Frigeridus*, who when he had mentioned that *Theodosius* Emperor of the *East* had sent grievous commands to *John*, who after the death of *Honorius* had usurped the crown of the *Western Empire*, he subjoins: *Iis permotus Johannes, Ætius id tempus curam palatii gerentem cum ingenti auri pondere ad Chunnos transmisit, notos sibi obsidiatûs, sui tempore et familiari amicitiæ devinctos*[22] — And a little after: *Ætius tribus annis Alarici obses, dehinc Chunnorum, postea Carpilionis gener ex Comite domesticorum et Joannis curopalatæ.*[23] Now *Bucher* shews that *Ætius* was hostage to *Alaric* till the year 410, when *Alaric* died, and to the *Hunns* between the years 411 and 415, and son-in-law to *Carpilio* about the year 417 or 418, and *Curopalates* to *John* about the end of the year 423. Whence 'tis probable that he became hostage to the *Hunns* about the year 412 or 413, when *Honorius* made leagues with almost all the barbarous nations, and granted them seats: but I had rather say with *Sigonius,** that *Ætius* became hostage to *Alaric* A.C. 403. It is further manifest out of *Prosper,** that the *Hunns* were in quiet possession of *Pannonia* in the year 432.

---

[21] [Trans.: `When the Goths quitted Illyricum, the Hunns took their place and first of all secured Pannonia, because Honorius was so beset by difficulties that he was without forces to meet them. But, adopting a better plan, he devoted his attention to a peaceable settlement and concluded an agreement with them, upon the mutual exchange of hostages. One of the hostages especially worthy of note was Ætius, who had also been a hostage to Alaric.']

[22] [Trans.: `Disturbed by these commands, Johannes sent Ætius - who at that time was in charge of the palace - across to the Hunns with a huge amount of gold, they being acquainted with 'tius since the time when he was a hostage among them, and were bound to him by intimate ties of friendship.']

[23] [Trans.: `Ætius was three years a hostage with Alaric; next a hostage with the Hunns, and subsequently son-in-law of Carpilio, after holding the offices of Comptroller of the household and governor of the palace for Johannes.']

For in the first book of *Eusebius's** Chronicle *Prosper* writes: *Anno decimo post obitum Honorii, cum ad Chunnorum gentem cui tunc Rugila præerat, post prælium cum Bonifacio se Ætius contulisset, impetrato auxilio ad Romanorum solum regreditur.*[24] And in the second book: *Ætio et Valerio Coss. Ætius depositâ potestate profugus ad Hunnos in Pannonia pervenit, quorum amicitiâ auxiloque usus, pacem principum interpellatæ obtinuit.*[25] Hereby it appears that at this time *Rugila*, or as as *Maximus** calls him, *Rechilla*, reigned over the *Hunns* in *Pannonia*; and that *Pannonia* was not now so much as accounted within the soil of the Empire, being formerly granted away to the *Hunns*; and that these were the very same body of *Hunns* with which *Ætius* had, in the time of his being an hostage, contracted friendship: by virtue of which, as he sollicited them before to the aid of *John* the Tyrant A.C. 430, so now he procured their intercession for himself with the Emperor. *Octar* died A.C. 430; for *Socrates** tells us, that about the same time the *Burgundians* having been newly vext by the *Hunns*, upon intelligence of *Octar's* death, seeing them without a leader, set upon them with so much vigour, that 3000 *Burgundians* slew 10000 *Hunns*. Of *Rugila's* being now King in *Pannonia* you have already heard. He died A.C. 433, and was succeeded by *Bleda*, as *Prosper** and *Maximus** inform us. This *Bleda* with his brother *Attila* were before this time Kings of the *Hunns* beyond the *Danube*, their father *Munzuc's* kingdom being divided between them; and now they united the kingdom of *Pannonia* to their own. Whence *Paulus Diaconus** saith, they did

---

[24] [Trans.: 'Ten years after the death of Honorius, and after his fight with Boniface, Ætius withdrew to the tribe of the Hunns, then governed by Rugila. Upon gaining the help he sought, Ætius then returned to Roman soil.']

[25] [Trans.: 'In the consulship of Ætius and Valerius. Ætius, resigning his office, came as an exile to the Hunns in Pannonia. By using their friendly assistance, he obtained the emperor's pardon for relinquishing his office.']

regnum intra Pannoniam Daciamque gerere.[26] In the year 441, they began to invade the Empire afresh, adding to the *Pannonian* forces new and great armies from *Scythia*. But this war was presently composed, and then *Attila*, seeing *Bleda* inclined to peace, slew him, A.C. 444, inherited his dominions, and invaded the Empire again. At length, after various great wars with the *Romans*, *Attila* perished A.C. 454; and his sons quarrelling about his dominions, gave occasion to the *Gepides*, *Ostrogoths* and other nations who were their subjects, to rebel and make war upon them. The same year the *Ostrogoths* had seats granted them in *Pannonia* by the Emperors *Marcian* and *Valentinian*; and with the *Romans* ejected the *Hunns* out of *Pannonia*, soon after the the death of *Attila*, as all historians agree. This ejection was in the reign of *Avitus* as is mentioned in the *Chronicum Boiorum*, and in *Sidonius*,* *Carm.* 7 *in Avitum*, which speaks thus of that Emperor.

> — *cujus solum amissas post sæcula multa*
> *Pannonias revocavit iter, jam credere promptum est*
> *Quid faciet bellis.*[27]

The Poet means, that by the coming of *Avitus* the *Hunns* yielded more easily to the *Goths*. This was written by *Sidonius** in the beginning of the reign of *Avitus*: and his reign began in the end of the year 455, and lasted not one full year.

*Jornandes** tells us: *Duodecimo anni regni Valiæ, quando et Hunni post pene quinquaginta annos invasa Pannonia, à Romanis et Gothis expulsi sunt.*[28]

---

[26] [Trans.: `they held sway within Pannonia and Dacia.']

[27] [Trans.: `It is easy to conceive what will be the exploits, in actual combat, of the man whose mere approach recovered the province of Pannonia, lost to us for many generations.']

[28] [Trans.: `In the twelfth year of the reign of Valia, almost fifty years after their invasion of

And *Marcellinus: Hierio et Ardaburio Coss. Pannoniæ, quæ per qunquaginta annos ab Hunnis retinebantur, à Romanis receptæ sunt*[29]: whence it should seem that the *Hunns* invaded and held *Pannonia* from the year 378 or 379 to the year 427, and then were driven out of it. But this is a plain mistake: for it is certain that the Emperor *Theodosius* left the Empire entire; and we have shewed out of *Prosper*,* that the *Hunns* were in quiet possession of *Pannonia* in the year 432. The *Visigoths* in those days had nothing to do with *Pannonia*, and the *Ostrogoths* continued subject to the *Hunns* till the the death of *Attila*, A.C. 454; and *Valia* King of the *Visigoths* did not reign twelve years. He began his reign in the end of the year 415 reigned three years, and was slain A.C. 419, as *Idacius*,* *Isidorus*,* and the *Spanish* manuscript Chronicles seen by *Grotius** testify. And *Olympiodorus*,* who carries his history only to the year 425, sets down therein the death of *Valia* King of the *Visigoths*, and conjoins it with that of *Constantius* which happened A.C. 420. Wherefore the *Valia* of *Jornandes*, who reigned at the least twelve years, is some other King. And I suspect that this name hath been put by mistake for *Valamir* King of the *Ostrogoths*: for the action recorded was of the *Romans* and *Ostrogoths* driving the *Hunns* out of *Pannonia* after the death of *Attila*; and it is not likely that the historian would refer the history of the *Ostrogoths* to the years of the *Visigothic* Kings. This action happened in the end of the year 455, which I take to be the twelfth year of *Valamir* in *Pannonia*, and which was almost fifty years after the year 406, in which the *Hunns* succeeded the *Vandals* and *Alans* in *Pannonia*. Upon the ceasing of the line of *Hunnimund* the son of *Hermaneric*, the *Ostrogoths* lived without Kings of their own nation about forty years together, being subject to the *Hunns*. And when *Alaric* began to

---

Pannonia, the Hunns were expelled from it by the Romans and the Goths.']

[29] [Trans.: `In the consulship of Hierus and Ardaburius, the provinces of Pannonia, which for fifty years had been in the possession of the Hunns, were recovered by the Romans.']

make war upon the *Romans*, which was in the year 444, he made *Valamir*, with his brothers *Theodomir* and *Videmir* the grandsons of *Vinethar*, captains or kings of these *Ostrogoths* under him. In the twelfth year of *Valamir's* reign dated from thence, the *Hunns* were driven out of *Pannonia*.

Yet the *Hunns* were not so ejected, but that they had further contests with the *Romans*, till the head of *Densix* the son of *Attila*, was carried to *Constantinople*, A.C. 469, in the Consulship of *Zeno* and *Marcian* as *Marcellinus** relates. Nor were they totally ejected from the Empire: for besides their reliques in *Pannonia*, *Sigonius** tells us, that when the Emperors *Marcian* and *Valentinian* granted *Pannonia* to the *Goths*, which was in the year 454, they granted part of *Illyricum* to some of the *Hunns* and *Sarmatians*. And in the year 526, when the *Lombards* removing into *Pannonia* made war there with the *Gepides*, the *Avares*, a part of the *Hunns*, who had taken the name of *Avares* from one of their kings, assisted the *Lombards* in that war; and the *Lombards* afterwards, when they went into Italy, left their seats in *Pannonia* to the *Avares* in recompence of their friendship. From that time the *Hunns* grew again very powerful; their Kings, whom they called *Chagan*, troubling the Empire much in the reigns of the Emperors *Mauritius*, *Phocas*, and *Heraclius*: and this is the original of the present kingdom of *Hungary*, from which these *Avares* and other *Hunns* mixed together, took the name of *Hun-Avaria*, and by contraction *Hungary*.

9. The *Lombards*, before they came over the *Danube*, were commanded by two captains, *Ibor* and *Ayon*: after whose death they had Kings *Agilmund, Lamisso, Lechu, Hildehoc, Gudehoc, Classo, Tato, Wacho, Walter, Audoin, Albion, Cleophis*, &c. *Agilmund* was the son of *Ayon*, who became their King, according to *Prosper*, in the Consulship of *Honorius* and *Theodosius* A.C. 389, reigned thirty three years, according to *Paulus Warnefridus*,* and was slain in the battle by the *Bulgarians*. *Prosper* places his death in the Consulship of *Marinianus* and

Asclepiodorus, A.C. 423. *Lamisso* routed the *Bulgarians*, and reigned three years, and *Lechu* almost forty. *Gudehoc* was contemporary to *Odoacer* King of the *Heruli* in Italy, and led his people from *Pannonia* into *Rugia*, a country on the north side of *Noricum* next beyond the *Danube*; from whence *Odoacer* then carried his people into *Italy*. *Tato* overthrew the kingdom of the *Heruli* beyond the *Danube*. *Wacho* conquered the *Suevians*, a kingdom then bounded on the east by *Bavaria*, on the west by *France*, and on the south by the *Burgundians*. *Audoin* returned into *Pannonia* A.C. 526, and there overcame the *Gepides*. *Alboin* A.C. 551 overthrew the kingdom of the *Gepides*, and slew their King *Chunnimund*: A.C. 563 he assisted the *Greek* Emperor against *Totila* King of the *Ostrogoths* in *Italy*; and A.C. 568 led his people out of *Pannonia* into *Lombardy*, where they reigned till the year 774.

According to *Paulus Diaconus*,* the *Lombards* with many other *Gothic* nations came into the Empire from beyond the *Danube* in the reign of *Arcadius* and *Honorius*, that is, between the years 395 and 408. But they might come in a little earlier: for we are told that the *Lombards*, under their captains *Ibor* and *Ayon*, beat the *Vandals* in battle; and *Prosper** placeth this victory in the Consulship of *Ausonius* and *Olybrius*, that is, A.C. 379. Before this war the *Vandals* had remained quiet forty years in the seats granted them in *Pannonia* by *Constantine* the great. And therefore if these were the same *Vandals*, this war must have been in *Pannonia*; and might be occasioned by the coming of the *Lombards* over the *Danube* into *Pannonia*, a year or two before the battle; and so have put an end to that quiet which had lasted forty years. After *Gratian* and *Theodosius* had quieted the *Barbarians*, they might either retire over the *Danube*, or continue quiet under the *Romans* till the death of *Theodosius*; and then either invade the Empire anew, or throw off all subjection to it. By their wars, first with the *Vandals*, and then with the *Bulgarians*, a *Scythian* nation so called from the river *Volga* whence they came; it appears that even in those days they were a kingdom not contemptible.

10. These nine kingdoms being rent away, we are next to consider the residue of the *Western Empire*. While this Empire continued entire, it was the Beast itself: but the residue thereof is only a part of it. Now if this part be considered as a horn, the reign of this horn may be dated from the translation of the imperial seat from *Rome* to *Ravenna*, which was in *October* A.C. 408. For then the Emperor *Honorius*, fearing that *Alaric* would besiege him in *Rome*, if he staid there, retired to *Millain*, and thence to *Ravenna*: and the ensuing siege and sacking of *Rome* confirmed his presence there, so that he and his sucessors ever made it their home. Accordingly *Macchiavel** in his *Florentine* history writes, that *Valentinian* having left Rome, translated the seat of the Empire to Ravenna.

Rhætia belonged to the *Western* Emperors, so long as that Empire stood; and then it descended, with *Italy* and the *Roman* Senate, to *Odoacer* King of the *Heruli* in *Italy*, and after him to *Theoderic* King of the *Ostrogoths* and his successors, by the grant of the *Greek* Emperors. Upon the death of *Valentinian* the second, the *Alemans* and *Suevians* invaded *Rhætia* A.C. 455. But I do not find they erected any settled kingdom there: for in the year 457, while they were yet depopulating *Rhætia*, they were attacked and beaten by *Burto* Master of the horse to the Emperor *Majoranus*; and I hear nothing more of their invading *Rhætia*. *Clodovæus* King of *France*, in or about the year 496, conquered a kingdom of the *Alemans*, and slew their last King *Ermeric*. But this kingdom was seated in *Germany*, and only bordered upon *Rhætia*: for its people fled from *Clodovæus* into the neighbouring kingdom of the *Ostrogoths* under *Theoderic*, who received them as friends, and wrote a friendly letter to *Clodovæus* in their behalf: and by this means they became the inhabitants of *Rhætia*, as subjects under the dominion of the *Ostrogoths*.

When the *Greek* Emperor conquered the *Ostrogoths*, he succeeded them in the kingdom of *Ravenna*, not only by right of conquest but also by right of inheritance, the *Roman* Senate still going along with this kingdom. Therefore we may reckon that this kingdom continued in the Exarchate of *Ravenna* and Senate of *Rome*: for the remainder of the Western Empire went along with the Senate of *Rome*, by reason of the right which this Senate still retained, and at length exerted, of chusing a new *Western* Emperor.

I have enumerated the ten kingdoms, into which the *Western Empire* became divided at its first breaking, that is, at the time of *Rome's* being besieged and taken by the *Goths*, Some of these kingdoms at length fell, and new ones arose: but whatever was their number afterwards, they are still called the *Ten Kingdoms* from their first number.

CHAPTER VII

Of the eleventh horn of Daniel's fourth Beast.

Now *Daniel considered the horns, and behold there came up among them another horn, before whom there were three of the first horns pluckt up by their roots; and behold in the horn were eyes like a the eyes of a man, and a mouth speaking great things,*[1] — and *his look was more stout than his fellows,*[2] — *and the same horn made war with the saints, and prevailed against them*: and one who stood by, and made *Daniel* know the interpretation of these things, told him, *that the ten horns were ten kings that should arise, and another should arise after them, and be diverse from the first, and he should subdue three kings,*[3] *and speak great words against the most High, and wear out the saints, and think to change times and laws: and that they should be given into his hands until a time and times and a half.*[4] Kings are put for kingdoms, as above; and therefore the little horn is a little kingdom. It was a horn of the fourth Beast, and rooted up three of his first horns; and therefore we are to look for it among the nations of the Latin Empire, after the rise of the ten horns. But it was a

---

[1]   Chap. vii. 8.

[2]   Ver. 20-21.

[3]   Ver. 24.

[4]   Ver. 25.

kingdom of a different kind from the other ten kingdoms, having a life or soul peculiar to itself, with eyes and a mouth. By its eyes it was a Seer; and by its mouth speaking great things and changing times and laws, it was a Prophet as well as a King. And such a Seer, a Prophet and a King, is the Church of *Rome*.

A Seer, Episkopos,[5] is a Bishop in the literal sense of the word; and this Church claims the universal Bishopric.

With his mouth he gives laws to kings and nations as an Oracle; and pretends to Infallibility, and that his dictates are binding to the whole world; which is to be a Prophet in the highest degree.

In the eighth century, by rooting up and subduing the Exarchate of *Ravenna*, the kingdom of the *Lombards*, and the Senate and Dukedom of *Rome*, he acquired *Peter's* Patrimony out of their dominions; and thereby rose up as a temporal Prince or King, or horn of the fourth Beast.

In a small book printed at *Paris* A.C. 1689, entitled, *An historical dissertation upon some coins of Charles the great*, Ludovicus Pius, Lotharius, *and their successors stamped at* Rome, it is recorded, that in the days of Pope *Leo X*, there was remaining in the *Vatican*, and till those days exposed to public view, an inscription in honour of Pipin the father of Charles the great, in these words: *Pipinum pium, primum fuisse qui aplificandæ Ecclesiæ Romanæ viam aperuerit Exarchatu Ravennate, et plurimus aliis oblatis;* "That *Pipin* the pious was the first who opened a way to the grandeur of the Church of *Rome*, conferring upon her the Exarchate of *Ravenna* and many other oblations." In and before the reign of the Emperors *Gratian* and *Theodosius*, the Bishop of *Rome* lived splendidly, but this was by the oblations of the *Roman* Ladies,

---

[5]   [Originally given in Greek characters.]

as *Ammianus** describes. After those reigns *Italy* was invaded by foreign nations, and did not get rid of her troubles before the fall of the kingdom of *Lombardy*. It was certainly by the victory of the see of *Rome* over the *Greek* Emperor, the King of *Lombardy*, and the Senate of *Rome*, that she acquired *Peter's* Patrimony, and rose up to her greatness. The donation of *Constantine* the Great is a fiction, and so is the donation of the *Alpes Cottiæ* to the Pope by *Aripert* King of the *Lombards*: for the *Alpes Cottiæ* were a part of the Exarchate, and in those days belonged to the *Greek Emperor*.

The invocation of the dead, and veneration of their images, being gradually introduced in the 4th, 5th, 6th and 7th centuries, the *Greek* Emperor *Philippicus* declared against the latter, A.C. 711 or 712. And the Emperor *Leo Isaurus*, put a stop to it, called a meeting of counsellors and Bishops in his palace, A.C. 726;[6] and by their advice put out an edict against that worship, and wrote to Pope *Gregory* II. that a general Council might be called. But the Pope thereupon called a Council at *Rome*, confirmed the worship of Images, excommunicated the *Greek* Emperor, absolved the people from their allegiance, and forbad them to pay tribute, or otherwise be obedient to him. Then the people of *Rome, Campania, Ravenna and Pentapolis*, with the cites under them, revolted and laid violent hands upon their magistrates, killing the Exarch *Paul* at *Ravenna*, and laying aside *Peter* Duke of *Rome* who was become blind: and when *Exhileratus* Duke of *Campania* incited the people against the Pope, the *Romans* invaded *Campania*, and slew him with his son *Hadrian*. Then a new Exarch, *Eutychius*, coming to *Naples*, sent some secretly to take away the lives of the Pope and the Nobles of *Rome*: but the plot being discovered, the *Romans* revolted

---

[6]   Sigonius, de Regno Italiæ, ad Ann. 726.

absolutely from the *Greek* Emperor, and took an oath to preserve the life of the Pope, to defend his state, and be obedient to his authority in all things. Thus Rome with its Duchy, including part of *Tuscany* and part of *Campania*, revolted in the year 726, and became a free state under the government of the Senate of this city. The authority of the Senate in civil affairs was henceforward absolute, the authority of the Pope extending hitherto no farther than to the affairs of the Church only.

At that time the *Lombards* also being zealous for the worship of images, and pretending to favour the cause of the Pope, invaded the cities of the Exarchate: and at length, *viz.* A.C. 752, took *Ravenna*, and put an end to the Exarchate.[7] And this was the first of the three kingdoms which fell before the little horn.

In the year 751 Pope *Zechary* deposed *Childeric*, a slothful and useless King of *France*, and the last of the race of the *Merovæus*; and absolving his subjects from their oath of allegiance, gave the kingdom to *Pipin* the major of the Palace; and thereby made a new and potent friend.[8] His successor Pope *Stephen* III, knowing better how to deal with the *Greek* Emperor than with the *Lombards*, went the next year to the King of the *Lombards*, to persuade him to return the Exarchate to the Emperor. But this not succeeding, he went into *France*, and persuaded *Pipin* to take the Exarchate and *Pentapolis* from the *Lombards*, and give it to *St. Peter*. Accordingly *Pipin* A.C. 754 came with an army into *Italy*, and made *Aistulphus* King of the *Lombards* promise the surrender: but the next year *Aistulphus*, on the contrary, to revenge himself on the Pope, besieged the city of *Rome* Whereupon the Pope sent letters to *Pipin*, wherein he told him that if he came not speedily against the

---

[7]   Sigon, ib. ad Ann. 726, 752.

[8]   Sigon, ib. Ann. 750.

Lombards, pro data sibi potentia, alienandum fore à regno Dei et vita æterna,[9] he should be excommunicated. *Pipin* therefore, fearing a revolt of his subjects, and being indebted to the Church of *Rome*, came speedily with an army into *Italy*, raised the siege, besieged the *Lombards* in *Pavia*, and forced them to surrender the Exarchate and region of *Pentapolis* to the Pope for a perpetual possession. Thus the Pope became Lord of *Ravenna*, and the Exarchate, some few cities excepted; and the keys were sent to *Rome*, and laid upon the confession of *St. Peter*, that is, upon his tomb at the high Altar, *in signum veri perpetuique dominii, sed pietate Regis gratuita,*[10] as the inscription of a coin of *Pipin* hath it. This was in the year of Christ 755.[11] And henceforward the Popes being temporal Princes, left off in their Epistles and Bulls to note the years of the *Greek* Emperors, as they had hitherto done.

After this the *Lombards* invading the Pope's countries, Pope *Adrian* sent to *Charles* the great, the son and successor of *Pipin*, to come to his assisstance. Accordingly *Charles* entered *Italy* with an army, invaded the *Lombards*, overthrew their kingdom, became master of their countries, and restored to the Pope, not only what they had taken from him, but also the rest of the Exarchate which they had promised *Pipin* to surrender to him, but had hitherto detained; and also gave him some cities of the Lombards, and was in return himself made *Patricius* by the *Romans*, and had the authority of confirming the elections of the Popes conferred upon him. These

---

[9]   [Trans.: `In accordance with the power given to him to prohibit entry into the Kingdom of God and life eternal.']

[10]   [Trans.: `as a token of true and perpetual dominion, and by the king's freely rendered devotion.']

[11]   Sigon. ib. Ann. 753-55.

things were done in the years 773 and 774.[12] This kingdom of the *Lombards* was the second kingdom which fell before the little horn. But *Rome*, which was to be the seat of his kingdom, was not yet his own.

In the year 796, *Leo* III being made Pope, notified his election to *Charles* the great by his Legates, sending to him for a present, the golden keys of the Confession of *Peter*, and the Banner of the city of *Rome*: the first as an acknowledgnment of the Popes's holding the cities of the Exarchate and *Lombardy* by the grant of *Charles*; the other as a signification that *Charles* should come and subdue the Senate and people of *Rome*, as he had done the Exarchate and the kingdom of the *Lombards*. For the Pope at the same time desired *Charles* to send some of his Princes to *Rome*, who might subject the *Roman* people to him, and bind them by oath *in fide et subjectione*, in fealty and subjection, as his words are recited by *Sigonius*.*[13] An anonymous poet, publish'd by *Boeclerus* at *Strasburg*, expresseth it thus:

> *Admonuitque piis precibus, qui mittere vellet*
> *Ex propriis aliquos primoribus, ac sibi plebem*
> *Subdere Romanam, servandaque foedera cogens*
> *Hanc fidei sacramentis promittere magnis.*[14]

Hence arose a misunderstanding between the Pope and the city: and the

---

[12] Sigon. ib. Ann. 773.

[13] Sigon. De Regno Ital. ad Ann. 796.

[14] [Trans.: `And he admonished him with pious treaties to send certain of his princes and subdue the Roman people to himself, and, by enforcing a treaty inviolate, to ensure such a measure of fealty on the guarantee of solemn oaths.']

Romans about two or three years after, by assistance of some of the Clergy, raised such tumults against him, as gave occasion to a new state of things in all the *West*. For two of the Clergy accused him of crimes, and the *Romans* with an armed force, seized him, stript him of his sacerdotal habit, and imprisioned him in a monastery. But by assistance of his friends he made his escape, and fled into *Germany* to *Charles* the great, to whom he complained of the *Romans* for acting against him out of a design to throw off all authority of the Church, and to recover their antient freedom. In his absence his accusers with their forces ravaged the possessions of the Church, and sent the accusations to *Charles*; who before the end of the year sent the Pope back to *Rome* with a large retinue. The Nobles and Bishops of *France* who accompanied him, examined the chief of his accusers at *Rome*, and sent them into *France* in custody. This was in the year 799. The next year *Charles* himself went to *Rome*, and upon a day appointed presided in a Council of *Italian* and *French* Bishops to hear both parties. But when the Pope's adversaries expected to be heard, the Council[15] declared that he who was the supreme judge of all men, was above being judged by any other than himself: whereupon he made a solemn declaration of his innocence before all the people, and by doing so was looked upon as acquitted.

Soon after, upon *Christmas*-Day, the people of *Rome*, who had hitherto elected their Bishop, and reckoned that they and their Senate inherited the rights of the antient Senate and people of *Rome*, voted Charles their *Emperor*, and subjected themselves to him in such a manner as the old *Roman* Empire and their Senate were subjected to the old *Roman* Emperors. The Pope crowned him, and anointed him with holy oil, and

---

[15]   Vide Anastasium.*

worshipped him on his knees after the manner of adoring the old *Roman* Emperors; as the aforesaid Poet thus relates:

> *Post laudes igitur dictas et summus eundem*
> *Præsul adoravit, sicut mos debitos olim*
> *Principibus fuit antiquis.*[16]

The Emperor, on the other hand, took the following oath to the Pope: *In nomine Christi spondeo atque polliceor, Ego Carolus Imperator coram Deo et beato Petro Apostolico me protectorem ac defensorem fore hujus santæ Romanæ Ecclesiæ in omnibus utilitatibus, quatenùs divino fultus fuero adjutorio, prout sciero poteroque.*[17] The Emperor was also made Consul of *Rome*, and his son *Pipin* crowned King of *Italy*: and henceforward the Emperor stiled himself: *Carolus serenissimus, Augustus, à Deo coronatus, magnus, pacifus, Romæ gubernans imperium, or Imperatorum Romanorum;*[18] and he was prayed for in the Churches of *Rome*. His image was henceforward put upon the coins of *Rome*: while the enemies of the Pope, to the number of three hundred *Romans* and two or three of the Clergy, were sentenced to death. The three hundred *Romans* were beheaded in one day in the *Lateran* fields: but

---

[16] [Trans.: `After the king's praises had been spoken, he was even worshipped by that highest prelate, as was the manner due to ancient emperors.']

[17] [Trans.: `In the name of Christ, I Charles, Emperor, before God and the Apostle Peter, vow and promise to protect and guard the Holy Roman Church to the best of my knowledge and ability in all times of need, in so far as I be upheld by divine help.']

[18] [Trans.: `Most serene Charles, Augustus, crowned by God, the mighty, the peacemaker, governor of the empire of Rome or Emperor of the Romans.']

the Clergymen at the intercession of the Pope, were pardoned, and banished into *France*. And thus the title of the *Roman* Emperor, which had hitherto been in the Greek Emperors, was by this act transferred in the *West* to the *Kings* of France.

After these things *Charles* gave the City and Duchy of *Rome* to the Pope, subordinately to himself as Emperor of the *Romans*; spent the winter in ordering the affairs of *Rome*, and those of the Apostolic see, and of all *Italy*, both civil and ecclesiastical, and in making new laws for them; and returned the next summer into *France*: leaving the city under its Senate, and both under the Pope and himself. But hearing that his new laws were not observed by the judges in dictating the law, nor by the people in hearing it; and that the great men took servants from free men, and from the Churches and Monasteries, to labour in their vineyards, fields, pastures and houses, and continued to exact cattle and wine of them, and to oppress those that served the Churches: he wrote to his son *Pipin* to remedy these abuses, to take care of the Church, and see his laws executed.[19]

Now the Senate and people and principality of *Rome* I take to be the third King the little horn overcame, and even the chief of the three. For this people elected the Pope and the Emperor; and now, by electing the Emperor and making him Consul, was acknowldged to retain the authority of the old *Roman* Senate and people. This city was the Metropolis of the old *Roman* Empire, represented in *Daniel* by the fourth Beast; and by subduing the Senate and people and Duchy, it became the Metropolis of the little horn of that Beast, and completed *Peter's* Patrimony, which was the kingdom of that horn. Besides, this victory was attended with greater consequences than those over the other two Kings. For it set up the *Western Empire*, which continues to this

---

[19]   Sigon. de Regno Ital.

day. It set up the Pope above the judicature of the *Roman* Senate, and above that of a council of *Italian* and *French* Bishops, and even above all human judicature; and gave him the supremacy over the *Western* Churches and their Councils in a high degree. It gave him *a look more stout than his fellows*; so that when this new religion began to be established in the minds of men, he grappled not only with Kings, but even with the *Western* Emperor himself. It is observable also, that the custom of kissing the Pope's feet, an honour superior to that of Kings and Emperors, began about this time. There are some instances of it in the ninth century: *Platina** tells us, that the feet of Pope *Leo* IV were kissed, according to antient custom, by all who came to him: and some say that *Leo* III began this custom, pretending that his hand was infected by the kiss of a woman. The Popes began also about this time to canonize saints, and to grant indulgences and pardons: and some represent that *Leo* III was the first author of all these things. It is further observable, that *Charles* the great, between the years 775 and 796, conquered all *Germany* from the *Rhine* and *Danube* northwards to the *Baltic* sea, and eastward to the river *Teis*; extending his conquests also into *Spain* as far as the river *Ebro*; and by these conquests he laid the foundation of the new Empire; and at the same time propagated the *Roman* Catholic religion into all his conquests, obliging the *Saxons* and *Hunns* who were heathens, to receive the *Roman* faith, and distributing his northern conquests into Bishopricks, granting tithes to the Clergy and *Peter-Pence** to the Pope: by all which the Church of *Rome* was highly enlarged, enriched, exalted and established.

In the forementioned *dissertation upon some coins of* Charles *the great*, Ludovicus Pius, Lotharius, *and their successors, stamped at* Rome, there is a draught of a piece of *Mosaic work* which Pope *Leo* III. caused to be made in his Palace near the Church of *John Lateran*, in memory of his sending the standard or banner of the city of *Rome* curiously wrought, to *Charles* the great; and which still remained there at the publishing of the said book. In the *Mosaic* work there appeared *Peter* with three keys in his lap, reaching the *Pallium* to the Pope with his right hand, and the banner of the city to *Charles* the great with his left. By the Pope was this inscription, SCISSIMUS D.N. LEO PP; by the King this, D.N. CARLO REGI; and under the feet of *Peter* this, BEATE PETRE, DONA VITAM LEONI PP, ET BICTORIAM CARLO REGI DONA. This Monument gives the title of King to *Charles*, and therefore was erected before he was Emperor. It was erected when *Peter* was reaching the *Pallium* to the Pope, and the Pope was sending the banner of the city to *Charles*, that is A.C. 796. The words above, *Sanctissimus Dominus noster Leo Papa domino nostro Carolo Regi*, relate to the message; and the words below, *beate Petre, dona vitam Leoni Papæ et victoriam Carolo regi dona*,[20] are a prayer that in this undertaking God would preserve the life of the Pope, and give victory to the King over the *Romans*. The three keys in the lap of *Peter* signify the keys of the three parts of his Patrimony, that of *Rome* with its Duchy, which the Pope claimed and was conquering, those of *Ravenna* with the Exarchate, and of the territories taken from the *Lombards*; both which he had newly conquered. These were the three dominions, whose keys were in the lap of St. *Peter*, and whose Crowns are now worn by the Pope, and by the conquest of which he became the little horn of the fourth Beast. By *Peter's* giving the *Pallium* to the Pope with his right hand, and the banner of the city to the king with his left, and by naming the Pope before the King in the inscription,

---

[20]   [Trans.: `OUR MOST HOLY LORD POPE LEO .... TO OUR LORD KING CHARLES ... BLESSED PETER, GRANT LIFE TO POPE LEO, AND VICTORY TO KING CHARLES.']

may be understood that the pope was then reckoned superior in dignity to the Kings of the earth.

After the death of *Charles* the great, his son and successor *Ludovicus Pius*, at the request of the Pope, confirmed the donations of his grandfather and father to the see of *Rome*. And in the confirmation he names first *Rome* with its Duchy extending into *Tuscany* and *Campania*; then the Exarchate of *Ravenna*, with *Pentapolis*; and in the third place, the territories taken from the *Lombards*.[21] These are his three conquests, and he was told to hold them of the Emperor for the use of the Church *sub integritate*, entirely, without the Emperor's meddling therewith, or with the jurisdiction or power of the Pope therein, unless called thereto in certain cases. This ratification the Emperor *Ludovicus* made under an oath: and as the King of the *Ostrogoths*, for acknowledging that he held his kingdom of *Italy* of the *Greek* Emperor, stamped the effigies of the Emperor on one side of his coins and his own on the reverse; so the Pope made the like acknowledgment to the *Western* Emperor. For the Pope began now to coin money, and the coins of Rome are henceforward found with the heads of the Emperors, *Charles*, *Ludovicus Pius*, *Lotharius*, and their successors, on the one side, and the Pope's inscription on the reverse, for many years.

---

[21] Confirmationem recitat Sigonius, lib. 4. de Regno Italiæ, ad An. 817.

CHAPTER VIII

Of the power of the eleventh horn of Daniel's fourth Beast, to change times and laws.

In the reign of the *Greek* Emperor *Justinian*, and again in the reign of *Phocas*, the Bishop of *Rome* obtained some dominion over the *Greek* Churches, but of no long continuance. His standing dominion was only over the nations of the *Western Empire*, represented by *Daniel's* fourth Beast. And this jurisdiction was set up by the following Edict of the Emperors *Gratian* and *Valentinian*. — *Volumus ut quicunque judicio Damasi, quod ille cum Concilio quinque vel septem habuerit Episcoporum, vel eorum qui Catholici sunt judicio vel Concilio condemnatus fuerit, si juste voluerit Ecclesiam retentare, ut qui ad sacerdotale judicium per contumeliam non ivisset: ut ab illustribus viris Præfectis Prætorio Galliæ atque Italiæ, authoritate adhibitâ, ad Episcopale judicium remittatur, sive â Consularibus vel Vicariis, ut ad Urbem Romam sub prosecutione perveniat. Aut si in longinquioribus partibus alicujus ferocitas talis emerserit, omnis ejus causæ edictio ad Metropolitæ in eadem Provincia Episcopi deduceretur examen. Vel si ipse Metropolitanus est, Romam necessariò, vel ad eos quos Romanus Episcopus judices dederit, fine delatione contendat. — Quod si vel Metropolitani Episcopi vel cujuscunque sacerdotis iniquitas est suspecta, aut gratis; ad Romanum Episcopum, vel as Concilium quindecim finitimorum Episcoporum accersitum liceat provocare; modo ne post examen habitum, quod definitum fuerit,* *integretur.*[1] This Edict wanting both the name of *Valens* and *Theodosius* in the Title, was made in the time between their reigns, that is, in the end of the year 378, or the beginning of 379. It was directed to the *Præfecti Prætorio Italiæ et Galliæ,* and therefore was general. For the *Præfectus Prætorio Italiæ* governed *Italy, Illyricum occidentale* and *Africa;* and the *Præfectus Prætorio Galliæ* governed *Gallia, Spain, and Britain.*

The granting of this jurisdiction to the Pope gave several Bishops occasion to write to him for his resolutions upon doubtful cases, whereupon he answered by decretal Epistles; and henceforward he gave laws to the *Western Churches* by such Epistles. *Himerius* Bishop of *Tarraco,* the head city of a province in *Spain,* writing to Pope *Damasus* for his direction about certain ecclesiastical matters, and the Letter not

---

[1] [Trans.: `— If anyone has been condemned by the court of Damasus, which he held with a council of five or seven bishops, or by a court or council consisting of Catholics; and if such a person duly wishes to cleave to the Church on the ground that he did not absent himself from the ecclesiastical court out of contempt for it, it is our will that he be remitted to the episcopal court by an exercise of authority on the part of the Prefects of the Praetorium of Gaul and Italy (or by its legates or their deputies) in order that he may come under escort to the City of Rome. Or if in districts more remote, an act of such recklessness be committed by anyone, let a full statement of his case be submitted to the examination of the Metropolitan Bishop. Or if he be a Metropolitan himself, let him without fail make all speed to come to Rome, or to whatever judges the Bishop of Rome shall direct. — But if the impartiality of the Metropolitan Bishop, or of any priest whatever, be questioned, or corruption suspected, let him have the right of appeal to the Bishop of Rome, or to a duly convened council of fifteen neighbouring bishops: only after the holding of the inquiry let not a matter which has been settled be opened again.'] See the Annales of Baronius, Anno 381. Sect. 6.

arriving at Rome till after the death of *Damasus*, A.C. 384; his successor *Siricius* answered the same with a legislative authority, telling him of one thing: *Cum hoc fieri — missa ad Provincias à venerandæ memoriæ prædecessore meo Liberio generalia decreta, prohibeant.*[2] Of another: *Noverint se ab omni ecclesiastico honore, quo indignè usi sunt, Apostolicæ Sedis auctoritate, dejectos.*[3] Of another: *Scituri posthac omnium Provinciarum summi Antistites, quod si ultrò ad sacros ordines quenquam de talibus esse assumendum, et de suo et de aliorum statu, quos contra Canones et interdicta nostra provexerint, congruam ab Apostolica Sede promendam esse sententiam.*[4] And the Epistle he concludes thus: *Explicuimus, ut arbitror, frater charissime, universa quæ digesta sunt in querelam; et ad singulas causas, de quibus ad Romanum Ecclesiam, utpote ad caput tui corporis, retulisti; sufficientia, quantum opinor, responsa reddidimus. Nunc fraternitatis tuæ animum ad servandos canones, et tenenda decretalia constituta, magis ac magis incitamus: ad hæc quæ ad tua consulta rescripsimus in omnium Coepiscoporum perferri facias notionem; et non solum*

---

[2] [Trans.: `Since the general decrees sent to the provinces by my predecessor Liberius of revered memory forbade this thing to be done.' (This and following quotations on this page do not properly relate to each other in context; Newton is using them only to indicate the extent of the jurisdiction of the popes in the late fourth century, so the page reads rather disjointedly.)]

[3] [Trans.: `Let them take note that by the authority of the Apostolic See, having made improper use of their ecclesiastical positions, they are deposed from them.']

[4] [Trans.: `The chief prelates of each province will hereafter bear in mind, that if it is further proposed to admit to holy orders any man of such a class, a suitable pronouncement must be issued by the Apostolic See, not only with regard to the status of such a person, but also with regard to that of those others whom they have already advanced contrary to canonical law and our interdicts.']

eorum, qui in tua sunt diocesi consituti, set etiam ad universos Carthaginen ac Boeticos, Lusitanos atque⁵ Gallicos, vel eos qui vicinis tibi collimitant hinc inde Provinciis, hæc quæ a nobis sunt salubri ordinatione disposita, sub literarum tuarum prosecutione mittantur. Et quanquam statuta sedis Apostolicæ vel Canonum venerabilia definita, nulli Sacerdotum Domini ignorare sit liberum: utilis tamen, atque pro antiquitate sacerdotii tui, dilectioni tuæ esse admodùm poterit gloriosum, si ea quæ ad te speciali nomine generaliter scripta sunt, per unamimitatis tuæ sollicitudinem in universorum fratrum nostrorum notitiam perferantur; quatenus et quæ à nobis non inconsultè sed providè sub nimia cautela et deliberatione sunt salubriter constituta, intemerata permaneant, et omnibus in posterum excusationibus aditus, qui jam ulli apud nos patere poterit, obstruatur. Dat 3 Id. Febr. Arcadio et Bautone viris clarissimus Consulibus, A.C. 385.⁶ Pope *Liberius* in the reign of *Jovian*

---

⁵   Populos Galliciæ [given as note `a']

⁶   [Trans.: `Dearest Brother, I have, as I think, explained those general matters which formed the body of your grievance; and with regard to those particular questions which you referred to the Roman Church - to the head of your body - the answers I have returned will, as far as I can see, prove sufficient. Now we do earnestly and yet more earnestly exhort you, and your brethren, to keep the canons and to hold fast by our decretal findings; moreover cause that these directions (which form our reply to your questions), be conveyed to the knowledge of all your fellow bishops: and not only to the knowledge of all those who are stationed in your own diocese; but also to all those of Carthage, Boetical, Lusitania and Gaul, that is, to your neighbours in the provinces on either side of you. Let these arrangements, ordained by us for your welfare, be sent under cover of your letters, and although it be not permissible for any priest of God to be ignorant of the statutes of the Holy See and the venerable enactments of the canons, yet it will not be without advantage and (in virtue of your long service to the Church) highly complimentary to your loving zeal towards ourselves, if those general

or *Valentinian* I. sent general Decrees to the Provinces, ordering that the *Arians* should not be rebaptized: and this he did in favour of the Council of *Alexandria*, that nothing more should be required of them than to renounce their opinions. Pope *Damasus* is said to have decreed in a Roman Council, that *Tithes* and *Tenths* should be paid upon the pain of an *Anathema*; and that *Glory be to the Father*, &c. should be said or sung at the end of the *Psalms*. But the first decretal Epistle now extant is this of *Siricius* to *Himerius*; by which the Pope made *Himerius* his Vicar over all *Spain* for promulging* his Decrees, and seeing them observed. The Bishop of *Sevill* was also the Pope's Vicar sometimes; for *Simplicius* wrote thus to *Zeno* Bishop of that place: *Talibus idcirco gloriantes indiciis, congruum duximus vicariâ Sedis nostræ te auctoritate fulciri: cujus vigore munitus, Apostolicæ institutionis Decreta, vel sanctorum terminos Patrum, nullatenus transcendi permittas.*[7] And Pope *Hormisda* made the Bishop of *Sevill* his Vicar over *Boetica* and *Lusitania*, and the Bishop of *Tarraco* his Vicar over all the rest of *Spain*, as appears by his Epistles to them.[8]

---

replies, sent specifically to yourself, should be brought to the notice of our brethren at large by your earnest sympathy with our objects. Thus, let those decisions which we have determined upon, not rashly, but with forethought and much caution and deliberation for the welfare of all, remain inviolate, and for the future let all possibility of claims for exemption be debarred, henceforth such pleas will not be accepted by us. Given on the 11th February in the consulship of the distinguished Arcadius and Bauto, A.C. 385.']

[7]   [Trans.: 'Rejoicing therefore in such evidence, we have thought it fitting that you should be supported by the vicarious authority of our See. Fortified with that strength, do not suffer the decrees ordained by the Apostolic See or the limits fixed by the Holy Fathers to be at all overstepped.']

[8]   Hormisd. Epist. 24, 26.

140

Pope *Innocent* the first, in his decretal Epistle to *Victricius* Bishop of *Rouen* in *France*, A.C. 404, in pursuance of the Edict of *Gratian*, made this Decree: *Si quæ autem causæ vel contentiones inter clericos tam superioris ordinis quam etiam inferioris fuerint exortæ; ut secundum Synodum Nicenum congregatis ejusdem Provinciæ Episcopis jurgium terminetur: nec alcui liceat,* [9] *Romanæ Ecclesiæ, cujus in omnibus causis debet reverentia custodiri, relictis his sacerdotibus, qui in eadem Provincia Dei Ecclesiam nutu Divino gubernant, ad alias convolare Provincias. Quod siquis fortè præsumpserit; et ab officio Clericatûs summotus, et injuriam reus judicetur. Si autem majores causæ in medium fuerint devolutae, ad Sedem Apostolicam sicut Synodus statuit, et beata consuetudo exigit, post judicium Episcopale referantur.* [10] By these Letters it seems to me that *Gallia* was now subject to the Pope, and had been so for some time, and that the Bishop of *Rouen* was then his Vicar or one of them: for the Pope directs him to refer the greater causes to the See of *Rome*, according to custom. But the Bishop of *Arles* soon after became the Pope's Vicar over all *Gallia*: for Pope *Zosimus*, A.C. 417, ordaining that none should have

---

[9]   The words, fine auctoritate, seem wanting. [should be sine auctoritate?; given as note `a'].

[10]   [Trans.: `If there shall arise any suits or differences between clerics, whether of high or low rank let the matter in dispute be settled before the bishops of that province assembled in council according to the directions of the Nicene Synod. Let it not be permitted, without the authority of the Roman Church (the reverence of which must ever be safeguarded) for any to absent themselves from those priests who are, by divine assent, the governors of the Church in that province, in order to seek shelter in other provinces. But if this be the case, let he who has so presumed be regarded as guilty of outrage and deposed from his office. But if cases of larger import be the subject of examination, subsequent to trial by the bishops, let them be referred to the Apostolic See in accordance with the decrees of the Synod and the exigencies of hallowed custom.']

access to him without the credentials of his Vicars, conferred upon *Patroclus* the Bishop of *Arles* this authority over all *Gallia*, by the following decree.

Zosimus universis Episcopis per Gallias et septem
Provincias constitutis.

Placuit Apostolicæ Sedi, ut siquis ex qualibet Galliarum parte sub quolibet ecclesiastico gradu ad nos Romæ venire contendit, vel aliò terrarum ire disponit, non aliter proficiscatur nisi Metropolitani Episcopi Formatas acceperit, quibus sacerdotium suum vel locum ecclesiasticum quem habet, scriptorum ejus adstipulatione perdoceat: quod ex gratia statuimus quia plures episcopi sive presbyteri sive ecclesiastici simulantes, quia nullum documentum Formatarum extat per quod valeant confutari, in nomen venerationis irrepunt, et indebitam reverantiam promerentur. Quisquis igitur, fratres charissimi, prætermissà supradicti Formatâ, sive episcopus, sive prebyter, sive diaconus, aut deinceps inferior gradu sit, ad nos venerit: sciat se omnino suscipi non posse. Quam auctoritatem ubique nos misisse manifestum est, ut cunctis regionibus innotescat id quod statuimus omnimodis esse servandum. Siquis autem hæc salubriter constituta temerare tentaverit sponte suâ, se a nostra noverit communione discretum. Hoc autem privilegium Formatarum sancto Patroclo fratri et coepiscopo nostro, meritorum ejus speciali contemplatione, concessimus.[11] And that the Bishop of *Arles* was sometimes the Pope's Vicar over all

---

[11]   [Trans.: `Zosimus to all the Bishops throughout the Province of Gaul and the Seven Provinces. The Apostolic See has resolved that if any one from any part of Gaul, or of any ecclesiastical rank wishes to come to us at Rome or go to any other place on earth, he may not do so without the having received credentials from his metropolitan bishop, in which his priestly office or ecclesiastical position may by affirmed.

France, is affirmed also by all the Bishops of the Diocese of *Arles* in their letter to Pope *Leo* I. *Cui id etiam honoris dignitatisque collatum est,* say they, *ut non tantum has Provincias potestate propriâ gubernaret; verum etiam omnes Gallias sibi Apostolicœ Sedis vice mandatas, sub omni ecclesiastica regula contineret.*[12] And Pope *Pelagius* I. A.C. 556, in his Epistle to *Sapaudus* Bishop of *Arles*: *Majorum nostrorum, operante Dei misericordiâ, cupientes inhœrere vestigiis et eorum actus divino examine in omnibus imitari: charitati tuœ per universam Galliam, Sanctœ Sedis Apostolicœ, cui divinâ gratiâ prœsidemus, vices injungimus.*[13]

By the influence of the same imperial Edict, not only *Spain* and *Gallia*, but

---

This decree we have graciously ordained on account of the many masquerading as bishops, presbyters or ecclesiastics who now steal into an honourable title and win unmerited respect because no documentary credentials exist by which they might be exposed. If anyone therefore, dearly beloved brethren, be he bishop, presbyter, deacon or of humbler position, come to us without the said credentials, be it known that he can by no means obtain recognition. This command we have sent everywhere, manifestly to the end, that all districts may know that our decree is to be observed. But if anyone chooses of his own accord to violate these decrees enacted for the common welfare, let it be known that he is banned from communion with us. This privilege of granting credentials, in special recognition of his services, we have conferred upon our holy brother and fellow bishop Patroclus.']

[12] [Trans.: `upon whom this further degree of honour and prestige had been conferred. He is not only to govern these provinces in virtue of his own authority, but also to keep in subjection to every ecclesiastical rule all the provinces of Gaul entrusted to his tutelage as vicar of the Holy See.']

[13] [Trans.: `By the efficacy of the mercy of God, we desire to tread in the footsteps of our predecessors, and under divine scrutiny to imitate their actions in all matters. Thus we entrust to you as our vicar, the authority of the Apostolic See - over which by the Grace of God we preside - as it applies to the whole of Gaul.']

also *Illyricum* became subject to the Pope. *Damasus* made *Ascholius*, or *Acholius*, Bishop of *Thessalonica* the Metropolis of *Oriental Illyricum*, his Vicar for hearing of causes; and in the year 382, *Acholius* being summond by Pope *Damasus*, came to a council at *Rome*. Pope *Siricius* the successor of *Damasus*, decreed that no Bishop should be ordained in *Illyricum* without the consent of *Anysius* the successor of *Acholius*. And the following popes gave *Rufus* the successor of *Anysius*, a power of calling Provincial Councils: for in the Collections of *Holstenius** there is an account of a Council of *Rome* convened under Pope *Boniface* II. in which were produced letters of *Damasus, Syricius, Innocent* I. *Boniface* I. and *Cælestine* Bishops of *Rome*, to *Ascholius, Anysius* and *Rufus*, Bishops of *Thessalonica*: in which Letters they commend to them the hearing of causes in *Illyricum*, granted by the Lord and the holy Canons to the Apostolic See thro'out that Province. And Pope *Siricius* saith in his Epistle to *Anysius*: *Etiam dudum, frater charissime, per Candidianum Episcopum, qui nos præcessit ad Dominum, hujusmodi literas dederamus, ut nulla licentia esset, sine consensu tuo in Illyrico. Episcopos ordinare præsumere, quæ utrum ad te pervenerint scire non potui. Multa enim gesta sunt per contentionem, ab Episcopis in ordinationibus faciendas, quod tua melius caritus novit.*[14] And a little after: *Ad omnem enim hujusmodi audaciam comprimendam vigilare debet instantia tua, Spiritu in te Sancto servente: ut vel ipse, si potes, vel quos judicaveris Episcopos idoneos,*

---

[14] [Trans.: 'It is long, my dearly belowed brother, since we sent you a letter by Bishop Candidianus (who has gone before us to the presence of God) to the effect that no licence should be granted for the ordination of bishops in Illyricum without your consent previously being obtained. I have never been able to learn, however, if this letter ever reached you or not. For many of the actions of the bishop in the matter of the filling of offices show a lack of harmony, a fact which you dear brother, know better than I.']

cum literis dirigas, dato consensu qui possit, in ejus locum qui defunctus vel depositus fuerit, Catholicum Episcopum vitâ et moribus probatum, secundum Nicœnœ Synodi statuta vel Ecclesiœ Romanœ, Clericum de Clero meritum ordinare.[15]   And Pope Innocent I. saith in his Epistle to *Anysius: Cui [Anysio] etiam anteriores tanti ac tales viri prœdecessores mei Episcopi, id est, sanctœ memoriœ Damasus, Siricius, atque supra memoratus vir ita detulerunt; ut omnia quœ in omnibus illis partibus gererentur, Sanctitati tuœ, quœ plena justitiœ est, traderent cognoscenda.*[16]   And in his Epistle to *Rufus* the successor of *Anysius: Ita longis intervallis disterminatis à me ecclesiis discat consulendum; ut prudentiœ gravitatique tuœ, committendam curam causasque, siquœ exoriantur, per Achaiœ, Thessaliœ, Epiri veteris, Epiri novœ, et Cretœ, Daciœ mediterraneœ, Daciœ ripensis, Moesiœ, Dardaniœ, et Prœvali ecclesias, Christo Domino annuante, censeam. Verè enim ejus sacratissimus monitus lectissimœ sinceritatis tuœ providentiœ et virtuti hanc injungimus sollicitudinem: non primitùs hœc statuentes, sed Prœcessores nostros Apostolicos imitati, qui beatissimis Acholio et Anysio injungi pro meritis ista voluerunt.*[17]   And *Boniface* I. in his decretal

---

[15]   [Trans.: 'You must never relax your diligence (the Holy Spirit working diligently within you) in suppressing all this outrageous conduct. Such that, you yourself, if possible (and otherwise those bishops you regard as suitable) must, in writing and with your full consent, indicate who is to be invested with powers to ordain - in the stead of those who have died or have been deposed from office - a Catholic bishop, a man of tried life and morals, a priest of merit, in accordance with the statutes of the Nicene Synod and of the Roman Church.']

[16]   [Trans.: 'My immediate predecessors in the Bishopric, men whose pre-eminence and qualities are well known, Damasus of sainted memory, Siricius and he whom I mentioned above, wrote to you to the effect that they consigned the supervision of all that was done in those parts to your Holiness and your abundant sense of justice.']

[17]   [Trans.: 'So let it be taken to heart, that the interest of the Churches separated from me by

Epistle to *Rufus* and the rest of the Bishops in *Illyricum*: *Nullus ut frequenter dixi, alicujus ordinationem citra ejus [Episocopi Thessalonicensis] conscientiam celebrare præsumat: cui, ut supra dictum est, vice nostrâ cuncta committamus.*[18] And Pope *Cælestine*, in his decretal Epistle to the Bishops thro'out *Ilyricum*, saith: *Vicem nostram per vestram Provinciam noveritis [Rufo] esse commissam, ita ut ad eum, fratres carissimi, quicquid de causis agitur, referatur. Sine ejus consilio nullis ordinetur. Nullus usurpet, eodem inconscio, commissam illi Provinciam; colligere nisi cum ejus voluntate Episcopus non præsumat.*[19] And in the cause of *Perigenes*, in the title of his Epistle, he thus enumerated the Provinces under the Bishop: *Rufo et cæteris Episcopis per Macedoniam, Achaiam, Thessalium, Epirum veterem, Epirum novam.*

---

long distances must be considered. It is my resolve (the Lord Christ approving thereof) that you, a man of prudence and and steadiness, should be entrusted with the care of any suits that may arise throughout the sphere comprising the Churches of Achæe, Thessaly, old and new Epirus, Crete, central Dacia, Dacia on the Danube, Moesia, Dardania and Prævalum. We say this with the approval of the Lord Jesus Christ, for, in truth, it is upon His most sacred injunctions that we place this charge upon your Holiness's most excellent prudence and virtue. Nor is our decision an innovation, for we act upon the precedent of our Apostolic predecessors, who decreed that a similar charge was laid upon the sainted Acholius and Anysius in reward of their services.']

[18]   [Trans.: `Let no one, as we have often said before, take upon it himself to celebrate the ordination of any cleric without the knowledge of the Bishop of Thessalonica, to whom, as previously we said, we entrust all our powers as our vicar.']

[19]   [Trans.: `You will know that our powers have been entrusted to Rufus as our vicar; and so my dearly beloved brethren, if there be any differences amongst you, let them be referred to his judgement. Without his cognizance let no one be admitted to clerical office. Let no one without his knowledge presume to appropriate these his peculiar duties or dare to convene a council except with his consent.']

Prævalin, et Daciam constitutis.[20] And Pope *Xistus* in a decretal Epistle to the same bishops: *Illyricanæ omnes Ecclesiæ, ut à decessoribus nostris recepimus, et nos quoque fecimus, ad curam nunc pertinent Thessalonicensis Antistitis, ut suâ sollicitudine, siquæ inter fratres nascantur, ut assolent, actiones distinguat atque definiat; et eum, quicquid à singulis sacerdotibus agiture, referatur. Sit Concilium, quotiens casæ fuerint, quotiens ille pro necessitatum emergentium ratione decreverit*[21]. And Pope *Leo* I in his decretal Epistle to *Anastasius* Bishop of Thessalonica: *Singulis autem Metropolitanis sicut potestas ista committitur, ut in suis Provinciis jus habeant ordinandi; ita eos Metropolitianos à te volumus ordinari; maturo tamen et decocto judicio.*[22]

Occidental *Illyricum* comprehended *Pannonia prima* and *secunda, Savia, Dalmatia, Noricum mediterraneum*, and *Noricum ripense*; and its Metropolis was *Sirmium*, till *Attila* destroyed this city. Afterwards *Laureacum* became the Metropolis of *Noricum* and both *Pannonias*, and *Salona* the Metropolis of *Dalmatia*. Now the

---

[20]   [Trans.: `To Rufus and other Bishops throughout Macedonia, Achæa, Thessaly, Old and New Epirus, Prævalum and Dacia.']

[21]   [Trans.: `In accordance with the precedents set by our predeccesors and with our own actions in the past, all the Churches of Illyricum do hereby fall under the supervision of the Bishop of Thessalonica. That by his earnest attention he may discriminate and give judgement in any disputes that arise - as arise they will - among the brethren and let any suit promoted by an individual priest be referred to his decision. Let a council be held as often as disputes arise, and as often as he shall so decree, in accordance with the exigencies of the situation.']

[22]   [Trans.: `In the same way as individual metropolitan bishops are invested with the power of ordination in their own provinces, so we decree that these metropolitan bishops be in turn ordained by you; only let your choice of them be the fruit of mature and considered judgement.']

Bishops of *Laureacum* and *Salona* received the *Pallium* from the Pope: and *Zosimus*, in his decretal Epistle to *Hesychius* Bishop of *Salona*, directed him to denounce the Apostolic decrees as well to the Bishops of his own as to those of the neigbouring Provinces.[23] The subjection of these Provinces to the See of *Rome* seems to have begun in *Anemius*, who was ordained Bishop of *Sirmium* by *Ambrose* Bishop of *Millain*, and who in the Council of *Aquileia* under Pope *Damasus*, A.C. 381, declared his sentence in these words: *Caput Illyrici non nisi civitas Sirmiensis: Ego igitur illius civitatis Episcopus sum. Eum qui non confitetur filium Dei æternum, et coeternum patri, qui est sempiternus, anathema dico.*[24] The next year *Anemius* and *Ambrose*, with *Valerian* Bishop of *Aquileia*, *Acholius* Bishop of *Thessalonica*, and many others, went to the Council of *Rome*, which met for overruling the *Greek* Church by majority of votes, and exalting the authority of the Apostolic See, as was attempted before in the Council of *Sardica*.

Aquileia was the second city of the *Western Empire*, and by some called the second *Rome*. It was the Metropolis of *Istria, Forum Julium*, and *Venetia*; and its subjugation to the See of *Rome* is manifest by the decretal Epistle of *Leo* I. directed to *Nicetas* Bishop of this city; for the Pope begins his Epistle thus: *Regressus ad nos filius meus Adeodatus Diaconus Sedis nostræ, dilectionem tuam poposcisse memorat, ut de his à nobis authoritatem Apostolicæ Sedis acciperes, quæ quidem magnam difficultatem dijudicationis videntur afferre.*[25] Then he sets down an answer to the

---

23   Vide Caroli a S. Paulo Geographicam sacram, p. 72-3.

24   [Trans.: `There is no capital of Illyricum but the City of Sirmium. I am, therefore, the Bishop of Illyricum. Whoever does not confess the Son of God as eternal and co-eternal with the Father (who is from everlasting to everlasting), I proclaim anathema.']

25   [Trans.: `Upon his return to us, my son Adeodatus, the Deacon of our See, reported to us

questions proposed by *Nicetas*, and concludes thus: *Hanc autem Epistolam nostram, quam ad consultationem tuæ fraternitatis emisimus, ad omnes fratres et comprovinciales tuos Episcopos facies pervenire, ut in omnium observantia, data profit authoritas. Data 12 Kal. Apr. Majorano Aug. Cos.*[26] A.C. 458. *Gregory* the great A.C. 591, cited *Severus* Bishop of *Aquileia* to appear before him in judgement a Council at *Rome.*[27]

The Bishops of *Aquileia* and *Millain* created one another, and therefore were of equal authority, and alike subject to the See of *Rome.* Pope *Pelagius* about the year 557, testified this in the following words: *Mos antiquus fuit,* saith he *ut quia pro longinquitate vel difficultate itineris, ab Apostolico illis onerosum fuerit ordinari, ipsi se invicem Mediolanensis et Aquileiensis ordinare Episcopos debuissent.*[28] These words[29] imply that the ordination of these two Bishops belonged to the See of *Rome.* When *Laurentius* Bishop of *Millain* had excommunicated *Magnus*, one of his Presbyters, and was dead, *Gregory* the great absolved *Magnus*, and sent the *Pallium* to

---

your request that to be vested with the authority of the Holy See to deal with matters which appear to present difficulty in decision.']

[26]   [Trans.: `Now as to this letter of ours which we have sent, in answer to your brotherly enquiries. You will see to it that it reaches all the brethren and the bishops of your province, so that by the universal observance thereof, the authority granted you may be of advantage. Given on the 21st March in the consulship of Majoranus Augustus A.C. 458.']

[27]   Greg. M. lib. I. Indic. 9. Epist. 16.

[28]   [Trans.: `It was the ancient custom' saith he, `in view of the burdensome length and difficulty of the journey to Rome for ordination of bishops by the Apostolic See, that they themselves should ordain each other in turn to the Bishopric of Aquileia or Millain.']

[29]   Apud Gratianum de Mediolanensi & Aquileiensi Episcopis.

the new elected Bishop *Constantius*;[30] whom the next year he reprehended of partiality in judging *Fortunatus*, and commanded him to send *Fortunatus* to *Rome* to be judged there:[31] four years after he appointed the Bishops of *Millain* and *Ravenna* to hear the cause of one *Maximus*;[32] and two years after, *viz.* A.C. 601, when *Constantius* was dead, and the people of *Millain* had elected another, *Gregory* wrote to the Notary, Clergy, and People of *Millain*, that by the authority of his Letters *Deusdedit* should be ordained, and that he whom the *Lombards* had ordained was an unworthy successor of *Ambrose*:[33] whence I gather, that the Church of *Millain* had continued in this state of subordination to the See of *Rome* ever since the days of *Ambrose*; for *Ambrose* himself acknowledged the authority of that See. *Ecclesia Romana,* saith he, *hanc consuetudinem non habet, cujus typum in omnibus sequimur, et formam. And a little after: In omnibus cupio sequi Ecclesiam Romanam.*[34] And in his commentary upon 1 *Tim.* iii. *Cum totus mundus Dei sit, tamen domus ejus Ecclesia dicitur, cujus hodie rector est Damasus.*[35] In his Oration on the death of his brother *Satyrus*, he relates how his brother coming to a certain city of *Sardinia, advocavit Episcopum loci, percontatusque est ex eo utrum cum Episcopis Catholicis hoc est cum Romana*

---

[30]   Greg. M. lib. 3. Epist. 26. & lib. 4. Epist 1.

[31]   Greg. lib. 5. Epist. 4.

[32]   Greg. lib. 9. Epist. 10 & 67.

[33]   Greg. lib. 11. Epist. 3-4.

[34]   [Trans.: ʿThe custom and model of the Church of Rome and no other do we follow in all things.ʾ And a little after: ʿIn all matters it is my desire to emulate the Church of Rome.ʾ] Ambros. 1. 3. de sacramentis, c. 1.

[35]   [Trans.: ʿThough the whole world be the Lord's, yet the Church is called His house, of which the present ruler is Damasus.ʾ]

Ecclesias conveniret?[36] And in conjunction with the Synod of Aquileia A.C. 381, in a synodical Epistle to the Emperor *Gratian*, he saith: *Totius orbis Romani caput Romanum Ecclesiam, atque illam sacrosanctam Apostolorum fidem, ne turbari sineret, obsecranda fuit clementia vestra; inde enim in omnes venerandæ communionis jura dimanant.*[37] The Churches therefore of *Aquileia* and *Millain* were subject to the See of *Rome* from the days of the Emperor *Gratian*. *Auxentius* the predecessor of *Ambrose* was not subject to the see of *Rome*, and consequently the subjection of the Church of *Millain* began in *Ambrose*. This Diocese of *Millain* contained *Liguria* with *Insubria*, the *Alpes Cottiæ* and *Rhœtia*; and was divided from the Diocese of *Aquileia* by the river *Addua*. In the year 844, the Bishop of *Millain* broke off from the See of *Rome*, and continued in this separation about 200 years, as is thus related by *Sigonius**: *Eodem anno Angilbertus Mediolanensis Archiepiscopus ab Ecclesia Romana parum comperta de causa descivit, tantumque exemplo in posterum valuit, ut non nisi post ducentos annos Ecclesia Mediolanensis ad Romanæ obedientiam auctoritatemque redierit.*[38]

The Bishop of *Ravenna*, the Metropolis of *Flaminia* and *Æmilia*, was also

---

[36] [Trans.: `he summoned the Bishop of the place and enquired whether he agreed with the Catholic Bishop or, in other words, with the Church of Rome?']

[37] [Trans.: `Claim had to be made upon your clemency not to permit the Roman Church, as head of the whole Roman world, or the sacred apostolic faith to be disturbed. For it is from your clemency that justice is assured to all of the Holy Communion.']

[38] [Trans.: `In the same year Angilbertus, Archbishop of Millain - for some reason not sufficiently authenticated - seceded from the See of Rome. Such a precedent he set his successors, that only after two hundred years did the See of Millain return to the obedience and authority of the See of Rome.'] Sigonius de Regno Itali', lib. 5.

subject to the Pope: for *Zosimus*, A.C. 417, excommunicated some of the Presbyters of that Church, and wrote a commonitory Epistle about them to the Clergy of that Church as a branch of the Roman Church: *In sua*, saith he, *hoc est, in Ecclesia nostra Romana*.[39] When those of *Ravenna*, having elected a new Bishop, gave notice thereof to Pope *Sixtus*, the Pope set him aside, and ordained *Peter Chrysologus* in his room.[40] *Chrysologus* in his Epistle to *Eutyches*, extant in the Acts of the Council of *Chalcedon*, wrote thus: *Nos pro studio pacis et fidei, extra consensum Romanæ civitatis Episcopi, causes fidei audire non possumus*.[41] Pope *Leo* I. being consulted by *Leo* Bishop of *Ravenna* about some questions, answered him by a decretal Epistle A.C. 451. And Pope *Gregory* the great, reprehending *John* Bishop of *Ravenna* about the use of the *Pallium*, tells him of a Precept of one of his predecessors, Pope *John*, commanding that all the Privileges formerly granted to the Bishop and Church of *Ravenna* should be kept: to this *John* returned a submissive answer; and after his death Pope *Gregory* ordered a visitation of the Church of *Ravenna*, confirmed the privileges heretofore granted them, and sent his *Pallium*, as of antient custom, to their new Bishop *Marinian*.[42] Yet this Church revolted sometimes from the Church of *Rome*, but returned again to its obedience.

The rest of *Italy*, with the Islands adjacent, containing the *suburbicarian* regions, or ten Provinces under the temporal vicar of *Rome*, viz. *Campania, Tuscia* and *Umbria, Picenum, Suburbicarium, Sicily, Apulia,* and *Calabria, Brutii* and

---

[39]   [Trans.: `In their Church, that is in our Roman Church.']

[40]   See Baronius,* Anno, 433. Sect. 24.

[41]   [Trans.: `On account of our zeal for peace and for the faith, we cannot hear cases on matters of faith without the consent of the Bishop of the City of Rome.']

[42]   Greg. M. lib. 3. Epist. 56-7. & lib. 5. Epist. 25-6, 56.

Lucania, Samnium, Sardinia, Corsica, and *Valeria,* constituted the proper Province of the Bishop of *Rome.* For the Council of *Nice* in their fifth Canon ordained that Councils should be held every spring and autum, in every Province; and according to this Canon, the Bishops of this Province met at *Rome* every half year. In this sense Pope *Leo* I. applied this Canon to *Rome,* in a decretal Epistle to the Bishops of *Sicily,* written *Alippio* et *Ardabure Coss.* A.C. 447. *Quia saluberrime,* saith he, *à sanctis patribus constitutum est, binos in annis singulis Episcoporum debere esse conventus, terni semper ex vobis ad diem tertium Kalendarum Octobrium Romam æterno concilio sociandi occurrant. Et indissimulanter à vobis hæc consuetudo servetur, quoniam adjuvante Dei gratiâ faciliùs poterit provideri, ut in Ecclesiis Christi nulla scandala, nulli nascantur errores; cum coram Apostolo Petro semper in communione tractatum fuerit, ut omnia Canonum Decreta apud omnes Domini sacerdotes inviolata permaneant.*[43] The Province of *Rome* therefore comprehended *Sicily,* with so much of *Italy* and the neighbouring Islands as sent Bishops to the annual Councils of *Rome;* but extended not into the Provinces of *Ravenna, Aquiliea, Millain, Arles,* &c. those Provinces having councils of their own. The Bishops in every Province of the *Roman* Empire were convened in Council by the Metropolitan or Bishop of the head city of the Province, and this Bishop presided in that Council: but the Bishop of *Rome* did not

---

[43]   [Trans.: `It having been most wisely decreed by the Holy Fathers, that two Councils of the Bishops must be convened every year, let three of your number always come to Rome for the 29th of September as associates with the permanent council. And let this custom be preserved by you without subterfuge, since (the Lord graciously assisting us) it would be the more easily effected that no scandals or heresies should arise in the Church; for (in the presence of the Apostle Peter it be said) it has always been the purpose of our coming together that all the canonical Decrees should remain inviolate with all the priests of God.']

only preside in his own Council of the Bishops of the *suburbicarian* regions, but also gave Orders to the Metropolitans of all the other Provinces in the *Western Empire*, as their universal governor; as may be further perceived by the following instances.

Pope *Zosimus* A.C. 417, cited *Proculus* Bishop of *Marseilles* to appear before a Council at *Rome* for illegitimate Ordinations; and condemned him, as he mentions in several of his Epistles. Pope *Boniface* I. A.C. 419, upon a complaint of the Clergy of *Valentia* against *Maximus* a Bishop, summoned the Bishops of all *Gallia* and the seven Provinces to convene in a Council against him; and saith in his Epistle, that his predecessors had done the like. Pope *Leo* I. called a general Council of all the Provinces of *Spain* to meet in *Gallæcia* against the *Manichees** and *Priscillianists**, as he says in his decretal Epistle to *Turribius* a *Spanish* Bishop. And in one of his decretal Epistles to *Nicetas* Bishop of *Aquileia*, he commands him to call a Council of the Bishop of that Province against the *Pelagians**, which might ratify all the Synodal Decrees which had been already ratified by the See of *Rome* against this heresy. And in his decretal Epistle to *Anastasius* Bishop of *Thesallonica*, he ordained that Bishop should hold two Provincial Councils every year, and refer the harder causes to the See of *Rome*: and if upon any extraordinary occasion it should be necessary to call a Council, he should not be troublesome to the Bishops under him, but content himself with two Bishops out of every Province, and not detain them above fifteen days. In the same Epistle he describes the form of the Church-Government then set up, to consist in a subordination of all the Churches to the See of Rome: *De qua forma*, saith he, *Episcoporum quoque est orta distinctio, et magna dispositione provisum est ne omnes sibi omnia vindicarent, sed essent in singulis Provinciis singuli quorum inter fratres haberetur prima sententia, et rursus quidam in majoribus urbibus constituti sollicitudinem sumerent ampliorem, per quos ad unam Petri Sedem universalis*

Ecclesiæ cura conflueret, et nihil usque à suo capite dissideret. Qui ergo scit se quibusdam esse præpositum, non moleste ferat aliquem sibi esse præpositum; sed obedientiam quam exigit etiam ipse dependat; et sicut non vult gravis oneris sarcinam ferre, ita non audeat aliis importabile pondus imponere.[44] These words sufficiently shew the monarchical form of government then set up in the Churches of the *Western Empire* under the Bishop of *Rome*, by means of the imperial Decree of *Gratian*, and the appeals and decretal Epistles grounded thereupon.

The same Pope *Leo*, having in a Council at *Rome* passed sentence upon *Hilary* Bishop of *Arles*, for what he had done by a Provincial Council in *Gallia*, took occasion from thence to procure the following Edict from the *Western* Emperor *Valentinian* III. for the more absolute establishing the authority of his See over all the Churches of the *Western Empire*.

Impp. Theodosius et Valentinianus AA. Aetio Viro illustri, Comiti et Magistro utriusque militiæ et Patricio.

---

[44] [Trans.: `As a result of this form of government,' saith he, `there has arisen a distinction of rank and authority between the bishops. By a broad arrangement, provision has been made against any conflict of interests, it being decreed that in the various provinces there should be individual bishops whose opinions should have precedence among their brethren. Further, that a yet larger responsibility should devolve upon certain bishops established in the larger cities, and that through them the government of the Church at large should ultimately centre in the See of Peter alone, to the end that no member of the ecclesiastical body should be at variance with its head. Whosoever, therefore, is set in authority over others, must not be indignant if another has authority over him. Rather he should render in turn the obedience he demands from others. Further, as he himself has no inclination to bear a heavy burden, let him not dare to lay on others a weight they cannot support.']

Certum est et nobis et imperio nostro unicum esse præsidium in supernæ Divinitatis favore, ad quem promerendum præcipue Christiana fides et veneranda nobis religio suffragatur. Cum igitur Sedis Apostolicæ Primatum sancti Petri meritum, qui princeps est Episcopalis coronæ et Romanæ dignitas civitatis, sacræ etiam Synodi firmavit auctoritas: ne quid præter auctoritatem Sedis istius illicitum præsumptio attemperare nitatur: tunc enim demum Ecclesiarum pax ubique servabitur, si Rectorem suum agnoscat Universitas. Hæc cum hactenus inviolabiliter fuerint custodita, Hilarius Arelatensis, sicut venerabilis viri Leonis Romani Papæ fideli relatione comperimus, contumaci ausu illicita quædam præsumenda tentavit, et ideo Transalpinas Ecclesias abominabilis tumultus invasit, quod recens maximè testatur exemplum. Hilarius enim qui Episcopus Arelatensis vocatur, Ecclesiæ Romanæ urbis inconsulto Pontifice indebitas sibi ordinationes Episcoporum solâ temeritate usurpans invasit. Nam alios incompetenter removit; indecenter alios, invitis et repugnantibus civibus, ordinavit. Qui quidem, quoniam non facile ab his qui non elegerant, recipiebantur, manum sibi contrahabet armatam, et claustra murorum in hostilem morem vel obsidione cingebat, vel aggressione referabat, et ad sedem quietis pacem prædicaturus per bella ducebat. His talibus contra Imperii majestatem, et contra reverentiam Apostolicæ Sedis admissis, per ordinem religiosi viri Urbis Papæ cognitione discussis, certa in eum, ex his quos malè ordinaverat, lata sententia est. Erat quidem ipsa sententia per Gallias etiam sine Imperiali Sanctione valitura: quid enim Pontificis auctoritate non liceret? Se nostram quoque præceptionem hæc ratio provocavit. Nec ulterius vel Hilario, quem adhuc Episcopum nuncupare sola mansueta Præsulis permittit humanitas, nec cuiquam alteri ecclesiasticis rebus arma miscere, aut præceptis Romani Antistitis, liceat obviare: ausibus enim talibus fides et reverentia nostri violatur Imperii. Nec hoc solum, quod est maximi criminis,

156

submovemus: verum ne levis saltem inter Ecclesias turba nascatur, vel in aliquo
minui religionis disciplina videatur, hoc perenni sanctione discernimus; nequid tam
Episcopis Gallicanis quam aliarum Provinciarum contra consuetudinem veterem
liceat, sine viri venerabilis Papæ Urbis æternæ auctoriate, tentare. Sed illis
omnibusque pro lege sit, quicquid sanxit vel sanxerit Apostolicæ Sedis auctoritas: ita
ut quisquis Episcoporum ad judicium Romani Antistitis evocatus venire neglexerit,
per Moderatorem ejusdem Provinciæ adesse cogatur, per omnia servatis quæ Divi
parentes nostri Romanæ Ecclesiæ detulerent, Aetî pater carissime Augusti. Unde
illustris et præclara magnificentia tua præsentis Edictalis Legis auctoritate faciet quæ
sunt superius statuta servari, decem librarum auri multa protinus exigenda ab
unoquoque Judice qui passus fuerit præcepta nostri violari. Divinitas te servet per
multos annos, parens carissime. Dat. viii. Id. Jun. Romæ, Valentiniano A. vi. Consule,
A.C. 445.[45] By this Edict the Emperor *Valentinian* enjoined an absolute obedience to

---

[45] [Trans.: The Emperors Theodosius and Valentinianus to the renowned Aetius, Count, Master
of Horse and Foot, and Patrician.

Assuredly the sole defence of our selves and of our Empire rests in the favour of Almighty
God, the meriting of which is especially promoted by the hallowed Christian faith and
religion. Since, therefore, the preeminence of the Holy See (as the tribute due to St Peter,
chief of the episcopate and the glory of the Roman State) - has received additional
confirmation from the authority of the Sacred Synod, let no one presume to make any
arrangement in any matter in which he has no power without the authority of the Holy See.
Peace will be secured throughout all the Churches only when the Church as a whole
acknowledges its governor. Though these rights have so far been guarded from violation, we
understand from the faithful report of the Venerable Pope Leo, that Hilary of Arles has
insolently and outrageously usurped certain offices to which he had no right. For this reason
the Transalpine Churches have been visited by an accursed tumult, of which a recent

example bears best witness.

Hilary, styling himself the Bishop of Arles, without consulting the Pontiff of the Church of Rome, assumed the prerogative of the ordination of bishops, so usurping on his own authority an office to which he had no claim. Some bishops he deposed on insufficient grounds; others he ordained with unseemly force against the will and opposition of the laity. When an electorate which had had no part in the election refused to receive those bishops, Hilary gathered an armed band. Like an enemy, he then laid seige to their defences or stoned them, forcibly installing a man by such acts of war who was to preach a gospel of peace. These and other such actions perpetrated against the Majesty of the Empire and in disrespect to the Apostolic See, have been reviewed and examined by the Court of the Pope of Rome. Consequently, with regard to those bishops whom he wrongly ordained, a definite decision against him has been reached.

This decision would undoubtedly have been valid throughout the Gallic Provinces even without our Imperial Sanction. For what the Pontiff approves could be condemned? But our additional authority hath been given for the following purpose: Be it henceforth illegal either for Hilary (who remains in possession of his title of bishop only by the kindly and considerate permission of the Holy Father) or any other clergyman to settle ecclesiastical matters by military force or to oppose the precepts of the Roman Pontiff. For by such presumption, the fealty and reverence due to our Empire are violated. Nor is this the only abuse (although it is the most criminal) that we order to cease. Lest any trivial quarrel arise between Churches or religious discipline be seen to relax, we resolve with a permanent sanction that no one, be he Bishop of Gaul or of the other provinces, attempt anything contrary to established custom without the authority of the reverend Pope of the Eternal City. Let all that the authority of the Apostolic See has sanctioned or will sanction be as law to all and sundry.

Thus, if any one of the bishops summoned to the Court of Rome fail to come, he must be compelled to do so by the governor of that same province. We charge thee Aetius, dearly beloved father of Augustus, that the rights which our sainted predecessors conceded to the See of Rome be maintained and protected. To assist your Highness in securing - by the

158

the will of the Bishop of *Rome* thro'out all the Churches of his Empire; and declares, that for the Bishops to attempt any thing without the Pope's authority is contrary to antient custom, and that the Bishops summoned to appear before his judicature must be carried thither by the Governor of the Province; and he ascribes these privileges of the See of *Rome* to the concessions of his dead Ancestors, that is, to the Edict of *Gratian* and *Valentinian* II. as above: by which reckoning the dominion of the Church of *Rome* was now of 66 years standing: and if in all this time it had not been sufficiently established, this new Edict was enough to settle it beyond all question thro'out the *Western Empire.*

Hence all the *Bishops of the Province of Arles* in their Letter to Pope *Leo*, A.C. 450, petitioning for a restitution of the privileges of their Metropolitan, say: *Per beatum Petrum Apostolorum principem, sacrosancta Ecclesiæ Romana tenebat supra omnes totius mundi Ecclesias principatum.*[46] And *Ceratius, Salonius and Veranus,* three Bishops of *Gallia,* say, in their Epistle to the same Pope: *Magna præterea et ineffabili quadam nos peculiares tui gratulatione succrescimus, quod illa specialis doctrinæ vestræ pagina ita per omnium Ecclesiarum conventicula celebratur, ut vere consona omnium sententia declaretur; merito illic principatum Sedis Apostolicæ constitutum, unde adhuc Apostolici spiritus oracula referentur.*[47] And *Leo* himself, in

---

means of the authority of our present law and edict - the observation of the above statutes, a fine of ten pounds in gold will be imposed upon every judge who permits the violation of our decrees. May heaven preserve you for many years dear father Aetius.

Given on the 6th June at Rome in the Consulship of Valentinianus Augustus A.C. 445.']

[46]   [Trans.: 'Through Blessed Peter, the Prince of Apostles, the Holy Roman Church has held the primacy over all the Churches of the whole world.']

[47]   [Trans.: 'We your servants cannot contain ourselves with great and inexpressible

his Epistle to the metropolitan Bishops thr'out *Illyricum*: *Quia per omnes Ecclesias cura nostra distenditur, exigente hoc à nobis Domino, qui Apostolicæ dignitatis beatissimo Apostolo Petro primatum, fidei sui remuneratione commisit, uiversalem Ecclesiam in fundamenti ipsius soliditate constituens.*[48]

While this Ecclesiastical Dominion was rising up, the northern barbarous nations invaded the *Western Empire*, and founded several kingdoms therein, of different religions from the Church of *Rome*. But these kingdoms by degrees embraced the *Roman* faith, and at the same time submitted to the Pope's authority. The *Franks* in *Gaul* submitted in the end of the fifth Century, the *Goths* in *Spain* in the end of the sixth; and the *Lombards* in *Italy* were conquered by *Charles* the great A.C. 774. Between the years 775 and 794, the same *Charles* extended the Pope's authority all over *Germany* and *Hungary* as far as the river *Theysse* and the *Baltic* sea; he then set him above all human judicature, and at the same time assisted him in subduing the City and Duchy of *Rome*. By the conversion of the ten kingdoms to the *Roman* religion, the Pope only enlarged his spiritual dominion, but did not yet rise up as a horn of the Beast. It was his temporal dominion which made him one of the

---

thanksgiving that the letter of private guidance which you gave to us, is in the Councils of all Churches acclaimed so heartily, that judgment thereon is unanimous in its declaration that the Primacy of the Holy See has been deservedly established in Rome. Whence it will be possible for the revelations of the apostolic spirit to be conveyed as far as here.'] Epist. 25. apud Holstenium.*

[48] [Trans.: Our supremacy has now extended over all the Churches, as is required of us by our Lord, who entrusted to the Blessed Apostle Peter (as the reward of his faith) the pre-eminence in apostolic rank, he being the secure foundation upon which the whole Church is built.']

160

horns: and this dominion he acquired in the latter half of the eighth century, by subduing three of the former horns as above. And now being arrived at a temporal dominion, and a power above all human judicature, he reigned *with a look more stout than his fellows*, and *times and laws were* henceforward *given into his hands, for a time times and half a time*, or three times and an half; that is, for 1260 solar years, reckoning a time for a calendar year of 360 days, and a day for a solar year.[49] After which *the judgment is to sit, and they shall take away his dominion*, not at once, but by degrees, *to consume, and to destroy it unto the end.*[50] *And the kingdom and dominion, and greatness of the kingdom under the whole heaven shall*, by degrees, *be given unto the people of the saints of the most High, whose kingdom is an everlasting kingdom, and all dominions shall serve and obey him.*[51]

Dan. vii. 20. Ver. 25.

[50] Ver. 26.

[51] Ver. 27.

CHAPTER IX

Of the kingdoms represented in Daniel by the Ram and He-Goat.

The second and third Empires, represented by the Bear and Leopard, are again represented by the Ram and He-Goat; but with this difference, that the Ram represents the kingdoms of the *Medes* and *Persians* from the beginning of the four empires, and the Goat represents the kingdom of the *Greeks* to the end of them. By this means, under the type of the Ram and He-Goat, the times of all the four Empires are again described: *I lifted up mine eyes*, saith *Daniel, and saw, and behold there stood before the river* [Ulai] *a Ram which had two horns, and the two horns were high, but one was higher than the other, and the higher came up last.*[1] — *And the Ram having two horns, are the kings of* Media *and* Persia: not two persons but two kingdoms, the kingdoms of *Media* and *Persia*; and the kingdom of *Persia* was the higher horn and came up last. The kingdom of *Persia* rose up when *Cyrus* having newly conquered *Babylon*, revolted from *Darius* King of the *Medes*, and beat him at *Pasargadæ*, and set up the *Persians* above the *Medes*. This was the horn which came up last. And the horn which came up first was the kingdom of the *Medes*, from the time that *Cyaxares* and *Nebuchadnezzar* overthrew *Nineveh*, and shared out the Empire of the *Assyrians* between them. The Empires of *Media* and *Babylon* were contemporary, and rose up together by the fall of the *Assyrian* Empire; and the

---

[1]   Chap. viii. 3.

Prophecy of the four Beasts begins with one of them, and that of the Ram and He-Goat with the other. As the Ram represents the kingdom of *Media* and *Persia* from the beginning of the four Empires; so the He-Goat represents the Empire of the *Greeks* to the end of those Monarchies. In the reign of his great horn, and of the four horns which succeeded it, he represents this Empire during the reign of the Leopard: and in the reign of his little horn, which stood up in the latter time of the kingdom of the four, and after their fall became mighty but not by his own power, he represents it during the reign of the fourth Beast.

The rough Goat, saith Daniel, *is the King of Grecia*, that is, the kingdom; and *the great horn between his eyes is the first King*: not the first Monarch, but the first kingdom, that which lasted during the reign of *Alexander* the great, and his brother *Aridæus* and two young sons, *Alexander* and *Hercules*. *Now that* [horn] *being broken off, whereas four* [horns] *stood up for it, four kingdoms shall stand up out of the nation* [of the *Greeks*], *but not in his* [the first horn's] *power.*[2] The four horns are therefore four kingdoms; and by consequence, the first great horn which they succeeded is the first great kingdom of the *Greeks*, that which was founded by *Alexander* the great, *An. Nabonass.** 414, and lasted till the death of his son *Hercules, An. Nabonass.* 441. And the four are those of *Cassander, Lysimachus, Antigonus*, and *Ptolemy*, as above.

And in the latter time of their kingdom, when the transgressors are come to the full, a King [or new kingdom] *of fierce countenance, and understanding dark sentences, shall stand up: and his power shall be mighty, but not by his own power.*[3] This King was the last horn of the Goat, the little horn which came up out of one of the four horns, and waxed exceeding great. The latter time of their kingdom was when the *Romans* began to conquer them, that is, when they conquered *Perseus* King

---

2   Ver. 22.

3   Ver. 23.

of *Macedonia*, the fundamental kingdom of the *Greeks*. And at that time the transgressors came to the full: for then the High-priesthood was exposed to sale, the Vessels of the Temple were sold to pay for the purchase; and the High-priest, with some of the Jews, procured a licence from *Antiochus Epiphanes* to do after the ordinances of the heathen, and set up a school at *Jerusalem* for teaching those ordinances. Then *Antiochus* took *Jerusalem* with an armed force, slew 4000 *Jews*, took as many prisoners and sold them, spoiled the Temple, interdicted the worship, commanded the Law of *Moses* to be burnt, and set up the worship of the heathen Gods in all *Judea*. In the very same year, *An. Nabonass.** 580, the *Romans* conquered *Macedonia*, the chief of the four horns. Hitherto the Goat was mighty by its own power, but henceforward began to be under the *Romans*. *Daniel* distinguishes the times, by describing very particularly the actions of the Kings of the north and south, those two of the four horns which bordered upon *Judea*, until the *Romans* conquered *Macedonia*; and thenceforward only touching upon the main revolutions which happened within the compass of the nations represented by the Goat. In this latter period of time the little horn was to stand up and grow mighty, but not by his own power.

The three first of *Daniel's* Beasts had their dominions taken away, each of them at the rise of the next Beast; but their lives were prolonged, and they are all of them still alive. The third Beast, or Leopard, reigned in his four heads, till the rise of the fourth Beast, or Empire of the *Latins*; and his life was prolonged under their power. This Leopard reigning in his four heads, signifies the same thing with the He-Goat reigning in his four horns: and therefore the He-Goat reigned in his four horns till the rise of *Daniel's* fourth Beast, or Empire of the *Latins*, but its life was prolonged under their power. The *Latins* are not comprehended among the nations represented by the He-Goat in this Prophecy: their power over the *Greeks* is only named in it, to distinguish the times in which the He-Goat was mighty by his own power, from the times he was mighty but not by his own power. He was mighty by his own power till his dominion was taken away by the *Latins*; after that, his life was prolonged under their dominion, and this prolonging of his life was in the days of his last horn: for in the days of this horn the Goat became mighty, but not by his own power.

Now because this last horn was a horn of the Goat, we are to look for it among the nations which composed the body of the Goat. Among those nations he was to rise up and grow mighty: he grew mighty *towards the south, and towards the east, and towards the pleasant land;*[4] and therefore he was to rise up in the northwest parts of those nations, and extend his dominion towards *Eygpt, Syria* and *Judea*. In the latter time of the kingdom of the four horns, it was to rise up out of one of them and subdue the rest, but not by its own power. It was to be assisted by a foreign power, a power superior to itself, the power which took away the dominion of the third Beast, the power of the fourth Beast. And such a little horn was the kingdom of *Macedonia*, from that time subject to the *Romans*. This kingdom, by the victory of the *Romans* over *Perseus* King of *Macedonia, Anno Nabonass*. 580, ceased to be one of the four horns of the Goat, and became a dominion of a new sort: not a horn of the fourth Beast, for *Macedonia* belonged to the body of the third; but a horn of the third beast of a new sort, a horn of the Goat which grew mighty but not by its own power, a horn which rose up and grew potent under a foreign power, the power of the *Romans*.

The *Romans*, by the legacy of *Attalus* the last King of *Pergamus, An. Nabonass*.* 615, inherited that kingdom, including all *Asia Minor* on this side mount *Taurus. An. Nabonass*. 684 and 685 they conquered *Armenia, Syria* and *Judea; An Nabonass*. 718, they subdued *Egypt*. And by these conquests the little horn waxed exceeding great towards the south, and towards the east, and towards the pleasant

---

[4]   Chap. viii. 9.

land. And it *waxed great even to the host of heaven; and cast down some of the host and of the stars to the ground and stamped upon them,*[5] that is, upon the people and great men of the *Jews. Yea, he magnified himself even to the Prince of the Host*, the *Messiah*, the Prince of the *Jews*, whom he put to death, *An. Nabonass.* 780.[6] *And by him the daily sacrifice was taken away, and the place of his sanctuary was cast down, viz.* in the wars which the armies of the *Eastern* nations under the conduct of the *Romans* made against *Judea*, when *Nero* and *Vespasian* were emperors, *An. Nabonass.* 816, 817, 818. *And an host was given him against the daily sacrifice by reason of transgression, and it cast down the truth to the ground, and it practised and prospered.*[7] This transgression is in the next words called *the transgression of desolation*; and in *Dan.* xi. 31. *the abomination which maketh desolate*; and in *Matth.* xxiv. 15, *the abomination of desolation, spoken of by* Daniel *the prophet, standing in the holy place*. It may relate chiefly to the worship of *Jupiter Olympius* in his Temple built by the Emperor *Hadrian*, in the place of the Temple of the *Jews*, and to the revolt of the *Jews* under *Barchochab* occasioned thereby, and to the desolation of *Judea* which followed thereupon; all the *Jews* being thenceforward banished *Judea* upon pain of death. *Then I heard*, saith Daniel, *one saint speaking, and another saint said unto that certain saint which spake, How long shall be the vision concerning the daily sacrifice, and the transgression of desolation, to give both the sanctuary and the host to be trodden under foot? And he said unto me, Unto two thousand and three hundred days; then shall the sanctuary be cleansed.*[8] *Daniel's* days are years; and these years may perhaps be reckoned either from the destruction of the Temple by the *Romans* in the reign of *Vespasian*, or from the pollution of the Sanctuary by the

---

5   Chap. viii. 9-10.

6   Ver. 11.

7   Ver. 12.

8   Ver. 13-14.

worship of *Jupiter Olympius*, or from the desolation of *Judea* made in the end of the *Jewish* war by the banishment of all the *Jews* out of their own country, or from some other period which time will discover. Henceforward the last horn of the Goat continued mighty under the *Romans*, till the reign of *Constantine* the great and his sons: and then by the division of the *Roman* Empire between the *Greek* and *Latin* Emperors, it separated from the *Latins*, and became the *Greek* Empire alone, but yet under the dominion of a *Roman* family; and at present it is mighty under the dominion of the *Turks*.

This last horn is by some taken for *Antiochus Epiphanes*, but not very judiciously. A horn of a Beast is never taken for a single person: it always signifies a new kingdom, and the kingdom of *Antiochus* was an old one. *Antiochus* reigned over one of the four horns, and the little horn was a fifth under its proper kings. This horn was at first a little one, and waxed exceeding great, but so did not *Antiochus*. It is described great above all the former horns, and so was not *Antiochus*. His kingdom on the contrary was weak, and tributary to the *Romans*, and he did not enlarge it. The horn was a *King of fierce countenance, and destroyed wonderfully, and prospered and practised*; that is, he prospered in his practises against the holy people: but *Antiochus* was frighted out of *Egypt* by a mere message of the *Romans*, and afterwards routed and baffled by the *Jews*. The horn was mighty by another's power, *Antiochus* acted by his own. The horn stood up against the Prince of the Host of heaven, the Prince of Princes; and this is the character not of *Antiochus* but of *Antichrist*. The horn cast down the Sanctuary to the ground, and so did not *Antiochus*; he left it standing. The Sanctuary and Host were trampled under foot 2300 days; and in *Daniel's* Prophecies days are put for years: but the profanation of the Temple in the reign of *Antiochus* did not last so many natural days. These were to last till the time of the end, till the last end of the indignation against the *Jews*; and this indignation is not yet at an end. They were to last till the Sanctuary which had been cast down should be cleansed, and the Sanctuary is not yet cleansed.

This Prophecy of the Ram and He-Goat is repeated in the last Prophecy of *Daniel*. There the Angel tells *Daniel, that he stood up to strengthen* Darius *the* Mede, *and that there should stand up yet three kings in* Persia, [*Cyrus, Cambyses,* and *Darius Hystaspis*] *and the fourth* [*Xerxes*] *should be far richer than they all; and by his wealth thro' his riches he should stir up all against the realm of* Grecia.[9] This relates to the Ram, whose two horns were the kingdoms of *Media* and *Persia*. Then he goes on to describe the horns of the Goat by the *standing up of a mighty king, which should rule with great dominion, and do according to his will;*[10] and by the breaking of his kingdom into four smaller kingdoms, and not descending to his own posterity. Then he describes the actions of two of those kingdoms which bordered on *Judea*, viz. *Egypt* and *Syria*, calling them the Kings of the *South* and *North*, that is, in respect of *Judea*; and he carries on the description till the latter end of the kingdoms of the four, and till the reign of *Antiochus Epiphanes*, when transgressors were to come to the full. In the eighth year of *Antiochus*, the year in which he profaned the Temple and set up the heathen Gods in all *Judea*, and the *Romans* conquered the kingdom of *Macedon*; the prophetic Angel leaves off describiing the affairs of the kings of the *South* and *North*, and begins to describe those of the *Greeks* under the dominion of the *Romans*, in these words: *And after him Arms* [the *Romans*] *shall stand up, and they shall pollute the sanctuary of strength.*[11] As mmlk[12] signifies *after the king*, Dan. xi. 8; so here mmno[13] may signify *after him*: and so mn-hachat[14] may

---

[9]   Dan. xi. 1, 2.

[10]   Ver. 3.

[11]   Dan. xi. 31.

[12]   [mmlk originally given in Hebrew characters.]

[13]   [mmno originally given in Hebrew characters.]

signify *after one of them*, Dan. viii. 9. Arms are everywhere in these Prophecies of *Daniel* put for the military power of a kingdom, and they stand up when they conquer and grow powerful. The *Romans* conquered *Illyricum, Epirus* and *Macedonia*, in the year of *Nabonassar* 580; and thirty five years after, by the last will and testament of *Attalus* the last King of *Pergamus*, they inherited that rich and flourishing kingdom, that is, all *Asia* on this side mount *Taurus*: and sixty nine years after, they conquered the kingdom of *Syria*, and reduced it into a Province: and thirty four years after did the like to *Egypt*. By all these steps the *Roman* arms stood up over the *Greeks*. And after 95 years more, by making war upon the *Jews, they polluted the sanctuary of strength, and took away the daily sacrifice, and*, in its room soon after, *placed the abomination which made* the Land *desolate*: for this abomination was placed after the days of Christ, *Matth.* xxiv. 15. In the 16th year of the Emperor *Hadrian*, A.C. 132, they placed this abomination by building a Temple to *Jupiter Capitolinus*, where the Temple of God in *Jerusalem* had stood. Thereupon the *Jews* under the conduct of *Barchochab* rose up in arms against the *Romans*, and in that war had 50 cities demolished, 985 of their best towns destroyed, and 580000 men slain by the sword: and in the end of the war, A.C. 136, they were all banished *Judea* upon pain of death; and that time the land hath remained desolate of its old inhabitants.

Now that the prophetic Angel passes in this manner from the four kingdoms of the *Greeks* to the *Romans* reigning over the *Greeks*, is confirmed from hence, that in the next place he describes the affairs of the *Christians* unto the time of the end, in these words: *And they that understand among the people shall instruct many, yet they shall fall by the sword and by flame, by captivity and by spoil many days. Now when they shall fall they shall be holpen* with a little help*, viz. in the reign of *Constantine* the great; *but many shall cleave to them with dissimulation. And some of them of understanding there shall fall to try them, and to purge* them from the dissemblers;

---

14   [mn-hachat originally given in Hebrew characters.]

and to make them white even to the time of the end.[15] And a little time after, the time of the end is said to be a *time, times, and half a time*: which is the duration of the reign of the last horn of *Daniel's* fourth Beast, and of the *Woman* and *Beast* in the *Apocalypse.*

---

[15]   Chap. xi. 3, &c.

CHAPTER X

Of the Prophecy of the Seventy Weeks.

The Vision of the Image composed of four Metals was given first to *Nebuchadnezzar*, and then to *Daniel* in a dream: and *Daniel* began then to be celebrated for revealing of secrets, *Ezek.* xxviii. 3. The Vision of the four Beasts, and of the *Son of Man* coming in the clouds of heaven, was also given to *Daniel* in a dream. That of the Ram and the He-Goat appeared to him in the day time, when he was by the bank of the river *Ulay*; and was explained to him by the prophetic Angel *Gabriel*. It concerns the *Prince of the host*, and the *Prince of Princes*: and now in the first year of *Darius* the *Mede* over *Babylon*, the same prophetic Angel appears to *Daniel* again, and explains to him what is meant by the *Son of Man*, by the *Prince of the Host*, and the *Prince of Princes*. The Prophecy of the *Son of Man* coming in the clouds of heaven relates to the second coming of *Christ*; that of the *Prince of the host* relates to his first coming: and this Prophecy of the *Messiah*, in explaining them, relates to both comings, and assigns the times thereof.

This Prophecy, like all the rest of *Daniel's*, consists of two parts, an introductory Prophecy and an explanation thereof; the whole I thus translate and interpret.

Seventy weeks are[1] cut out upon thy people, and upon thy holy city, to finish

---

[1]   Cut upon. A phrase in Hebrew, taken from the practise of numbring by cutting notches. [given as note `a']

172

transgression, and[2] to make an end of sins, to expiate iniquity, and to bring in everlasting righteousness, to consummate the Vision and[3] the Prophet, and to anoint the most Holy.

Know also and understand, that from the going forth of the commandment to cause to return and to build Jerusalem, unto[4] the Anointed the Prince, shall be seven weeks.

Yet threescore and two weeks shall it[5] return, and the street be built and the wall; but in troublesome times: and after the threescore and two weeks, the Anointed shall be cut off, and[6] it shall not be his; but the people of a Prince to come shall destroy the city and the sanctuary: and the end thereof shall be with a flood, and unto the end of the war, desolations are determined.

Yet shall he confirm the covenant with many for one week: and in half a week he shall cause the sacrifice and oblation to cease: and upon a wing of abominations he shall make it desolate, even until the consummation, and that which is determined be poured upon the desolate.[7]

Seventy weeks are cut out upon thy people, and upon thy holy city, to finish transgression, &c. Here, by putting a week for seven years, are reckoned 490 years from the time that the dispersed *Jews* should be re-incorporated into[8] a people and a

---

[2]   Heb. to seal, i.e. to finish or consummate: a metaphor taken from sealing what is finished. So the Jews compute, ad obsignatum Misnam as ibsignatum Talmud, that is ad absolutum. [given as note 'b']

[3]   Heb. the Prophet, not the Prophecy. [given as note 'c']

[4]   Heb. the Messiah, that is, in Greek, the Christ; in Engish, the Anointed. I use the English word, that the relation of this clause to the former may appear. [given as note 'd']

[5]   Jersualem. [given as note 'e']

[6]   Jersualem. [given also as note 'e']

[7]   Chap. ix. 24-27.

[8]   See Isa. xxiii. 13.

holy city, until the death and resurrection of *Christ*; whereby *transgression should be finished, and sins ended, iniquity be expiated, and everlasting righteousness brought in, and this Vision be accomplished and the Prophet consummated,* that Prophet whom the *Jews* expected; and whereby *the most Holy* should be *anointed,* he who is therefore in the next words called the *Anointed,* that is, the *Messiah,* or the *Christ.* For by joining the accomplishment of the vision with the expiation of sins, the 490 years are ended with the death of *Christ.* Now the dispersed *Jews* became a people and city when they first returned into a polity or body politick; and this was in the seventh year of *Artaxerxes Longimanus,* when *Ezra* returned with a body of *Jews* from captivity and revived the *Jewish* worship; and by the king's commission created Magistrates in all the land, to judge and govern the people according to the laws of God and the King, *Ezra* vii. 25. There were but two returns from captivity, *Zerubbabel's* and *Ezra's*; in *Zerubbabel's* they had only commission to build the Temple, in *Ezra's* they first became a polity or city by a government of their own. Now the years of this *Artaxerxes* began about two or three months after the summer solstice, and his seventh year fell with the third year of the eightieth *Olympiad*;* and the latter part thereof, wherein *Ezra* went up to *Jerusalem,* was in the year of the *Julian Period** 4257. Count the time from thence to the death of *Christ,* and you will find it just 490 years. If you count in *Judaic* years commencing in autumn, and date the reckoning from the first autumn after *Ezra's* coming to *Jerusalem,* when he put the King's decree in execution; the death of *Christ* will fall on the year of the *Julian Period** 4747, *Anno Domini* 34; and the weeks will be *Judaic* weeks, ending with sabbatical years; and this I take to be the truth: but if you had rather place the death of *Christ* in the year before, as is commonly done, you may take the year of *Ezra's* journey into the reckoning.

Know also and understand, that from the going forth of the commandment to cause to return and build Jerusalem, unto the Anointed the Prince, shall be seven *weeks*. The former part of the Prophecy related to the first coming of *Christ*, being dated to his coming as a Prophet; this being dated to his coming to be Prince or King, seems to relate to his second coming. There the Prophet was consummate, and the most holy anointed: here, he that was anointed comes to be Prince and to reign. For *Daniel's* Prophecies reach to the end of the world; and there is scarce a Prophecy in the Old Testament concerning *Christ*, which doth not in something or other relate to his second coming. If divers of the antients, as *Irenæus*,[9] *Julius Africanus*,[10] *Hippolytus** the martyr, and *Apollinaris** Bishop of *Laodicea*, applied the half week to the times of the *Antichrist*; why may not we, by the same liberty of interpretation, apply the the seven weeks to the time when *Antichrist* shall be destroyed by the brightness of *Christ's* coming?

The *Israelites* in the days of the antient Prophets, when the ten Tribes were led into captivity, expected a double return; and that at the first the *Jews* should build a new Temple inferior to Solomon's, until the time of that age should be fulfilled; and afterwards they should return from all places of their captivity, and build *Jerusalem* and the Temple gloriously, *Tobit* xiv. 4, 5, 6: and to express the glory and excellence of this city, it is figuratively said to be built of precious stones, *Tobit* viii. 16, 17. 18. *Isa*. liv. 11, 12. *Rev*. xi. and called the *New Jerusalem*, the *Heavenly Jerusalem*, the *Holy City*, the *Lamb's Wife*, the *City of the Great King, the City into which the Kings of the earth do bring their glory and honour*. Now while such a return from captivity was the expectation of *Israel*, even before the times of *Daniel*, I know not why *Daniel* should omit it in his Prophecy. This part of the Prophecy being therefore not yet fulfilled, I shall not attempt a particular interpretation of it, but content myself with observing, that as the *seventy* and the *sixty two weeks* were *Jewish* weeks, ending with sabbatical years; so the seven weeks are the compass of a

---

[9]   Iren. 1. 5. Hær. c. 25. [given as note 'a']

[10]   Apud Hieron. in h. 1. [given as note 'b']

Jubilee, and begin and end with actions proper for a *Jubilee*, and of the highest nature for which a *Jubilee* can be kept; and that since *the commandment to return and to build* Jerusalem, precedes the *Messiah the Prince* 49 years; it may perhaps come forth not from the *Jews* themselves, but from some other kingdom friendly to them, and precede their return from captivity and give occasion to it; and lastly, that this rebuilding of *Jerusalem* and the waste places of *Judah* is predicted in *Micah* vii. 11. *Amos* ix. 11, 14. *Ezek.* xxxvi. 33, 35, 36, 38. *Isa.* liv. 3. 11, 12. lv. 12. lxi. 4. lxv. 18, 21, 22. and *Tobit* xiv. 5. and that the return from captivity and coming of the *Messiah* and his kingdom are described in *Daniel* vii. *Rev.* xix. *Acts* i. *Mat.* xxiv. *Joel* iii. *Ezek.* xxxvi. xxxvii. *Isa.* lx. lxii. lxiii. lxv and lxvi. and many other places of scripture. The manner I know not, let time be the Interpreter.

Yet threescore and two weeks shall it return, and the street be built and the wall, but in troublesome times: and after the threescore and two weeks the Messiah *shall be cut off, and it shall not be his; but the people of a Prince to come shall destroy the city and the sanctuary*, &c. Having foretold both comings of *Christ*, and dated the last from their returning and building *Jerusalem*; to prevent the applying that to the building *Jerusalem* by *Nehemiah*, he distinguishes this from that, by saying that from this period to the *Anointed* shall be, not seven weeks, but threescore and two weeks, and this not in prosperous but in troublesome times; and at the end of these weeks the *Messiah* shall not be the Prince of the *Jews*, but be cut off; and *Jerusalem* not be his, but the city and sanctuary be destroyed. Now *Nehemiah* came to *Jerusalem* in the 20th year of this same *Ataxerxes*, while *Ezra* still continued there, *Nehem.* xii. 36, and found the city lying waste, and the houses and wall unbuilt, *Nehem.* ii, 17. vii. 4, and finished the wall the 25th day of the month *Elul, Nehem.* vi. 15, in the 28th year of the King, that is, in *September* in the year of the *Julian Period** 4278. Count now from this year threescore and two weeks of years, that is 434 years, and the reckoning will end in *September* in the year of the *Julian Period**

4712 which is the year in which *Christ* was born, according to *Clemens Alexandrinus,* Irenæus,* Eusebius,* Epiphanius,* Jerome,* Orosius,* Cassiodorus,** and other antients; and this was the general opinion, till *Dionysius Exiguus** invented the vulgar account, in which *Christ's* birth is placed two years later. If with some you reckon that *Christ* was born three or four years before the vulgar account, yet his birth will fall in the latter part of the last week, which is enough. How after these weeks *Christ* was cut off, and the city and sanctuary destroyed by the *Romans*, is well known.

Yet shall he confirm the covenant with many for one week. He kept it, notwithstanding his death, till the rejection of the *Jews*, and calling of *Cornelius* and the *Gentiles* in the seventh year after his passion.

And in half a week he shall cause the sacrifice and oblation to cease; that is, by the war of the *Romans* upon the *Jews*: which war, after some commotions, began in the 13th year of *Nero*, A.D. 67. in the spring, when *Vespasian* with an army invaded them; and ended in the second year of *Vespasian*, A.D. 70, in autumn, Sept. 7, when *Titus* took the city, having burnt the Temple 27 days before: so that it lasted three years and a half.

And upon a wing of abominations he shall cause desolation, even until the consummation, and that which is determined be poured upon the desolate. The Prophets, in representing kingdoms by Beasts and Birds, put their wings stretcht out over any country for their armies sent out to invade and rule over that country. Hence a wing of abominations is an army of false Gods: for abomination is often put in scripture for a false God; as where *Chemosh* is called the abomination of *Moab*, and *Molech* the abomination of *Ammon*.[11] The meaning therefore is, that the people of a Prince to come shall destroy the sanctuary, and abolish the daily worship of the true God, and overspread the land with an army of false gods; and by setting up their

---

[11]   1. Kings xi. 7.

dominion and worship, cause desolation to the *Jews*, until the times of the *Gentiles* be fulfilled. For *Christ* tells us, that the abomination of desolation spoken of by *Daniel* was to be set up in the times of the *Roman Empire, Matth.* xxiv. 15.

Thus we have in this short Prophecy, a prediction of all the main periods relating to the coming of the *Messiah*; the time of his birth, that of his death, that of the rejection of the *Jews*, the duration of the *Jewish* war whereby he caused the city and sanctuary to be destroyed, and the time of his second coming: and so the interpretation here given is more full and complete and adequate to the design, than if we should restrain it to his first coming only, as Interpreters usually do. We avoid also the doing violence to the language of *Daniel*, by taking the *seven weeks* and *sixty two weeks* for one number. Had that been *Daniel's* meaning, he would have said *sixty and nine weeks*, and not *seven weeks* and *sixty two weeks*, a way of numbring used by no nation. In our way the years are *Jewish Luni-solar years*,[a] as they ought to be; and the *seventy weeks of years* are *Jewish weeks* ending with *sabbatical years*, which is very remarkable. For they end either with the year of the birth of *Christ*, two years before the vulgar account, or with the year of his death, or with the seventh year after it: all which are *sabbatical years*. Others either count by Lunar years, or by weeks not *Judaic*: and, which is worst, they ground their interpretations or erroneous Chronology, excepting the opinion of *Funccius** about the *seventy weeks*, which is the same with ours. For they place *Ezra* and *Nehemia* in the reign of *Artaxerxes Mnemon*, and the building of the Temple in the reign of *Darius Nothus*, and date the weeks of *Daniel* from those two reigns.

a   The ancient solar years if the eastern nations consisted of 12 months, and every month of 30 days: and hence came the division of the circle into 360 degrees. This year seems to be used by *Moses* in his history of the Flood, and by *John* in the *Apocalypse*, where a time, times and a half time, 42 months and 1260 days, are put equipollent. But in reckoning by many of these years together, an account is to be kept of the odd days which were added to the end of these years. For the

Egyptians added five days to end this year; and so did the *Chaldeans* long before the times of *Daniel*, as appears by the *Æra* of *Nabonassar**; and the *Persian* magi used the same year of 365 days, till the empire of the *Arabians*. The antient *Greeks* also used the same solar year of 12 equal months, or 360 days; but every other year added an intercalary* month, consisting of 10 days and 11 days alternately.

The year of the *Jews*, even from their coming out of *Egypt*, was Luni-solar, for the passover always followed the Passover, and the fruits of the land were gathered before the feast of the Tabernacles, *Levit.* xxii. But the months were lunar, the people were commanded by *Moses* in the beginning of every month to blow trumpets, and offer burnt offerings with their drink offerings, *Num.* x. 10. xxviii. 11, 14. And this solemnity was kept of the new moons, *Psal.* lxxxi. 3, 4, 5, 1. *Chon.* xxiii. 31. These months were called by *Moses* the first, second, third, fourth month, &c. and the first month was also called *Abib*, the second *Zif*, the seventh *Ethanim*, the eighth *Bull*, *Exod.* xii. 4. 1. *Kings* vi. 37, 38, viii. 2. But in the *Babylonian* captivity the *Jews* used the names of the *Chaldean* months, and by those names understood the months of their own year, so that the *Jewish* months then lost their old names, and are now called by those of the *Chaldeans*.

The *Jews* began their civil year from the autumnal Equinox, and their sacred year from the vernal: and the first day of the first month was on the visible new moon, which was nearest to the equinox.

Whether *Daniel* used the *Chaldaick* or *Jewish* year, is not material; the differernce being but six hours in a year, and 4 months in 480 years. But I take his month to be *Jewish*: first, because *Daniel* was a *Jew*, and the *Jews* even by the names of the *Chaldean* months understood the months of their own year: secondly, because this prophecy is grounded on *Jeremiah's* concerning the 70 years captivity, and therefore must be understood of the same sort of years with the seventy; and those are *Jewish*, since that Prophecy was given in *Judae* before the captivity: and lastly, because *Daniel* reckons by weeks of years, which is a way of reckoning peculiar to the *Jewish* years. For as their own days ran by sevens, and the last year of every seven was a sabbatical year, and seven such weeks of years made a *Jubilee*.

The grounds of the Chronology here followed, I will now set down as briefly as I can.

The *Peloponnesian* war began in spring *An.* 1. *Olymp.** 87, as *Diodorus,** *Eusebius,** and all other authors agree. It began two months before *Pythodorus* ceased to be *Archon, Thucyd.* 1. 2. that is, in *April,* two months before the end of the *Olympic* year. Now the years of this war are most certainly determined by the 50 years distance of its first year from the transit of *Xerxes* inclusively, *Thucyd.* 1. 2. or 48 years exclusively, *Eratosth. apud Clem. Alex.** by the 69 years distance of its end, or 27th year, from the beginning of *Alexander's* reign in *Greece*; by the acting of the *Olympic* games in its 4th and 12th years, *Thucyd.** 1. 5; and by three eclipses of the sun, and one of the moon, mentioned by *Thucydides** and *Xenophon.** Now *Thucydides,* an unquestionable witness, tells us, that the news of the death of *Artaxerxes Longimanus* was brought to *Ephesus,* and from thence by some *Athenians* to *Athens,* in the 7th year of this *Peloponnesian* war, when the winter half year was running; and therefore he died *An.* 4. *Olymp.** 88, in the end of *An. J.P.** 4289, suppose a month or two before midwinter; for so long the news would be in coming. Now *Artaxerxes Longimanus* reigned 40 years, by the consent of *Diodorus,** *Eusebius,** *Jerome,** *Sulpitius;** or 41, according to *Ptol.** *in can. Clem. Alexander.** 1. 1. *Strom. Chron. Alexandr. Abulpharagius, Nicephorus,* including therein the reign of his successors *Xerxes* and *Sogdian, as Abulpharagius* informs us. After *Artaxerxes* reigned his son *Xerxes* two months, and *Sogdian* seven months; but their reign is not reckonded apart in summing the years of the Kings, but is included in the 40 or 41 years reign of *Artaxerxes*: omit these nine months, and the precise reign of *Artaxerxes* will be thirty nine years and three months. And therefore since his reign ended in the beginning of winter *An. J.P.* 4289, it began between midsummer and autumn, *An. J.P.* 4250.

The same thing I gather also thus. *Cambyses* began his reign in spring *An. J.P.** 4185, and reigned eight years, including the five months of *Smerdes*; and then *Darius Hystaspis* began in spring *An. J.P.* 4193, and reigned thirty six years, by the unamimous consent of all Chronologers. The reigns of these two Kings are determined by three eclipses of the moon observed at *Babylon*, and recorded by *Ptolemy*; so that it cannot be disputed. One was in the seventh year of Cambyses, *An. J.P.* 4191, *Jul.* 16, at 11 at night; another in the 20th year of *Darius, An. J.P.* 4212, *Nov.* 19, at 11^h. 45' at night; a third in the 31st year of *Darius, An. J.P.* 4223, *Apr.* 25, at 11^h. 30' at night. By these eclipses, and the Prophecies of *Haggai* and *Zechary* compared together, it is manifest that his years began after the 24th day of the 11th *Jewish* month, and before the 25th day of *April*, and by consequence about *March*. *Xerxes* therfore began in spring An. J.P. 4229: for *Darius* died in the fifth year after the battle at *Marathon*, as *Herodotus*,* *lib.* 7, and *Plutarch** mention; and that battle was in *October An. J.P.* 4224, ten years before the battle at *Salamis*. *Xerxes* therefore began within less than a year after *October An. J.P.* 4228, suppose in the spring following: for he spent his first five years, and something more, in preparations for his expedition against the *Greeks*; and this expedition was in the time of the *Olympic* games, *An.* 1. *Olymp.** 75, *Calliade Athenis Archonte*, 28 years after the *Regifuge** and Consulship of the first Consul *Junius Brutus, Anno Urbes Conditæ** 273, *Fabio et Furio Coss.* The passage of *Xerxes* army over the *Hellespont* began in the end of the fourth year of the 74th *Olympiad*,* that is, in *June An. J.P.** 4234, and took up one month: and in autumn, three months after, on the full moon, the 16th day of the month *Munychion*, was the battle at *Salamis*, and a little after that an eclipse of the sun, which by calculation fell on *Octob.* 2. His sixth year therefore began a little before *June*, suppose in spring *An. J.P.* 4234, and his first year consequently in spring *An. J.P.* 4229, as above. Now he reigned almost twenty one years, by the consent of all writers. Add the 7 months of *Artabanus*, and the sum will be 21 years and about four or five months, which end between midsummer and autumn *An. J.P.* 4250. At this time therefore began the reign of his successor *Artaxerxes*, as was to be proved.

The same thing is also confirmed by *Julius Africanus*,* who informs us out of former writers, that the 20th year of this *Artaxerxes* was the 115th year from the beginning of the reign of *Cyrus* in *Persia*, and fell in with *An.* 4. *Olymp.** 83. It began therefore with the *Olympic* year, soon after the summer Solstice, *An. J.P.* 4269. Subduct nineteen years, and his first year will begin at the same time of the year *An. J.P.* 4250, as above.

His 7th year therefore began after midsummer *An. J.P.* 4256; and the Journey of *Ezra* to *Jerusalem* in the spring following fell on the beginning of *An. J.P.* 4257, as above.

CHAPTER XI

Of the Times of the Birth and Passion of Christ.

The times of the Birth and Passion of *Christ*, with such like niceties, being not material to religion, were little regarded by the *Christians* of the first age. They who began first to celebrate them, placed them in the cardinal periods of the year; as the annunciation of the Virgin *Mary*, on the 25th *March*, which when *Julius Cæsar* corrected the Calendar was the vernal Equinox; the feast of *John* Baptist on the 24th of *June*, which was the summer Solstice; the feast of St. *Michael* on *Sept.* 29, which was the autumnal Equinox; and the birth of *Christ* on the winter Solstice, Decemb. 25, with the feast of St. *Stephen*, St *John* and the *Innocents*, as near it as they could place them. And because the Solstice in time removed from the 25th of *December* to the 24th, the 23rd, the 22nd, and so on backwards, hence some in the following centuries placed the birth of *Christ* on *Decemb.* 23, and at length on *Decemb.* 20: and for the same reason they seem to have set the feast of St. *Thomas* on *Decemb.* 21, and that of St. *Matthew* on Sept. 21. So also at the entrance of the Sun into all the signs in the *Julian* Calendar, they placed the days of other Saints; as the conversion of *Paul* on *Jan.* 25, when the Sun entred Aquarius;[1] St. *Matthias* on *Feb.* 25, when he entred Pisces; St. *Mark* on Apr. 25, when he entred Taurus; *Corpus Christi* on May 26, when he entred Gemini; St. *James* on July[2] 25, when he entred Cancer; St.

---

[1]   [All the divisions of the Zodiac were given here by Newton in their usual pictorial form.]

[2]   [There seems to be a typographic error here: July 25th should indicate Leo, rather than Cancer.]

Bartholomew on Aug. 24, when he entred Virgo; *Simon* and *Jude* on *Oct*. 28, when he entred Scorpio: and if there were any other remarkable days in the Julian calender, they placed Saints upon them, as St. *Barnabas* on *June* 11, where *Ovid** seems to place the feast of *Vesta* and *Fortuna*, and the goddess *Matuta*; and St. *Philip* and *James* on the first of *May*, a day dedicated to both the *Bona Dea* or *Magna Mater*, and to the goddess *Flora*, and still celebrated with her rites. All which shews that these days were fixed in the first *Christian* Calendars by Mathematicians at pleasure, without any ground in tradition; and that the *Christians* afterwards took up with what they found in the Calendars.

Neither was there any certain tradition about the years of *Christ*. For the *Christians* who first began to enquire into these things, as *Clemens Alexandrinus,** *Origen,** *Tertullian,** *Julius Africanus,** *Lactantius,** *Jerome,** St. *Austin,** *Sulpicius Severus*, *Prosper,** and as many as place the death of *Christ* in the 15th or 16th year of *Tiberius*, make *Christ* to have preached but one year, or at most but two. At length *Eusebius** discovered four successive Passovers in the Gospel of *John*, and thereupon set on foot an opinion that he preacht three years and an half; and so died in the 19th year of *Tiberius*. Others afterwards, finding the opinion that he died in the Equinox Mar. 25, more consonant to the times of the *Jewish* Passover, in the 17th and 20th years, have placed his death in one of those two years. Neither is there any greater certainty in the opinions about the time of his birth. The first *Christians* placed his baptism near the beginning of the 15th year of *Tiberius*; and thence reckoning thirty years backwards, placed his birth in the 43rd *Julian* year, the 42nd of *Augustus* and 28th of the *Actiac* victory. This was the opinion which obtained in the first ages, till *Dionysius Exiguus,** placing the baptism of *Christ* in the 16th year of *Tiberius*, and misinterpreting the text of *Luke*, iii. 23. as if *Jesus* was only beginning to be 30 years old when he was baptized, invented the vulgar account, in which his birth is placed two years later than before. As therefore relating to these things there is no tradition worth considering; let us lay aside all and examine what prejudices can be gathered from records of good account.

The fifteenth year of *Tiberius* began *Aug*. 28, *An. J.P*.* 4727. So soon as the winter was over, and the weather beame warm enough, we may reckon that *John* began to baptize; and that before next winter his fame went abroad, and all the people came to his baptism, and *Jesus* among the rest. Whence the first Passover after his baptism mentioned *John* ii. 13. was in the 16th year of *Tiberius*. After this feast *Jesus* came into the land of *Judea*, and staid there baptizing, whilst *John* was baptizing in *Ænon*, *John* iii. 22, 23. But when he heard that *John* was cast into prison, he departed into *Galilee, Mat*. iii. 12. being afraid, because the Pharisees had heard that he baptized more disciples than *John, John* iv. 1. and in his journey he passed thro' *Samaria* four months before the harvest, *John* iv. 35. that is, about the time of the winter Solstice. For their harvest was between *Easter* and *Whitsunday*, and began about a month after the vernal Equinox. *Say not* ye, saith he, *there are yet four months and then cometh harvest? Behold I say unto you, lift up your eyes, and look on the fields, for they are white already to harvest;* meaning, that the people in the fields were ready for the Gospel, as his next words shew.[a] *John* therefore was imprisoned about *November*, in the 17th year of *Tiberius*; and *Christ* thereupon went from *Judea* to *Cana* of *Galilee* in *December*, and was received there of the *Galileans*, who had seen all he did at *Jerusalem* at the Passover: and when a Nobleman of *Capernaum* heard he was returned into *Galilee*, and went to him and desired him to come and cure his son, he went not hither yet, but only said, *Go thy way, thy son liveth; and the Nobleman returned and found it so, and believed, he and his house, John* iv. This is the beginning of his miracles in *Galilee*; and thus far *John* is full and distinct in relating the actions of his first year, omitted by the other Evangelists. The rest of his history is from this time related more fully by the other Evangelists than by *John*; for what they relate he omits.

a   I observe, that *Christ* and his forerunner *John* in their parabolical* discourses were wont to allude
to things present. The old Prophets, when they would describe things emphatically, did not only
draw parables from things which offered themselves, as from the rent of a garment, 1 Sam. xv.
from the sabbatic year, *Isa*. xxxvii. from the vessels of a Potter, *Jer*. xviii, &c. but also when such
fit objects were wanting, they supplied them by their own actions, as by rending a garment, 1
Kings xi. by shooting, 2 *Kings* xiii. by making bare their body, *Isa*. xx. by imposing significant
names to their sons, *Isa*. viii. *Hos*. i. by hiding a girdle in the bank of *Euphrates*, *Jer*. xiii. by
breaking a potter's vessel, *Jer*. xix. by putting on setters and yokes, *Jer*. xxvii. by binding a book
to a stone, and casting them both into *Euphrates*, *Jer*. li. by besieging a painted city, *Ezek*. iv. by
dividing hair into three parts, *Ezek*. v. by making a chain, *Ezek*. vii. by carrying out houshold fluff
like a captive and trembling, *Ezek*. xii, &c. By such kind of types the prophets loved to speak.
And *Christ* being endued with a nobler prophetic spirit than the rest, excelled also in this kind of
speaking, yet so as not to speak by his own actions, that was less grave and decent, but to turn into
parables such things as offered themselves. On occasion of the harvest approaching, he
admonishes his disciples once and again of the spiritual harvest, *John* iv. 35. *Matth*. ix. 37. Seeing
the lilies of the field, he admonishes his disciples about gay clothing, *Matth*. vi. 28. In allusion to
the present season of fruits, he admonishes his disciples about knowing men by their fruits, *Matth*.
vii.16. In the time of the Passover, when trees put forth leaves, he bids his disciples *learn a*
parable from the fig-tree: when its branch is yet tender and putteth forth leaves, ye know that
sumnmer is nigh, &c. *Matth*. xxiv. *Luke* xxi. 29. The same day, alluding both to the season of the
year and to his passion, which was to be two days after, he formed a parable of the time of the
fruits approaching, and the murdering of the heir, *Matth*. xxi. 33. Alluding at the same time, both
to the money-changers whom he had newly driven out of the Temple, and to his passion at hand;
he made a parable of a Noble-man going to a far country to receive a kingdom and return, and
delivering his goods to his servants, and at his return condemning the slothful servant because he
put not his money to the exchangers, *Matth*. xxi. 14. *Luke* xix. 12. Being near the Temple where
sheep were kept in folds to be sold for the sacrifices, he spake many things parabolically of sheep,
of the shepherd, and of the door of the sheepfold; and discovers that he alluded to the sheepfolds
which were to be hired in the market-place, by speaking of such folds as a thief could not enter by
the door, nor the shepherd himself open, but a porter opened to the shepherd, *John* x. 1. 3. Being
in the mount of *Olives, Matth*. xxxvi. 30. *John* xiv. 31. a place so fertile that it could not want
vines, he spake many things mystically to the Husbandman, and of the vine and its branches, *John*

xv. Meeting a blind man, he admonished of spiritual blindness, *John* ix. 39. At the sight of little children, he described once and again the innocence of the elect, *Matth*. xviii. 2. xix. 13. Knowing that *Lazarus* was dead and should be raised again, he discoursed of the resurrection and life eternal, *John* xi. 25, 26. Hearing of the slaughter of some whom *Pilate* had slain, he admonished of eternal death, *Luke* xiii. 1. To his fishermen he spake of fishers of men, *Matth*, iv. 10 and composed another parable about fishes, *Matth*. xiii. 47. Being by the Temple, he spake of the Temple of his body, *John* ii. 19. At supper he spake a parable about the mystical supper to come in the kingdom of heaven, *Luke* xiv. On occasion of temporal food, he admonished his disciples of spiritual food, and of eating his flesh and drinking his blood mystically, *John*. vi. 27, 53. When his disciples wanted bread, he bad them beware of the leven of the Pharisees, *Matth*. xvi. 6. Being desired to eat, he answered that he had other meat, *John*. iv. 31. In the great day of the feast of the Tabernacles, when the *Jews*, as their custom was, brought a great quantity of waters from the river *Shiloah* into the Temple, Christ stood and cried, saying, *If any man thirst let him come unto me and drink. He that believeth in me, out of his belly shall flow rivers of living water*, John vii. 37. The next day, in allusion to the servants who by reason of the sabbatical year were newly set free, he said, *If ye continue in my word, the truth shall make you free*. Which the *Jews* understanding literally with respect to the present manumission of servants answered, *We be Abraham's seed, and were never in bondage to any man: how sayest thou, ye shall be made free?* John viii. They assert their freedom by a double argument: first, because they were the seed of *Abraham* and therefore newly made free, had they ever been in bondage; and then, because they never were in bondage. In the last Passover, when Herod led his army thro' *Judea* against *Aretas* King of *Arabia*, because *Aretas* was aggressor and the stronger in military forces, as appeared by the event; *Christ* alluding to that state of things, composed the parable of a weaker King leading his army against a stronger who made war upon him, *Luke* xiv. 31. And I doubt not but divers other parables were formed upon other occasions, the history of which we have not.

From this time therefore *Jesus* taught in the Synagogues of *Galilee* on the sabbath-days, being glorified of all: and coming to his own city *Nazareth*, and preaching in their Synagogue, they were offended, and thrust him out of the city, and led him to the brow of the hill on which the city was built and cast him headlong; but he passing thro' the midst of them, went his way, and came and dwelt at *Capernaum*. *Luke* iv. And by this time we may reckon the second Passover was either past or at hand.

All this time *Matthew* passeth over in few words, and here begins to relate the preaching and miracles of *Christ*. *When* Jesus, saith he, *had heard that* John *was cast into prison, he departed into* Galilee; *and leaving* Nazareth, *he came and dwelt at* Capernaum, *and from that time began to preach and say, Repent, for the kingdom of heaven is at hand,* Matth. iv. 12. Afterwards he called his disciples *Peter, Andrew, James* and *John*; and *then went about all* Galiliee, *teaching in the Synagogues,* — *and healing all manner of sickness:* — *and his fame went thr'out all Syria; and they brought unto him all sick people,* — *and there followed him great multitudes of people from* Galilee, *and from* Decapolis, *and from* Jerusalem, *and* Judea, *and from beyond* Jordan, Matth. iv. 18, 25. All this was done before the sermon in the mount: and therefore we may certainly reckon that the second Passover was past before the preaching of that sermon. The multitudes that followed him from *Jerusalem*, and *Judea*, shew that he had lately been there at the feast. The sermon in the mount was made when great multitudes came to him from all places, and followed him in the open fields; which is an argument of the summer-season: and in this sermon he pointed at the lilies of the field then in flower before the eyes of his auditors. *Consider, saith he, the lilies of the field, how they grow; they toil not, neither do they spin; and yet* Solomon *in all his glory was not arayed like one of these; Wherefore if God so clothe the grass of the field, which to day is and to morrow is cast into the oven,* &c. *Matth.* vi. 28. So therefore the grass of the field was now in the flower, and by consequence the month of *March* with the Passover was past.

Let us see therefore how the rest of the feasts follow in order in *Matthew's* Gospel: for he was an eye-witness of what he relates, and so tells all things in due order of time, which *Mark* and *Luke* do not.

Some time after the sermon in the mount, when the time came that he should be received, that is, when the time of a feast came that he should be received by the *Jews*, he set his face to go to *Jerusalem*: and as he went with his disciples in the way, when the *Samaritans* in his passage thro' *Samaria* had denied him lodgings, and a certain Scribe said unto him, *Master, I will follow thee whithersoever thou goest,* Jesus *said unto him, The foxes have holes, and birds of the air have nests, but the Son of man hath not where to lay his head,* Matth. viii. 19. Luke ix. 51, 57. The Scribe told Christ he would bear him company in his journey, and *Christ* replied that he wanted a lodging. Now this feast I take to be the feast of Tabernacles, because soon after I find *Christ* and his Apostles on the sea of *Tiberias* in a storm so great, that the ship was covered with water and in danger of sinking, till *Christ rebuked the winds and the sea,* Matth. viii. 23. For this storm shews that winter was now come on.

After this *Christ* did many miracles, *and went about all the cities and villages of* Galilee, *teaching in their Synagogues, and preaching the gospel of the kingdom, and healing every sickness, and every disease among the people,* Matth. ix. he then sent forth the twelve to do the like, *Matth.* x. and at length when he had received a message from *John*, and answered it, he said to the multitudes, *From the days of* John *the Baptist until now the kingdom of heaven suffereth violence*; and upbraided the cities, *Chorazin, Bethsaida*, and *Capernaum*, wherein most of his mighty works were done, because they repented not, *Matth.* xi. Which several passages shew, that from the imprisonment of *John* till now there had been a considerable length of time: the winter was now past, and the next Passover was at hand; for immediately after this, *Matthew*, in chap. xii. subjoins, that *Jesus went on the sabbath-day thro' the corn, and his disciples were an hungred, and began to pluck the ears of corn and to eat,* — *rubbing them*, saith *Luke, in their hands*: the corn therefore was not only in the ear, but ripe; and consequently the Passover, in which the first-fruits were always offered before the harvest, was now come or past. *Luke* calls this sabbath deuteroproton,[3] the second prime sabbath, that is, the second of the two great feasts of the Passover. As we call *Easter* day high *Easter*, and its octave low *Easter* or *Lowsunday:* so *Luke* calls the feast on the seventh day of the unleavened bread, the second of the two prime sabbaths.

In one of the sabbaths following he went into a Synagogue, and healed a man with a withered hand, *Matth.* xii. 9. *Luke* vi. 6. And when the Pharisees took counsel to destroy him, *he withdrew himself from thence, and great multitudes followed him; and he healed them all, and charged them that they should not make him known.* Matth. xii. 14. Afterwards, being in a ship, and the multitude standing on the shore, he spake to them three parables together, taken from the seeds-men sowing the fields, *Matth.* xiii, by which we may know that it was now seed-time, and by consequence that the feast of Tabernacles was past. After this he went *into his own country, and taught them in their Synagogue, but did not many mighty works there because of their unbelief.* Then the twelve having been abroad a year, returned, and told *Jesus* all that they had done: and at the same time *Herod* beheaded *John* in prison, and his disciples came and told *Jesus*; and when *Jesus* heard it, he took the twelve and departed thence privately by ship into a desert place belonging to *Bethsaida*: and the people when they knew it, followed him on foot out of the cities, the winter now being past; and he healed their sick, and in the desert fed them to the number of five thousand men, besides women and children, with only five loaves and two fishes, *Matth.* xiv. *Luke* ix. at the doing of which miracle the Passover of the *Jews* was nigh, *John* vi. 4. But *Jesus* went not up to this feast; but *after these things walked in* Galilee, *because the* Jews at the Passover before had taken counsel to destroy him, and still *sought to kill him,* John vii. 1. Henceforward therefore he is found first in the coast of *Tyre* and

---

[3]   [Deuteroproton originally given in Greek characters.]

Sidon, then by the sea of *Galilee*, afterwards in the coast of *Cæsarea Philippi*; and lastly at *Capernaum, Matth.* xv. 21, 29. xvi. 13. xvii. 34.

Afterwards when the feast of Tabernacles was at hand, his brethren upbraided him for walking secretly, and urged him to go up to the feast. But he went not till they were gone, and then went up privately, *John* vii. 2. and when the *Jews* sought to stone him, he escaped, John viii. 59. After this he was at the feast of the Dedication* in winter, *John* x. 22. and when they sought again to take him, he fled beyond *Jordan, John* x. 39, 40. *Matth.* xix. 1. where he stayed till the death of *Lazarus*, and then came to *Bethany* near *Jerusalem*, and raised him, *John* xi. 7, 18. whereupon the *Jews* took counsel from that time to kill him: and *therefore he walked no more openly among the* Jews, *but went thence into a country near to the wilderness, into a city called Ephraim; and there continued with his disciples* till the last Passover in which the *Jews* put him to death, *John* xi. 53, 54.

Thus have we, in the Gospels of *Matthew* and *John* compared together, the history of *Christ's* actions in continual order during five Passover's. *John* is more distinct in the beginning and end; *Matthew* in the middle: what either omits, the other supplies. The first Passover was between the baptism of *Christ* and the imprisonment of *John, John* ii. 13. the second within four months after the inprisonment of *John* and *Christ's* beginning to preach in *Galilee, John* iv. 35. and therefore it was either that feast to which *Jesus* went up, when the Scribe desired to follow him, *Matth.* viii.19. *Luke* ix. 51, 57. or the feast before it. The third was the next feast after it, when the corn was eared and ripe, *Matth.* xii. 1. *Luke* vi. 1. The fourth was that which was nigh at hand when *Christ* wrought the miracle of the five loaves, *Matth.* xiv. 14. *John* vi. 4, 5. and the fifth was that in which *Christ* suffered, *Matth.* xx. 17. *John* xii. 1.

Between the first and the second Passover *John* and *Christ* baptized together, till the imprisonment of *John*, which was four months before the second. Then *Christ* began to preach, and call his disciples; and after he had instructed them a year, sent them to preach in the cities of the *Jews*: at the same time *John* hearing of the fame of *Christ*, sent to him to know who he was. At the third, the chief Priests began to consult about the death of *Christ*. A little before the fourth, the twelve after they had preached a year in all the cities, returned to *Christ*; and at the same time *Herod* beheaded *John* in prison, after he had been in prison two years and a quarter: and thereupon *Christ* fled into the desert for fear of *Herod*. The fourth *Christ* went not up to *Jerusalem* for fear of the *Jews*, who at the Passover before had consulted his death, and because his time was not yet come. Thenceforward therefore till the feast of Tabernacles he walked in *Galilee*, and that secretly for fear of *Herod*: and after the feast of Tabernacles he returned no more into *Galilee*, but sometimes was at *Jerusalem*, and sometimes retired beyond *Jordan*, or to the city *Ephraim* by the wilderness, till the Passover in which he was betrayed, apprehended, and crucified.

John therefore baptized two summers, and *Christ* preached three. The first summer *John* preached to make himself known, in order to give testimony to *Christ*. Then, after *Christ* came to his baptism and was made known to him, he baptized another summer, to make *Christ* known by his testimony; and *Christ* also baptized the same summer, to make himself the more known: and by reason of *John's* testimony there came more to *Christ's* baptism than to *John's*. The winter following *John* was imprisoned; and now his course being at an end, *Christ* entred upon his proper office of preaching in the cities. In the beginning of his preaching he completed the number of the twelve Apostles, and instructed them all the first year in order to send them abroad. Before the end of this year, his fame by his preaching and miracles was so far spread abroad, that the *Jews* at the Passover following consulted how to kill him. In the second year of his preaching, it being no longer safe for him to converse openly in *Judea*, he sent the twelve to preach in all their cities: and in the end of the year they returned to him, and told him all they had done. All the last year the twelve continued with him to be instructed more perfectly, in order to their preaching to all nations after his death.[4] And upon the news of *John's* death, being afraid of *Herod* as well as of the *Jews*, he walked this year more secretly than before; frequenting desarts, and spending the last half of the year in *Judea*, without the dominions of *Herod*.

Thus have we in the Gospels of *Matthew* and *John* all things told in due order, from the beginning of John's preaching to the death of *Christ*, and the years distinguished from one another by such essential characters that they cannot be mistaken. The second Passover is distinguished from the first, by the interposition of *John's* imprisonment. The third is distinguished from the second, by a double character: first, by the interposition of the feast to which *Christ* went up. *Matt.* viii. 19. *Luke* ix. 57. and secondly, by the distance of time from the beginning of *Christ's* preaching: for the second was in the beginning of his preaching and the third so long after, that before it came Christ said, *from the days of* John *the Baptist until now*, &c. and upbraided the cities of *Galilee* for their not repenting at his preaching, and mighty works done in all that time. The fourth is distinguished from the third, by the mission of the twelve from *Christ* to preach in the cities of *Judea* in all the interval. The fifth is distinguished from all the former by the twelve's being returned from preaching, and continuing with *Christ* during all the interval, between the fourth and fifth, and by the passion and other infallible characters.

Now since the first summer of *John's* baptizing fell in the fifteenth year of the Emperor *Tiberius*, and by consequence the first of these five Passovers in his sixteenth year; the last of them, in which *Jesus* suffered, will fall on the twentieth year of the same Emperor; and by consequence in the Consulship of *Fabius* and *Vitellius*, in the 79th *Julian* year, and year of *Christ* 34, which was the sabbatical year of the *Jews*. And that it did so, I further confirm by these arguments.

---

[4]   [This sentence does not read well; but it is the sentence as it appears in the text.]

I take it for granted that the passion was on friday the 14th day of the month Nisan, the great feast of the Passover on saturday the 15th day of *Nisan*, and the resurrection on the day following. Now the 14th day of *Nisan* always fell on the full moon next after the vernal Equinox; and the month began at the new moon before, not at the true conjunction, but at the first appearance of the new moon: for the *Jews* referred all the time of the silent moon, as they phrased it, that is, of the moon's disappearing, to the old moon; and because the first appearance might usually be about 18 hours after the true conjunction, they therefore began their month from the sixth hour at evening, that is, at sun set, next after the eighteenth hour from the conjunction. And this rule they called *Jah*,[5] designing by the letters j and h[6] the number 18.

I know that *Epiphanius** tells us, if some interpret his words rightly, that the *Jews* used a vicious cycle, and thereby anticipated the legal moon by two days. But this surely he spake not as a witness, for he neither understood *Astronomy* nor *Rabbinical* learning, but as arguing from his erroneous hypothesis about the time of the passion. For the *Jews* did not anticipate, but postpone their months: they thought it lawful to begin their months a day later than the first appearance of the new moon, because the new moon continued for more days than one; but not a day sooner, lest they should celebrate the new moon before there was any. And the *Jews* still keep a tradition in their books, that the *Sanhedrin** used diligently to define the new moons by sight: sending witnesses into mountainous places, and examining them about the moon's appearing, and translating the new moon from the day they had agreed on to the day before, as often as witnesses came from distant regions, who had seen it a day sooner that it was seen at *Jerusalem.* Accordingly *Josephus,** one of the *Jewish* Priests who had ministred in the temple, tells us that the Passover was kept on the

---

5   [The word Jah originally given also in Hebrew characters.]

6   [Jah, J and H originally given in Hebrew characters.]

14th day of *Nisan, kata selene,*[7] *according to the moon, when the sun was in* Aries. This is confirmed also by two instances, recorded by him, which totally overthrow the hypothesis of the *Jews* using a vicious cycle. For that year in which *Jerusalem* was taken and destroyed, he saith, the Passover was on the 14th day of the month *Xanticus*, which according to *Josephus* is our April; and that five years before, it fell on the 8th day of the same month. Which two instances agree with the course of the moon.[8]

Computing therefore the new moons of the first month according to the course of the moon and the rule *Jah*, and thence counting 14 days, I find that the 14th day of this month of the year of *Christ* 31, fell on tuesday *March* 27; in the year 32, on sunday *Apr.* 13; in the year 33, on friday *Apr.* 3; in the year 34, on wednesday *March* 24, or rather, for avoiding the Equinox which fell on the same day, and for having a fitter time for harvest, on thursday *Apr.* 22. also in the year 35, on tuesday *Apr.* 12. and in the year 36, on saturday *March* 31.

But because the 15th and 21st days of *Nisan*, and a day or two of *Pentecost*, and the 10th, 15th, and 22nd of *Tisri*, were sabbatical days or days of rest, and it was inconvenient on two sabbaths together to be prohibited burying their dead and making ready fresh meat, for in that hot region their meat would be apt in two days to corrupt: to avoid these and such like inconveniences, the *Jews* postponed their months a day, as often as the first day of the month *Tisri*, or, which is all one, the third day of the month *Nisan*, was sunday, wednesday or friday: and this rule they called *Adu*,[9] by the letters A D U,[10] signifying the numbers 1, 4, 6; that is, the 1st, 4th, and 6th days of the week; which days we call sunday, wednesday and friday.

---

[7] [kata selene originally given in Greek characters.]

[8] Joseph.* Antiq. Lib. 3. c. 10.

[9] [Adu originally given also in Hebrew characters.]

[10] [A D U originally given in Hebrew characters.]

Postponing therefore by this rule the months found above; the 14th day of the month *Nisan* will fall in the year of *Christ* 31, on wednesday *March* 28; in the year 32, on monday *Apr.* 14; in the year 33, on friday *Apr.* 3; in the year 34, on friday *Apr.* 23; in the year 35, on wednesay *Apr.* 13; and in the year 36, on saturday *March* 31.

By this computation therefore the year 32 is absolutely excluded, because the Passion cannot fall on friday without making it five days after the full moon, or two days before it; whereas it ought to be upon the day of the full moon, or the next day. For the same reason the years 31 and 35 are excluded, because in them the Passion cannot fall on friday, without making it three days after the full moon, or four days before it: errors so enormous, that they would be very conspicuous in the heavens to every vulgar eye. The year 36 is contended for by few or none, and both this and the year 35 may thus be excluded.

Tiberius in the beginning of his reign made *Valerius Gratus* President of *Judea*; and after 11 years, substituted *Pontius Pilate*, who governed 10 years. Then *Vitellius*, newly made President of Syria, deprived him of his honour, substituting *Marcellus*, and at length sent him to *Rome*: but, by reason of delays, *Tiberius* died before *Pilate* got thither. In the mean time *Vitellius*, after he had deposed *Pilate*, came to *Jerusalem* in the time of the Passover, to visit that Province as well as others in the beginning of his office; and in the place of *Caiaphas*, then High Priest, created *Jonathas* the son of *Ananus*, or *Annas* as he is called in scripture. Afterwards, when *Vitellius* was returned to *Antioch*, he received letters form *Tiberius*, to make peace with *Artabanus* king of the *Parthians*. At the same time the *Alans*, by the sollicitation of *Tiberius*, invaded the kingdom of *Artabanus*; and his subjects also, by the procurement of *Vitellius*, soon after rebelled: for *Tiberius* thought that *Artabanus*, thus pressed with difficulties, would more readily accept the conditions of peace. *Artabanus* therefore straightaway gathering a greater army, opprest the rebels; and then meeting *Vitellius* at *Euphrates*, made a league with the *Romans*. After this

Tiberius commanded *Vitellius* to make war upon *Aretas* King of *Arabia*. He therefore leading his army against *Aretas*, went together with *Herod* to *Jerusalem*, to sacrifice at the publick feast which was then to be celebrated. Where being received honourably, he stayed three days, and in the mean while translated the high Priesthood from *Jonathas* to his brother *Theophilus*: and the fourth day, receiving letters of the death of *Tiberius*, made the people swear allegiance to *Caius* the new Emperor; and recalling his army, sent them into quarters. All this is related by *Jospehus* Antiq.* lib. 18. c. 6, 7. Now *Tiberius* reigned 22 years and 7 months, and died *March* 16, in the beginning of the year of *Christ* 37; and the feast of the Passover fell on *April* 20 following, that is, 35 days after the death of *Tiberius*: so that there were about 36 or 38 days, for the news of his death to come from *Rome* to *Vitellius* at *Jerusalem*; which being a convenient time for that message, confirms that the feast which *Vitellius* and *Herod* now went up to was the Passover. For had it been the Pentecost, as is usually supposed, *Vitellius* would have continued three months ignorant of the Emperor's death: which is not to be supposed. However, the things done between this feast and the Passover which *Vitellius* was at before, namely, the stirring up a sedition in *Parthia*, the quieting that sedition, the making a league after that with the *Parthians*, the sending news of that league to *Rome*, the recieving new orders from thence to go against the *Arabians*, and the putting those orders in execution; required much more time than the fifty days between the Passover and Pentecost of the same year: and therefore the Passover which *Vitellius* first went up to, was in the year before. Therefore *Pilate* was deposed before the Passover of A.C. 36, and by consequence the passion of *Christ* was before that Passover: for he suffered not under *Vitellius*, nor under *Vitellius* and *Pilate* together, but under *Pilate* alone.

Now it is observable that the high Priesthood was at his time become an annual office, and the Passover was the time of making a new high Priest. For *Gratus* the predecessor of *Pilate*, saith *Josephus*, made *Ismael* high Priest after *Ananus*; and a while after, suppose a year, deposed him, and substituted *Eleazar*, and a year after *Simon*, and after another year *Caiaphas*; and then gave way to *Pilate*. So *Vitellius* at one Passover made *Jonathas* successor to *Caiaphas*, and at the next *Theophilus* to *Jonathas*. Hence *Luke* tells us, that in the 15th year of *Tiberius*, *Annas* and *Caiaphas* were high Priests, that is, *Annas* till the Passover, and *Caiaphas* afterwards. Accordingly *John* speaks of the high Priesthood as an annual office: for he tells us again and again, in the last year of *Christ's* preaching, that *Caiaphas* was high Priest for that year, *John* xi. 49, 51. xviii. 13. And the next year *Luke* tells you, that *Annas* was high Priest, *Acts* iv. 6. *Theophilus* was therefore made high Priest in the first year of *Caius*, *Jonathas* in the 22d year of *Tiberius*, and *Caiaphas* in the 21st year of the same Emperor: and therefore, allotting a year to each, the Passion, when *Annas* succeeded *Caiaphas*, could not be later that the 20th year of *Tiberius*, A.C. 34.

Thus there remain only the years 33 and 34 to be considered; and the year 33 I exclude by this argument. In the Passover two years before the Passion, when *Christ* went thro' the corn, and his disciples pluckt the ears, and rubbed them with their hands to eat; this ripeness of the corn shews that the Passover then fell late: and so did the Passover A.C. 32, *April* 14. but the Passover A.C. 31, *March* 28th, fell very early. It was not therefore two years after the year 31, but two years after 32 that *Christ* suffered.

Thus all the characters of the Passion agree to the year 34; and that is the only year to which they all agree.

CHAPTER XII

Of the Prophecy of the Scripture of Truth.

The kingdoms represented by the second and third Beasts, or the Bear and Leopard, are again described by *Daniel* in his last Prophecy written in the third year of *Cyrus* over *Babylon*, the year in which he conquered *Persia*. For this Prophecy is a commentary upon the Vision of the Ram and He-Goat.

Behold, saith he, *there shall stand up yet three kings in Persia, [Cyrus, Cambyses, and Darius Hystaspes] and the fourth [Xerxes] shall be far richer than they all: and by his strength thro' his riches he shall stir up all against the realm of Grecia. And a mighty king [Alexander* the great*] shall stand up, that shall rule with great dominion, and do according to his will. And when he shall stand up, his kingdom shall be broken, and shall be divided towards the four winds of heaven; and not to his posterity* [but after their death,] *nor according to his dominion which he ruled: for his kingdom shall be pluckt up, even for others besides those. Alexander* the great having conquered all the *Persian* Empire, and some part of *India*, died at *Babylon* a month before the summer Solstice, in the year of *Nabonassar** 425: and his captains gave the monarchy to his bastard brother *Philip Aridæus*, a man disturbed in his understanding; and made *Perdiccas* administrator of the kingdom. *Perdiccas* with their consent made *Meleager* commander of the army, *Seleucus* master of the horse, *Craterus* treasurer of the kingdom, *Antipater* governor of *Macedon* and *Greece, Ptolemy* governor of *Egypt; Antigonus* governor of *Pamphylia, Lycia, Lycaonia*, and *Phrygia* major; *Lysimachus* governor of *Thrace*, and other captains governors of other Provinces; as many as had been so before in the days of *Alexander* the great. The *Babylonians* began now to count a new Æra, which they called the Æra of *Phillip*, using the years of *Nabonassar*,* and reckoning the 425th year of *Nabonassar* to be the first year of *Philip*. *Roxana* the wife of *Alexander* being left big with cild, and about three or four months after brought to bed of a son, they called him *Alexander*, saluted him King, and joined him with *Philip*, whom they had before placed in the throne. *Philip* reigned three years under the administratorship of *Perdiccas*, two years more under the administratorship of *Antipater*, and above a year more under that of *Polyperchon*; in all six years and four months; and then was slain with his Queen *Eurydice* in September by the command of *Olympias* the mother of *Alexander* the great. The *Greeks* being disgusted at the cruelties of *Olympias*, revolted to *Cassander* the son of and successor of *Antipater*. *Cassander* affecting the dominion of *Greece*, slew *Olympias*; and soon after shut up the young king *Alexander*, with his mother *Roxana*, in the castle of *Amphipolis*, under the charge of *Glaucias, An. Nabonass*. 432. The next year *Ptolemy, Cassander* and *Lysimachus*, by means of *Seleucus*, form'd a league against *Antigonus*; and after certain wars made peace with him, *An. Nabonass*. 438, upon these certain conditions: that *Cassander* should command the forces of *Europe* till *Alexander* the son of *Roxana* came to age; and that *Lysimachus* should govern *Thrace*, *Ptolemy Egypt* and *Lybia*, and *Antigonus* all *Asia*. *Seleucus* had possest himself of *Mesopotamia, Babylonia, Susiana* and *Media* the year before. About three years after *Alexander's* death he was made governor of *Babylon* by *Antipater*; then was expelled by *Antigonus*; but now he recovered and enlarged his government over a great part of the *East*: which gave occasion to a new *Æra*, called *Æra Seleucidarum*. Not long after the peace made with *Antigonus*, *Diodorus* saith the same *Olympic* year; *Cassander*, seeing that *Alexander* the son of *Roxana* grew up, and that it was discoursed thro' out *Macedonia* that it was fit he should be set at liberty, and take upon him the government of his father's kingdom, commanded *Glaucias* the governor of the castle to kill *Roxana* and the young king *Alexander* her son, and conceal their deaths. Then *Polyperchon* set up *Hercules*, the son of *Alexander* the great by *Barsinè*, to be king; and soon after, at the sollicitation of *Cassander*, caused him to be slain. Soon after that, upon a great victory at sea got by *Demetrius* the son of *Antigonus* over *Ptolemy*, *Antigonus* took upon himself the title of king, and gave the same title to his son. This was *An. Nabonass.* 441. After his example, *Seleucus*, *Cassander*, *Lysimachus* and *Ptolemy*, took upon themselves the title and dignity of kings, having abstained from this honour while there remained any of *Alexander's* race to inherit the crown. Thus the monarchy of the *Greeks* for want of an heir was broken into several kingdoms; four of which, seated *to the four winds of heaven*, were very eminent. For *Ptolemy* reigned over *Egypt*, *Lybia* and *Ethiopia*; *Antigonus* over *Syria* and the lesser *Asia*; *Lysimachus* over *Thrace*; and *Cassander* over *Macedon*, *Greece* and *Epirus*, as above.

Seleucus at this time reigned over the nations which were beyond *Euphrates*, and belonged to the bodies of the two first Beasts; but after six years he conquered *Antigonus*, and thereby became possest of one of the four kingdoms. For *Cassander* being afraid of the power of *Antigonus*, combined with *Lysimachus*, *Ptolemy* and *Seleucus*, against him: and while *Lysimachus* invaded the parts of *Asia* next to the *Hellespont*, *Ptolemy* subdued *Phoenicia* and *Coelosyria*, with the sea-coasts of *Asia*.

Seleucus came down with a powerful army into *Cappadocia*, and joining the confederate forces, fought *Antigonus* in *Phrygia* and slew him, and seized his kingdom, *An. Nabonass.* 447. After which *Seleucus* built *Antioch*, *Seleucia*, *Laodicea*, *Apamea*, *Berrhœa*, *Edessa*, and other cities in *Syria* and *Asia*; and in them granted the *Jews* equal privileges with the *Greeks*.

Demetrius the son of *Antigonus* retained but a small part of his father's dominions, and at length lost *Cyprus* to *Ptolemy*; but afterwards killing *Alexander*, the son and successor of *Cassander* king of *Macedon*, he seized his kingdom, *An. Nabonass.** 454. Sometime after, preparing a very great army to recover his father's dominions in *Asia; Seleucus, Ptolemy, Lysimachus* and *Pyrrhus* king of *Epirus*, combined against him; and *Pyrrhus* invading *Macedon*, corrupted the army of *Demetrius*, put him to flight, seized his kingdom, and shared it with *Lysimachus*. After seven months, *Lysimachus* beating *Pyrrhus*, took *Macedon* from him, and held it five years and a half, uniting the kingdoms of *Macedon* and *Thrace*. *Lysimachus* in his wars with *Antigonus* and *Demetrius*, had taken from them *Caria, Lydia* and *Phrygia*; and had a treasury in *Pergamus*, a castle on the top of a conical hill in *Phrygia*, by the river *Caicus*, the custody of which he had committed to one *Philetærus*, who was at first faithful to him, but in the last year of his reign revolted. For *Lysimachus*, having at the instigation of his wife *Arsinoe*, slain first his own son *Agathocles*, and then several that lamented him; the wife of *Agathocles* fled with her children and brothers, and some others of their friends, and sollicited *Seleucus* to make war upon *Lysimachus*; whereupon *Philetærus* also, who grieved at the death of *Agathocles*, and was accused thereof by *Arsinoe*, took up arms, and sided with *Seleucus*. On this occasion *Seleucus* and *Lysimachus* met and fought in *Phrygia*; and *Lysimachus* being slain in the battel, lost his kingdom to *Seleucus, An. Nabonass.* 465. Thus the empire of the *Greeks*, which at first brake into four kingdoms, became now reduced into two notable ones, henceforward called by *Daniel* the kings of the *South* and *North*. For *Ptolemy* now reigned over *Egypt, Lybia, Ethiopia, Arabia, Phoenicia, Coelosyria*, and *Cyprus*; and *Seleucus*, having united three of the four kingdoms, had a dominion scarce inferior to that of the *Persian* Empire, conquered by *Alexander* the great. All which is thus represented by *Daniel*: *and the king of the South* [*Ptolemy*] *shall be strong, and one of his Princes* [*Seleucus*, one of *Alexander's*

Princes] *shall be strong above him, and have dominion; his dominion shall be a great dominion.*[1]

After *Seleucus* had reigned seven months over *Macedon, Greece, Thrace, Asia, Syria, Babylonia, Media,* and in all the *East* as far as *India; Ptolemy Ceraunus,* the younger brother of *Ptolemy Philadelphus* king of *Egypt,* slew him treacherously, and seized his dominions in *Europe:* while *Antiochus Soter,* the son of *Seleucus,* succeeded his father in *Asia, Syria,* and most of the *East;* and after nineteen or twenty years was succeeded by his son *Antiochus Theos;* who having a lasting war with *Ptolemy Philadelphus,* at length composed the same by marrying *Berenice* the daughter of *Philadelphus:* but after a reign of fifteen years, his first wife *Laodice* poisoned him, and set her son *Seleucus Callinicus* upon the throne. *Callinicus* in the beginning of his reign, by the impulse of his mother *Laodice,* besieged *Berenice* in *Daphne* near *Antioch,* and slew her with her young son and many of her women. Whereupon *Ptolemy Euergetes,* the son and successor of *Philadelphus,* made war upon *Callinicus;* took from him *Phoenicia, Syria, Cilicia, Mesopotamia, Babylonia, Susiana,* and some other regions; and carried back to *Egypt* 40000 talents of silver, and 2500 images of the Gods, amongst which were the Gods of *Egypt* carried away by *Cambyses. Antiochus Hierax* at first assisted his brother *Callinicus,* but afterwards contended with him for *Asia.* In the mean time *Eumenes* governor of *Pergamus* beat *Antiochus,* and took from them both all *Asia* westward of mount *Taurus.* This was in the fifth year of *Callinicus,* who after an inglorious reign of 20 years was succeeded by his son *Seleucus Ceraunus;* and *Euergetes* after four years more, *An. Nabonass.* 527, was succeeded by his son *Ptolemy Philopator.* All which is thus signified by *Daniel: And in the end of years they* [the kings of the *South* and North] *shall join themselves together: for the king's daughter of the* South [*Berenice*] *shall come to the king of the North to make an agreement, but she shall not retain the power of the*

---

[1]   Chap. xi. 5

arm; neither shall she stand, nor her seed, but she shall be delivered up, and he [Callinicus] that brought her, and he whom she brought forth, and they that strengthened her in [those] *times,* [or defended her in the siege of *Daphne*]. *But out of a branch of her roots shall one stand up in his feet* [her brother *Euergetes*] *who shall come with an army, and shall enter into the fortress* [or fenced cities] *of the king of the* North, *and shall act against them and prevail: and shall carry captives into* Egypt, *their Gods with their Princes and precious vessels of silver and gold; and he shall continue some years after the king of the* North.[2]

Seleucus Ceraunus, inheriting the remains of his father's kingdoms, and thinking to recover the rest, raised a great army against the governor of *Pergamus*, now King thereof, but died in the third year of his reign. His brother and successor, *Antiochus Magnus*, carrying on the war, took from the king of *Pergamus* almost all the lesser *Asia*, recovering also the provinces of *Media, Persia and Babylonia*, from the governors who had revolted: and in the fifth year of his reign invading *Coelosyria*, he with little opposition possest himself of a good part thereof; and the next year returning to invade the rest of *Coelosyria* and *Phoenicia*, beat the army of *Ptolemy Philopator* near *Berytus*; he then invaded *Palestine* and the neighbouring parts of *Arabia*, and the third year returned with an army of 78000: but *Ptolemy* coming out of *Egypt* with an army of 75000, fought and routed him at *Raphia* near *Gaza*, between *Palestine* and *Egypt*; and recovered all *Phoenicia* and *Coelosyria, An. Nabonass.** 532. Being puffed up with this victory, and living in all manner of luxury, the *Egyptians* revolted, and had wars with him, but were overcome; and in the broils sixty thousand *Egyptian Jews* were slain. All which is thus described by *Daniel: But his sons* [*Seleucus Ceraunus*, and *Antiochus Magnus*, the sons of *Callinicus*] *shall be stirred up, and shall gather a great army; and he* [*Antiochus Magnus*] *shall come effectually and overflow, and pass thro' and return, and* [again

---

[2]   Chap. xi. 6-8.

the next year] *be stirred up* [marching even] *to his fortress,* [the frontier towns of *Egypt*;] *and the King of the South shall be moved with choler, and come forth* [the third year] *and fight with him, even with the King of the* North; *and he* [the King of the North] *shall lead forth a great multitude, but the multitude shall be given into his hand. And the multitude being taken away, his heart shall be lifted up, and he shall cast down many ten thousands; but he shall not be strengthened by it: for the king of the* North *shall return,* &c.[3]

About twelve years after the battle between *Philopator* and *Antiochus, Philopator* died; and left his kingdom to his young son *Ptolemy Epiphanes,* a child of five years old. Thereupon *Antiochus Magnus* confederated with *Philip* king of *Macedon,* that they should each invade the dominions of *Epiphanes* which lay next to them. Hence arose a various war with *Antiochus* and *Epiphanes,* each of them seizing *Phoenicia* and *Coelosyria* by turns; whereby those countries were much afflicted by both parties. First *Antiochus* seized them; then one *Scopas* being sent with the army of *Egypt,* recovered them from *Antiochus*: the next year, *An. Nabonass.* 550, *Antiochus* fought and routed *Scopas* near the fountains of *Jordan,* besieged him in *Sidon,* took the city, and recovered *Syria* and *Phoenicia* from *Egypt,* the *Jews* coming over to him voluntarily. But about three years after, preparing for a war against the *Romans,* he came to *Raphia* on the borders of *Egypt*; made peace with *Epiphanes,* and gave him his daughter *Cleopatra*: next autumn he passed the *Hellespont* to invade the cities of *Greece* under *Roman* protection, and took some of them; but was beaten by the *Romans* the summer following, and forced to return back with his army into *Asia.* Before the end of the year the fleet of *Antiochus* was beaten by the fleet of the *Romans* near *Phocœa*: and at the same time *Epiphanes* and *Cleopatra* sent an embassy to Rome to congratulate the *Romans* on their success against their father *Antiochus,* and to exhort them to prosecute the war against him into *Asia.* The

---

[3]   Chap. xi. 10, &c.

Romans beat *Antiochus* again at sea near *Ephesus*, past their army over the *Hellespont*, and obtain'd a great victory over him by land, took from him all *Asia* westward of mount *Taurus*, gave it to the King of *Pergamus* who assisted them in the war; and imposed a large tribute upon *Antiochus*. Thus the King of *Pergamus*, by the power of the *Romans*, recovered what *Antiochus* had taken from him; and *Antiochus* retiring into the remainder of his kingdom, was slain two years after by the *Persians*, as he was robbing the Temple of *Jupiter Belus* in *Elymais*, to raise money for the *Romans*. All which is thus described by *Daniel*. *For the King of the North* [*Antiochus*] *shall return, and shall set forth a multitude greater than the former; and shall certainly come, after certain years, with a great army and with much riches. And in those times there shall many stand up against the King of the* South, [particularly the *Macedonians*;] *also the robbers of thy people* [the *Samaritans*, &c.] *shall exalt themselves to establish the vision, but they shall fall. So the King of the* North *shall come, and cast up a mount, and take the most fenced cities; and the arms of the* South *shall not withstand, neither his chosen people, neither shall there be any strength to withstand. But he that cometh against him shall do according to his own will, and none shall stand before him: and he shall stand in the glorious land, which shall fail*[4] *into his hand. He shall also set his face to go with the strength* [or army] *of all his kingdom, and make an agreement with him* [at *Raphia*;] *and he shall give him the daughter of women corrupting her; but she shall not stand his side, neither be for him. After this he shall turn his face unto the Isles, and shall take many: but a Prince for his own behalf* [the *Romans*] *shall cause the reproach offered by him to cease; without his own reproach he shall cause it to turn upon him. Then he shall turn his*

---

[4]   [This - fail - seems to be a typographical error; presumably it should read 'fall into his hand'?]

face towards the fort of his own land: but he shall stumble and fall, and not be found.[5]

Seleucus Philopator succeeded his father *Antiochus, Anno Nabonass.* 561, and reigned twelve years, but did nothing memorable, being sluggish, and intent upon raising money for the *Romans* to whom he was tributary. He was slain by *Heliodorus*, whom he had sent to rob the temple of *Jerusalem. Daniel* thus describes his reign. *Then shall stand up in his estate a raiser of taxes in the glory of the kingdom, but within few days he shall be destroyed, neither in anger nor in battle.*[6] A little before the death of *Philopator*, his son *Demetrius* was sent hostage to *Rome*, in the place of *Antiochus Epiphanes*, the brother of *Philopator*; and *Antiochus* was at *Athens* in his way home from *Rome*, when *Philopator* died: whereupon *Heliodorus* the treasurer of the kingdom, stept into the throne. But *Antiochus* so managed his affairs, that the *Romans* kept *Demetrius* at *Rome*; and their ally the King of *Pergamus* expelled *Heliodorus*, and placed *Antiochus* in the throne, while *Demetrius* the right heir remained an hostage at *Rome*. *Antiochus* being thus made King by the friendship of the King of *Pergamus* reigned powerfully over *Syria* and the neighbouring nations: but carried himself much below his dignity, stealing privately out of his palace, rambling up and down the city in disguise with one or two of his companions; conversing and drinking with people of the lowest rank, foreigners and strangers; frequenting the meetings of dissolute persons to feast and revel; clothing himself like the *Roman* candidates and officers, acting their parts like a mimick, and in publick festivals jesting and dancing with servants and light people, exposing himself by all manner of ridiculous gestures. This conduct made some take him for a madman, and call him *Antiochus Epimenes*.[7] In the first year of his reign he deposed *Onias* the

---

[5]   Chap. xi. 13-19.

[6]   Chap. xi. 20.

[7]   [Epimenes originally given in Greek characters.]

high-Priest, and sold the high-Priesthood to *Jason* the younger brother of *Onias*: for *Jason* had promised to give him 440 talents of silver for that office, and 150 more for a licence to erect a place of exercise for the training up of youth in the fashions of the heathen; which licence was granted by the King, and put in execution by *Jason*. Then the King sending one *Apollonius* into *Egypt* to the coronation of *Ptolemy Philometor*, the young son of *Philometor* and *Cleopatra* and knowing *Philometor* not to be well affected to his affairs in *Phoenicia*, provided for his own safety in those parts; and for that end came to *Joppa* and *Jersusalem* where he was honourably received; from thence he went in like manner with his little army to the cities of *Phoenicia*, to establish himself against *Egypt*, by courting the people, and distributing extraordinary favours amongst them. All which is thus represented by *Daniel. And in his* [*Philometor's*] *estate shall stand up a vile person, to whom they* [the *Syrians* who set up *Heliodorus*] *shall not give the honour of the kingdom. Yet he shall come in peaceably and obtain the kingdom by flatteries* [made principally to the King of *Pergamus*;] *and the arms* [which in favour of *Helioforus* oppose him] *shall be overflowed with a flood from before him, and be broken; yea also* [*Onias* the high-Priest] *the Prince of the covenant. And after the league made with him,* [the King of *Egypt*, by sending *Apollonius* to his coronation] *he shall work deceitfully* [against the King of *Egypt*,] *for he shall come up and shall become strong* [in *Phoenicia*] *with a small people. And he shall enter into the quiet and plentiful cities of the Province* [of *Phoenicia*;] *and* [to ingratiate himself with the *Jews* of *Phoenicia* and *Egypt*, and with their friends] *he shall do that which his fathers have not done, nor his fathers fathers: he shall scatter among them the prey and the spoil, and the riches* [exacted from other places;] *and shall forecast his devices against the strong holds* [of *Egypt*] *even for a time.*[8]

These things were done in the first year of his reign, *An. Nabonass.** 573.

---

[8]   Chap. xi. 21, &c.

And thenceforward he forecast his devices against the strong holds of *Egypt*, until the sixth year. For three years after, that is in the fourth year of his reign, *Menelaus* bought the high-Priesthood from *Jason*, but not paying the price was sent for by the King; and the King, before he could hear the cause, went into *Cilicia* to appease a sedition there, and left *Andronicus* his deputy at *Antioch*; in the mean time the brother of *Menelaus*, to make up the money, conveyed several vessels out of the Temple, selling some of them at *Tyre*, and sending others to *Andronicus*. When *Menelaus* was reproved for this by *Onias*, he caused *Onias* to be slain by *Andronicus*: for which fact the King at his return from *Cilicia* caused *Andronicus* to be put to death. Then *Antiochus* prepared his second expedition against *Egypt*, which he performed in the sixth year of his reign, *An Nabonass.* 578: for upon the death of *Cleopatra*, the governors of her son the young King of *Egypt* claimed *Phoenicia* and *Coelosyria* from him as her dowry; and to recover those countries raised a great army. *Antiochus* considering that his father had not quitted the possession of those countries, denied they were her dowry; and with another great army met and fought the *Egyptians* on the borders of *Egypt*, between *Pelusium* and the mountain *Casius*. He there beat them, and might have destroyed their whole army, but that he rode up and down, commanding his soldiers not to kill them, but to take them alive: by which humanity he gained *Pelusium*, and soon after all *Egypt*; entring it with a vast multitude of foot and chariots, elephants and horsemen, and a great navy. Then seizing the cities of *Egypt* as a friend, he marched to *Memphis*, laid the whole blame of the war upon *Elæus* the King's governor, entred into outward friendship with the young King, and took upon him to order the affairs of the kingdom. While *Antiochus* was thus employ'd, a report being spread in *Phoenicia* that he was dead, *Jason* to recover the high-Priesthood assaulted *Jerusalem* with above a thousand men, and took the city: hereupon the King thinking *Judea* had revolted, came out of *Egypt* in a furious manner, re-took the city, slew forty thousand of the people, made as many prisoners, and sold them to raise money; went into the Temple, spoiled it of its treasures, ornaments, utensils, and vessels of gold and silver, amounting to 1800 talents; and carried all away to *Antioch*.[9] This was done in the year of *Nabonassar* 578, and is thus described by *Daniel*. *And he shall stir up his power, and his courage against the King of the* South *with a great army; and the King of the* South *shall be stirred up to battle with a very great and mighty army; but he shall not stand: for they*, even *Antiochus* and his friends, *shall forecast devices against him*, as is represented above; *yea, they that feed of the portion of his meat, shall betray and destroy him, and his army shall be overthrown, and many shall fall down slain. And both these Kings hearts shall be to do mischief; and they, being now made friends, shall speak lyes at one table*, against the *Jews* and against the holy covenant; *but it shall not prosper: for yet the end*, in which the setting up of the abomination of desolation is to prosper, *shall be at the time appointed. Then shall he return into his land with great riches, and his heart shall be against the holy covenant; and he shall act*, against it by spoiling the Temple, *and return into his own land*.[10]

The *Egyptians* of *Alexandria* seeing *Philometor* first educated in luxury by the Eunuch *Eulæus*, and now in the hands of *Antiochus*, gave the kingdom to *Euergetes*, the yonger brother of *Philometor*. Whereupon *Antiochus* pretending to restore *Philometor*, made war upon *Euergetes*; beat him at sea, and besieged him and his sister *Cleopatra* in *Alexandria*: while the besieged Princes sent to *Rome* to implore the assistance of the Senate. *Antiochus* finding himself unable to take the city that year, returned into *Syria*, leaving *Philometor* at *Memphis* to govern *Egypt* in his absence. But *Philometor* made friendship with his brother that winter; and *Antiochus*, returning the next spring *An. Nabonass*.* 580, to besiege both the brothers in *Alexandria*, was met in the way by the Roman Ambassadors. *Popilius Læna, C.*

---

[9]   2. Maccab. iii. 5, 8, & iv. 4.

[10]   Chap. xi. 25, &c.

Decimus, and *C. Hostilius*: he offered them his hand to kiss, but *Popilius* delivering to him the tables wherein the message of the Senate was written, bad him read those first. When he had read them, he replied he would consider with his friends what was fit to be done; but *Popilius* drawing a circle about him, bad him answer it before he went out of it: *Antiochus*, astonished at this blunt and unusual imperiousness, made answer he would do what the *Romans* demanded; and then *Popilius* gave the King his hand to kiss, and he returned out of *Egypt*. The same year, *An. Nabonass.* 580, his captains by his order spoiled and slaughtered the *Jews*, profaned the Temple, set up the worship of the heathen Gods in all *Judea*, and began to persecute and make war upon those who would not worship them: which actions are thus described by *Daniel*. *At the time appointed he shall come again towards the* South, *but the latter shall not be as the former. For the ships of* Chittim *shall come*, with an embassy from *Rome, against him. Therefore he shall be grieved, and return, and have indignation against the holy covenant. So shall he do; he shall even return, and have intelligence with them that forsake the holy covenant.*[11]

In the same year that *Antiochus* by the command of the *Romans* retired out of *Egypt*, and set up the worship of the *Greeks* in *Judea*; the *Romans* conquered the kingdom of *Macedon*, the fundamental kingdom of the Empire of the *Greeks* and reduced it into a *Roman* Province; and thereby began to put an end to the reign of *Daniel's* third Beast. This is thus exprest by *Daniel*. *And after him Arms*, that is the *Romans, shall stand up.* As mmlk signifies after the King, Dan. xi. 8; so mmno[12] may signify *after him*. *Arms* are everywhere in this Prophecy of *Daniel* put for the military power of a kingdom: and they stand up when they conquer and grow powerful. Hitherto *Daniel* described the actions of the Kings of the *North* and *South*; but upon the conquest of *Macedon* by the *Romans*, he left off describing the actions

---

[11]   Chap. xi. 29-30.

[12]   [Both mmlk and mmno originally given in Hebrew characters.]

of the *Greeks*, and began to describe those of the *Romans* in *Greece*. They conquered *Macedon, Illyricum* and *Epirus*, in the year of *Nabonassar* 580. 35 years after, by the last will and testament of *Attalus* the last King of *Pergamus*, they inherited that rich and flourishing kingdom, that is, all *Asia* westward of mount *Taurus*; 69 years after they conquered the kingdom of *Syria*, and reduced it into a Province, and 34 years after they did the like to *Egypt*. By all these steps the *Romans* Arms stood up over the *Greeks*: and after 95 years more, by making war upon the *Jews*, they polluted the sanctuary of strength, and took away the daily sacrifice, and then placed the abomination of desolation. For this abomination was placed after the days of *Christ, Math.* xxiv. 15. In the 16th year of the Emperor *Adrian*, A.C. 132, they placed this abomination by building a Temple to *Jupiter Capitolinus*, where the Temple of God in *Jerusalem* had stood. Thereupon the *Jews* under the conduct of *Barchochab* rose up in arms against the *Romans*, and in the war had 50 cities demolished, 985 of their best towns destroyed, and 580000 men slain by the sword; and in the end of the war, A.C. 136, were banished *Judea* upon pain of death, and thenceforward the land remained desolate of its old inhabitants.

In the beginning of the *Jewish* war in *Nero's* reign, the Apostles fled out of *Judea* with their flocks; some beyond *Jordan* to *Pella* and other places, some into *Egypt, Syria, Mesopotamia, Asia minor*, and elsewhere. *Peter* and *John* came into *Asia*, and *Peter* went thence by *Corinth* to *Rome*; but *John* staying in *Asia*, was banished by the *Romans* into *Patmos*, as the head of a party of the *Jews*, whose nation was in war with the *Romans*. By this dispersion of the *Christian Jews*, the *Christian* religion, which was already propagated westward as far as *Rome*, spred fast into all the *Roman* Empire, and suffered many persecutions under it till the days of *Constantine* the great and his sons: all which is thus described by *Daniel. And such as do wickedly against the covenant, shall he*, who places the abomination, *cause to dissemble*, and worship the heathen Gods; *but the people* among them *who do know* *their God, shall be strong and act. And they that understand among the people, shall instruct many: yet they shall fall by the sword, and by flame, and by captivity, and by spoil many days. Now when they shall fall, they shall be holpen* with a little help, viz.* in the reign of *Constantine* the great; *and* at that time by reason of their prosperity, *many shall* come over to them from among the heathen, and *cleave to them with dissimulation. But of those of understanding there shall* still *fall to try* God's people *by them, and to purge* them from the dissemblers, *and to make them white even to the time of the end: because it is yet for a time appointed.*[13]

Hitherto the *Roman* Empire continued entire; and under this dominion, the little horn of the He-Goat continued *mighty, but not by his own power.* But now, by the building of *Constantinople,* and endowing it with a Senate and other like privileges with *Rome*; and by the division of the *Roman* Empire into the two Empires of the *Greeks* and *Latins,* headed by those two cities; a new scene of things commences, in which a King, the Empire of the *Greeks, doth according to his will, and,* by setting his own laws above the laws of God, *exalts and magnifies himself above very God, and speaks marvellous things against the God of Gods, and shall prosper till the indignation be accomplished. — Neither shall he regard the God of his fathers, nor the* lawful *desire of women in* matrimony, *nor any God, but shall magnify himself above all. And in his seat he shall honour* Mahuzzims, that is, strong guardians, the souls of the dead; *even with a God whom his fathers knew not shall he honour them,* in their Temples, *with gold and silver, and with precious stones and valuable things.*[14] All which relates to the overspreading of the *Greek* Empire with Monks and Nuns, who placed holiness in abstinence from marriage; and to the invocation of the saints and veneration of their reliques, and such like superstitions, which these men introduced in the fourth and fifth centuries. *And at the time of the*

---

[13]   Chap. xi. 32, &c.

[14]   Chap. xi. 36, &c.

end the King of the South, *or the Empire of the* Saracens, *shall push at him; and the King of the* North, *or Empire of the* Turks, *shall come against him like a whirlwind, with chariots and with horsemen, and with many ships; and he shall enter into the countries of the Greeks, and shall overflow and pass over. He shall enter also into the glorious land, and many countries shall be overthrown; but these shall escape out of his hand, even* Edom *and* Moab, *and the chief of the children of* Ammon: that is, those to whom his Caravans pay tribute. *He shall stretch forth his hand also upon the countries, and the land of* Egypt *shall not escape; but he shall have power over the treasures of gold and silver, and over all the precious things of* Egypt; *and the* Lybians *and* Ethiopians *shall be at his steps.*[15] All these nations compose the Empire of the *Turks*, and therefore this Empire is here to be understood by the King of the *North*. They compose also the body of the He-Goat; and therefore the Goat still reigns in his last horn, but not by his own power.

---

[15]   Chap. xi. 40, &c.

CHAPTER XIII

Of the King who did according to his will, and magnified himself above every God, and honoured Mahuzzims, and regarded not the desire of women.*

In the first ages of the Christian religion the Christians of every city were governed by a Council of Presbyters, and the President of the Council was the Bishop of the city. The Bishop and Presbyters of one city meddled not with the affairs of another city, except by admonitory letters or messages. Nor did the Bishops of several cities meet together in Council before the time of the Emperor *Commodus*:* for they could not meet together without the leave of the *Roman* governors of the Provinces. But in the days of that Emperor they began to meet in Provincial Councils, by the leave of the governors; first in *Asia*, in opposition to the *Cataphrygian** heresy, and soon after in other places and upon other occasions. The Bishop of the chief city, or Metropolis of the *Roman* Province, was usually made President of the Council; and hence came the authority of Metropolitan Bishops above that of other Bishops within the same Province. Hence also it was that the Bishop of *Rome* in *Cyprian's** days called himself the Bishop of Bishops. As soon as the Empire became Christian, the *Roman* Emperors began to call general Councils out of all the Provinces of the Empire; and by prescribing to them what points they should consider, and influencing them by their interest and power, they set up what party they pleased. Hereby the *Greek* Empire, upon the division of the *Roman* Empire into the *Greek* and *Latin* Empires, became the *King who*, in matters of religion, *did according to his will; and, in legislature, exalted and magnified himself above every other God*: and at length, by the seventh general Council,* established the worship of the images and souls of dead men, here called *Mahuzzims*.

The same King placed holiness in abstinence from marriage. *Eusebius** in his Ecclesiastical history tells us, that *Musanus* wrote a tract against those who fell away to the heresy of the *Encratites*,* which was then newly risen, and had introduced pernicious errors; and that *Tatian*,* the disciple of *Justin*,* was the author thereof; and that *Irenæus** in his first book against heresies teaches this, writing of *Tatian* and his heresy in these words: *A Saturnino & Marcione profecti qui vocantur Continentes, docuerunt non contrahendum esse matrimonium; reprobantes scilicet primitivum illud opificium Dei, & tacitè accusantes Deum qui masculum & fœminam condidit ad procreationem generis humani. Induxerunt etiam abstinentiam ab esu eorum quæ animalia appellant, ingratos se exhibentes erga eum qui universa creavit Deum. Negant etiam primi hominis salutem. Atque hoc nuper apud illos excogitatum est, Tatiano quodam omnium primo hujus impietatis auctore: qui Justini auditor, quamdiu cum illo versatus est, nihil ejusmodi protulit. Post martyrium autem illius, ad Ecclesia se abrumpens, doctoris arrogantia elatus ac tumidus, tanquam præstantior cæteris, novam quandam formam doctrinæ conflavit: Æonas* invisibles commentus perinde ac Valentinus:* asserens quoque cum Saturnino* & Marcione,* matrimonium nihil aliud esse quam corruptionem ac stuprum: nova præterea argumenta ad subvertendam Adami salutem excogitans. Hæc Irenæus de Hæresi quæ tunc viguit Encratitarum.*[1] Thus far *Eusebius*. But altho the followers of *Tatian* were

---

[1]   Lib. 4. c. 28-29. [Trans.: `A certain branch of the school of Saturninus* and Marcion* who call themselves Continentes made it a point of doctrine that matrimony should be avoided, plainly by their teaching rejecting the ancient work of God, and by innuendo finding fault with God who created male and female for the procreation of the human race. They also

at first condemned as hereticks by the name of *Encratites*,* or *Continentes*; their principles could not be yet quite exploded: for *Montanus** refined upon them, and made only second marriages unlawful; he also introduced frequent fastings, and annual fasting days, the keeping of *Lent*, and feeding upon dried meats. The *Apostolici*, about the middle of the third century, condemned marriage, and were a branch of the disciples of *Tatian*. The *Hierocitæ* in *Egypt*, in the latter end of the third century, also condemned marriage. *Paul** the *Eremite* fled into the wilderness from the persecution of *Decius*, and lived there a solitary life till the reign of *Constantine* the great, but made no disciples. *Antony** did the like in the persecution of *Dioclesian*, or a little before, and made disciples; and many others soon followed his example.

Hitherto the principles of the *Encratites** had been rejected by the Churches; but now being refined by the Monks, and imposed not upon all men, but only upon those who would voluntarily undertake a monastic life, they began to be admired, and to overflow first the *Greek* Church, and then the *Latin* also, like a torrent. *Eusebius** tells us, that *Constantine* the great had those men in the highest veneration, who dedicated themselves wholly to the divine philosophy; and that he almost venerated

---

introduced abstinence from the flesh of those creatures they term animals, displayng their ingratitude toward God, who is the creator of all things. They also deny the salvation of the first man. This impious assertion has only recently been evolved among them, the one chiefly responsible for it being a certain Tatian,* a disciple of Justin;* though as long as he associated with his master he propounded nothing so erroneous. But after the martydom of Justin he broke away from the Church; and being elated and puffed up with his professional importance, assuming his superiority to all others, he trumped up a new scheme of doctrine, inventing invisible æons* exactly like Valentinus.* He also asserted with Saturninus and Marcion that marriage was mere lechery and lust; and invented original and novel arguments to overthrow the doctrine of Adams's salvation. Such is the statement of Irenæus* on the heresy of Encratites* which was then in vogue'.]

the most holy company of Virgins perpetually devoted to God; being certain that the God to whom he had consecrated himself did dwell in their minds. In his time and that of his sons, this profession of a single life was propagated in *Egypt* by *Antony,** and in *Syria* by *Hilarion;** and spred so fast, that soon after the time of *Julian* the Apostate a third part of the *Egyptians* were got into the desarts of *Egypt*. They lived first singly in cells, then associated into *coenobia* or convents; and at length came into towns, and filled the Churches with Bishops, Presbyters and Deacons. *Athanasius** in his younger days poured water upon the hands of his master *Antony*; and finding the Monks faithfull to him, made many of them Bishops and Presbyters in *Egypt*: and these Bishops erected new Monasteries, out of which they chose Presbyters of their own cities, and sent Bishops to others. The like was done in Syria, the superstition being quickly propagated thither out of *Egypt* by *Hilarion* a disciple of *Antony*. *Spiridion* and *Epiphanes* of *Cyprus*, *James* of *Nisibis*, *Cyril* of *Jerusalem*, *Eustathius* of *Sebastia* in *Armenia*, *Eusebius* of *Emisa*, *Titus* of *Bostra*, *Basilius* of *Ancyra*, *Acacius* of *Cæsarea* in *Palestine*, *Elpidius* of *Laodicea*, *Melitius* and *Flavian* of *Antioch*, *Theodorus* of *Tyre*, *Protogenes* of *Carrhæ*, *Acacius* of *Berrhæa*, *Theodotus* of *Hieropolis*, *Eusebius* of *Chalcedon*, *Amphilochius* of *Iconium*, *Gregory Nazianzen*, *Gregory Nyssen*, and *John Chrysostom* of *Constantinople*, were both Bishops and Monks in the fourth century. *Eustathius, Gregory Nazianzen,** *Gregory Nyssen,** *Basil,** &c had Monasteries of Clergymen in their cities, out of which Bishops were sent to other cities; who in like manner erected Monasteries there, till the Churches were supplied with Bishops out of these Monasteries.[2] Hence *Jerome,** in a Letter written about the year 385, saith of the Clergy: *Quasi & ipsi aliud sint quam Monachi, & non quicquid in Monachos dicitur redundet in Clericos qui patres sunt Monachorum. Detrimentum pecoris pastoris est.*[3] And in his book against

---

[2]   In Vita Constantini, l. 4.c. 28.

[3]   Epist. 10. [Trans.: `As if they themselves were anything but monks and as if anything said

Vigilantius:* *Quid facient Orientis Ecclesiæ? Quæ aut Virgines Clericos accipiunt, aut Continentes si uxores habuerint mariti esse desistunt.*[4] Not long after even the Emperors commanded the Churches to chuse Clergymen out of the Monasteries by this Law.

Impp. Arcad. & Honor. AA. Cæsario PF. P.

Si quos forte Episcopi deesse sibi Clericos arbitrantur, ex monachorum numero rectius ordinabunt: non obnoxios publicis privatisque rationibus cum invidia teneant, sed habeant jam probatos. Dat. vii. Kal. Aug. A. iv. & Eutychianio Coss. A.C. 398.[5] The *Greek* Empire being now in the hands of these *Encratites,** and having them in great admiration, *Daniel* makes it a characteristick of the King who doth according to his will, that *he should not regard the desire of women.*

Thus the Sect of the *Encratites*, set on foot by the *Gnostics*, and propagated by *Tatian** and *Montanus** near the end of the second century, which was condemned by the Churches of that and the third century, and refined upon by their followers; overspread the *Eastern* Churches in the fourth century, and before the end of it began to overspread the *Western*. Henceforward the *Christian* Churches having a form of godliness, but denying the power thereof, came into the hands of the *Encratites*: and the Heathens, who in the fourth century came over in great numbers to the Christians, embraced more readily this sort of Christianity, as having a greater affinity with their old superstitions, than that of the sincere Christians; who by the

---

against the monks did not rebound against the clergy who are the fathers of the monks. An injury to the flock is an injury to the shepherd.']

4   [Trans.: `What are the Eastern Churches for doing? They either accept celibate clergy, or continentes; or if they are married they cease to be husbands.']

5   L. 32. de Episcopis. [Trans.: `If the bishops think that they require priests, it will be the better plan to ordain them from the ranks of the monks. Let them not from public or private reasons keep weaklings (though their action be unpopular) but let them have men who are already tried.']

lamps of the seven Churches of *Asia*, and not by the lamps of the Monasteries, had illuminated the Church Catholic during the three first centuries.

The *Cataphrygians** brought in also several other superstitions: such as were the doctrine of *Ghosts*, and of their punishment in Purgatory, with prayers and oblations for mitigating that punishment, as *Tertullian** teaches in his books *De Anima* and *De Monogamia*. The used also the sign of the cross as a charm. So *Tertullian* in his book *de Corona militis: Ad omnem progressum atque promotum, ad omnem aditum & exitum ad vestitum, ad calceatum, ad lavacra, ad mensas, ad lumina, ad cubilia, ad sedilia, quacunque nos conversatio exercet, frontem crucis signaculo terminus*.[6] All these superstitions the Apostle refers to, where he saith: *Now the Spirit speaketh expressly, that in the latter times some shall depart from the faith, giving heed to seducing spirits, and doctrines of devils*, the *Dæmons and* Ghosts worshipped by the heathens, *speaking lyes in hypocrisy*, about their apparitions, the miracles done by them, their reliques, and the sign of the cross, *having consciences seared with a hot iron; forbidding to marry, and commanding to abstain from meats*, &c. 1. Tim. iv. 1, 2, 3. From the *Cataphrygians* these principles and practices were propagated down to posterity. *For the mystery of iniquity did already work* in the *Apostles* days in the *Gnosticks*, continued to work very strongly in their offspring the *Tatianists* and *Cataphrygians*, and was to work *till that man of sin should be revealed; whose coming is after the working of Satan, with all power and signs, and lying wonders, and all deceivableness of unrighteousness*; coloured over with a form of *Christian* godliness, but without the power thereof, 2 *Thess*. ii. 7-10.

---

[6]   [Trans.: `At every advancement or promotion, at every going out and coming in, with our clothes, shoes, at the baths, at the table, with the lights, in rooms, with the furniture, in a word at whatever our daily life brings us into contanct with, we imprint on our forhead the sign of the Cross.']

For tho some stop was put to the *Cataphrygian* Christianity, by Provincial Councils, till the fourth century; yet the *Roman* Emperors then turning *Christians*, and great multitudes of heathens coming over in outward profession, these found the *Cataphrygian* Christianity more suitable to their old principles, of placing religion in outward forms and ceremonies, holy-days, and doctrines of Ghosts, than the religion of the sincere *Christians*: wherefore they readily sided with the *Cataphrygian Christians*, and established that *Christianity* before the end of the fourth century. By this means those of understanding, after they had been persecuted by the heathen Emperors in the three first centuries, and were holpen with a little help, by the conversion of *Constantine* the great and his sons to the *Christian* religion, fell under new persecutions, *to purge them from the dissemblers, and to make them white, even to the time of the end.*

CHAPTER XIV

Of the Mahuzzims, honoured by the King who doth according to his will.

In Scripture we are told of some *trusting in God* and others *trusting in idols*, and that *God is our refuge, our strength, our defense.* In this sense God is *the rock of his people,* and false Gods are called *the rock of those that trust in them,* Deut. xxxii. 4, 15, 18, 30, 31, 37. In the same sense the Gods of *the King who shall do according to his will* are called *Mahuzzims,** munitions, fortresses, protectors, guardians, or defenders. *In his estate,* saith *Daniel, shall he honour* Mahuzzims; *even with a God whom his fathers knew not, shall he honour them with gold and silver, and with precious stones, and things of value. Thus shall he do in the most strong holds* or temples; — *and he shall cause them to rule over many, and divide the land among them for a possession.*[1] Now this came to pass by degrees in the following manner.

*Gregory Nyssen** tells us, that after the persecution of the Emperor *Decius, Gregory* Bishop of *Neocæsarea** in Pontus, *instituted among all people, as an addition or corollary of devotion towards God, that festival days and assemblies should be celebrated to them who had contended for the faith,* that is, to the Martyrs. And he adds this reason for the institution: *When he observed,* saith, *Nyssen, that the simple and unskilful multitude, by reason of corporeal delights, remained in the error of the idols; that the principal thing might be corrected among them, namely, that*

instead of their vain worship they might turn their eyes upon God; he permitted that
at the memories of the holy Martyrs they might make merry and delight themselves,
and be dissolved into joy. The heathens were delighted with the festivals of their
Gods, and unwilling to part with those delights; and therefore *Gregory*, to facilitate
their conversion, instituted annual festivals to the *Saints and Martyrs*.[2] Hence it
came to pass, that for exploding the festivals of the heathens, the principal festivals of
the *Christians* succeeded in their room: as the keeping of *Christmas* with ivy and
feasting, and playing and sports, in the room of the *Bacchanalia* and *Saturnalia*; the
celebrating of *May-day* with flowers, in the room of the *Floralia*; and the keeping of
festivals to the Virgin *Mary*, *John* the Baptist, and divers of the Apostles, in the room
of the solemnities at the entrance of the Sun into the signs of the *Zodiac* in the old
Julian Calendar. In the same persecution of *Decius*, *Cyprian** ordered the passions of
the Martyrs in *Africa* to be registred, in order to celebrate their memories annually
with oblation and sacrifices: and *Felix* Bishop of *Rome*, a little after, as *Platina**
relates, *Martyrum gloriæ consulens, constituit ut quotannis sacrificia eorum nomine*
celebrarentur; "consulting the glory of the Martyrs, ordained that sacrifices should be
celebrated annually in their name." By the pleasures of these festivals the *Christians*
increased much in number, and decreased as much in virtue, until they were *purged*
and made white by the persecution of *Dioclesian*. This was the first step made in the
Christian religion towards the veneration of the Martyrs: and tho it did not yet
amount to an unlawful worship; yet it disposed the *Christians* towards such a further
veneration of the dead, as in a short time ended in the invocation of the Saints.

    The next step was the affecting to pray at the sepulchres of the Martyrs: which
practice began in *Dioclesian's* persecution. The Council of *Eliberis* in *Spain*,
celebrated in the third or fourth year of *Dioclesian's* persecution, A.C. 305, hath

---

[1]   Chap. xi. 38-39. [Daniel does not, however, use the term Mahuzzims.]

[2]   Orat. de vita Greg. Thaumaturg. T. 3. p. 574.

these Canons. Can. 34. *Cereos per diem placuit in Coemeterio non incendi: inquietandi enim spiritus sanctorum non sunt. Qui hæc non observârint, arceantur ab Ecclesiæ communione. Can. 35. Placuit prohiberi ne fæminæ in Coemeterio pervigilent, eò quod sæpe sub obtentu orationis latentèr scelera committant.*[3] Presently after that persecution, suppose about the year 314, the Council of *Laodicea* in *Phrygia*, which then met for restoring the lapsed discipline of the Church, has the following Canons. Can. 9. *Those of the Church are not allowed to go into the* Coemeteries or Martyries, *as they are called, of hereticks, for the sake of prayer or recovery of health: but such as go, if they be of the faithful, shall be excommunicated for a time.* Can. 34. A Christian *must not leave the Martyrs of* Christ, *and go to false Martyrs,* that is, to the Martyrs of the hereticks; *for these are alien from* God: *and therefore let those be anathema who go to them.* Can. 51. *The birth-days of the Martyrs shall not be celebrated in* Lent, *but their commemoration shall be made on the Sabbath-days and Lords days.* The Council of *Paphlagonia,* celebrated in the year 324, made this canon: *If any man being arrogant, abominates the congregations of the Martyrs, or the Liturgies performed therein, or the memories of the martyrs, let him be anathema.* By all which it is manifest that the *Christians* in the time of *Dioclesian's* persecution used to pray in the *Coemeteries* or burying-places of the dead; for avoiding the danger of the persecution, and for want of Churches, which were all thrown down: and after the persecution was over, continued that practice in honour of the Martyrs, till new Churches could be built: and by use affected it as advantageous to devotion, and for recovering the health of those that were sick. It also appears that in these burying-places they commemorated the Martyrs yearly

---

[3]   [Trans.: Can. 34. 'That wax tapers not be burned by day in the cemetery, for the spirits of the saints must not be disturbed. Whosoever disobeys this command will be excommunicated.' Can. 35. 'That women be prohibited from night vigils in the cemetary, because often under the pretence of prayer they secretly commit sin.']

upon days dedicated to them, and accounted all these practices pious and religious, and anathematized those men as arrogant who opposed them, or prayed in the *Martyries* of the hereticks. They also lighted torches to the Martyrs in the day-time, as the heathens did to their Gods; which custom, before the end of the fourth century, prevailed much in the *West*. They sprinkled the worshipers of the Martyrs with holy-water, as the heathens did the worshipers of their Gods; and went in pilgrimage to see *Jerusalem* and other holy places, as if those places conferred sanctity on the visiters. From the custom of praying in the *Coemeteries* and *Martyries*, came the custom of translating the bodies of the Saints and Martyrs into such Churches as were new built: the Emperor *Constantius* began this practice about the year 359, causing the bodies of *Andrew* the Apostle, *Luke* and *Timothy*, to be translated into a new Church at *Constantinople*: and before this act of *Constantius*, the *Egyptians* kept the bodies of their Martyrs and Saints unburied upon beds in their private houses, and told stories of their souls appearing after death and ascending up to heaven, as *Athanasius** relates in the life of *Antony.** All which gave occasion to the Emperor *Julian*, as *Cyril** relates, to accuse the *Christians* in this manner: *Your adding to that antient dead man, Jesus, many new dead men, who can sufficiently abominate? You have filled all places with sepulchres and monuments, altho you are no where bidden to prostrate yourselves to sepulchres, and to respect them officiously.* And a little after: *Since Jesus said that sepulchres are full of filthiness, how do you invoke God upon them?* and in another place he saith, that if *Christians* had adhered to the precepts of the *Hebrews, they would have worshiped one God instead of many, and not a man, or rather not many unhappy men*: and that they *adored the wood of the cross, making its images on their foreheads, and before their houses.*

After the sepulchres of Saints and Martyrs were thus converted into places of worship like the heathen temples, and the Churches into sepulchres, and a certain sort of sanctity attributed to the dead bodies of the Saints and Martyrs buried in them, and annual festivals were kept to them, with sacrifices offered to God in their name; the next step towards the invocation of Saints, was the attributing to their dead bodies, bones and other reliques, a power of working miracles by means of the separate souls, who were supposed to know what we do or say, and to be able to do us good or hurt, and to work those miracles. This was the very notion the heathens had of the separate souls of their antient Kings and Heroes, whom they worshiped under the names of *Saturn, Rhea, Jupiter, Juno, Mars, Venus, Bacchus, Ceres, Osiris, Isis, Apollo, Diana,* and the rest of their Gods. For these Gods being male and female, husband and wife, son and daughter, brother and sister, are thereby discovered to be antient men and women. Now as the first step towards the invocation of Saints was set on foot by the perscution of *Decius,* and the second by the persecution of *Dioclesian;* so this third seems to have been owing to the proceedings of *Constantius* and *Julian* the Apostate. When *Julian* began to restore the worship of the heathen Gods, and to vilify the Saints and Martyrs; the *Christians of Syria* and *Egypt* seem to have made a great noise about the miracles done by the reliques of the *Christian* Saints and Martyrs, in opposition to the powers attributed by *Julian* and the heathens to their Idols. For *Sozomen** and *Ruffinus** tell us, that when he opened the heathen Temples, and consulted the Oracle of Apollo *Daphnæus* in the suburbs of *Antioch,* and pressed by many sacrifices for an answer; the Oracle at length told him that the bones of the Martyr *Babylas* which were buried there hinder'd him from speaking. By which answer we may understand that some *Christian* was got into the place where the heathen Priests used to speak thro' a pipe in delivering their Oracles: and before this, *Hilary,** in his book against *Constantius,* written in the last year of that Emperor, makes the following mention of what was then doing in the East where he was. *Sine martyrio persequeris. Plus crudelitate vestræ Nero, Deci, Maximiane, debemus Diabolum enim per vos vicimus. Sanctus ubique beatorum martyrum sanguis exceptus est, dum in his Dæmones mugiunt, dum ægritudines depelluntur,* *dum miraculorum opera cernuntur, elevari sine laqueis corpora, & dispensis pede fœminis vestes non defluere in faciem, uri sine ignibus spiritus, confiteri sine interrogantis incremento fidei.*[4] And *Gregory Nazianzen,** in his first Oration against the Emperor *Julian* then reigning, writes thus: *Martyres non extimuisti quibus præclari honores & festa constituta, à quibus Dæmones propelluntur & morbi curantur; quorum sunt apparitiones & prædictiones; quorum vel sola corpora idem possunt quod animæ sanctæ, sive manibus contrectentur, sive honorentur: quorum vel solæ sanguinis guttæ atque exigua passionis signa idem possunt quod corpora. Hæc non colis sed contemnis & aspernaris.*[5] These things made the heathens in the reign of the same Emperor demolish the sepulchre of *John* the Baptist in *Phoenicia,* and burn his bones; when several *Christians* mixing themselves with the heathens, gathered up some of his remains, which were sent to *Athanasius,** who hid them in the wall of a Church; foreseeing by a prophetic spirit, as *Ruffinus** tells us, that they might be profitable to future generations.

The cry of these miracles being once set on foot, continued for many years, and encreased and grew more general. *Chrysostom,** in his second Oration on St.

---

[4] [Trans.: `You would persecute without martyrdom? We owe a deeper debt to the cruelty of Nero, Decius and Maximianus. For by them we overcame the devil. The sacred blood of the martyrs has been received everywhere, while demons cry out because of them, diseases are banished and miraculous works are beheld: bodies float in the air without support, female figures are seen hanging by the feet and their garments do not flow down over their faces, spirits burn without fire and make confession without increasing the belief of the catechizer.']

[5] [Trans.: `You have paid no respect to the martyrs, to who illustrious honours and festivals have been decreed, by whom demons are cast out and diseases cured, and whose apparitions can be seen and teachings heard. Their mere bodies are as efficacious as their blessed souls, whether the one be touched or the other worshipped. A few drops of their blood and some scanty tokens of their suffering can do as much as their whole bodies; and these it is that, refusing to esteem, you scorn and despise.']

Babylas, twenty years after the silencing of the Oracle of *Apollo Daphnæus* as above, viz. A.C. 382, saith of the miracles done by the Saints and their reliques: *Nulla est nostri hujus Orbis seu regio, seu gens, sue urbs, ubi nova & inopinata miracula hæc non decantentur; quæ quidem si figmenta fuissent, prorsus in tantam hominum admirationem non venissent.* And a little after: *Abunde orationi nostræ fidem faciunt quæ quotidiana à martyribus miracula eduntur, magna affatim ad illa hominum multitudine affluente.*[6] And in his 66th Homily, describing how the Devils were tormented and cast out by the bones of the Martyrs, he adds: *Ob eam causam multi plerumque Reges peregrè profecti sunt, ut hoc spectaculo fruerentur. Siquidem sanctorum martyrum templa futuri judicii vestigia & signa exhibent, dum nimirum Dæmones flagris cæduntur, hominesque torquentur & liberantur. Vide quæ sanctorum vitâ functorum vis sit?*[7] And *Jerom* in his Epitaph on *Paula*, thus mentions the same things. *Paula vidit Samariam: ibi siti sunt Elisæus & Abdias prophetæ, & Joannes Baptista, ubi multis intremuit consternata miraculis. Nam cernebat variis dæmones rugire cruciatibus, & ante sepulchra sanctorum ululare, homines more luporum vocibis latrare canum, fremere leonum, sibilare serpentum, mugire taurorum, alios rotare caput & post tergum terram vertice tangere, suspensisque pede fæminis vestes non defluere in faciem.*[8] This was about the year 384: and

---

[6] Vide Hom. 47. in S. Julian. [Trans.: `There is no district or race, or city of this world of ours where these strange and unexpected miracles are not recounted. Indeed, had they been mere inventions, they would hardly have attained such universal renown.' And a little after: `My words have ample support in those miracles which our martyrs are daily working, to which no small throng of people constantly crowd.']

[7] [Trans.: `A considerable number of kings came from foreign parts to enjoy this sight, for the reason that the temples of the holy marytrs display tokens and signs of coming judgment. The demons doubtless being tormented with scourges, and men, though agonizing, finding release. Behold the power inherent in the life of the holy dead.']

[8] Epist. 27. ad Eustochium. [Trans.: `Paula saw Samaria, where the prophets Elisha and

Chrysostom in his Oration on the *Egyptian* Martyrs, seems to make *Egypt* the ringleader in these matters, saying: `Benedictus Deus quandoquidem ex ægypto prodeunt martyres, ex ægypto illa cum Deo pugnante ac insanissima, & unde impia ora, unde linguæ blasphemæ; ex ægypto martyres habentur; non in ægypto tantum, nec in finitima vicinaque regione, sed UBIQUE TERRARUM. Et quemadmodum in annonæ summa ubertate, cum viderunt urbium incolæ majorem quam usus habitatorum postulat esse proventum, ad peregrinas etiam urbes transmittunt: cum & suam comitatem & liberalitatem ostendat, tum ut præter horum abundantiam cum facilitate res quibus indigent rursus ad illis sibi comparent: sic et ægyptii, quod attinet ad religionis athletas, fecerunt. Cum apud se multam eorum Dei benignitate copiam cernerent, nequaquam ingens Dei munus sua civitate concluserunt, sed in OMNES TERRÆ PARTES bonorum thesauros effuderent: cum ut suum in fratres amorem ostenderent, tum ut communem omnium dominum honore afficerent, ac civitati suæ gloriam apud omnes compararent, totiusque terrarum ORBIS esse METROPOLIN declararent. — Sanctorum enim illorum corpora quovis adamantino & inexpugnabili muro tutiùs nobis urbem communiunt, & tanquam excelsi quidam scopuli undique prominentes, non horum qui sub sensus cadunt & oculis cernuntur hostium impetus propulsant tantùm, sed etiam invisibilium dæmonum insidias, omnesque diaboli fraudes subvertunt ac dissipant — Neque vero tantùm adversus hominum insidias aut adversas fallacias dæmonum utilis nobis est hæc possessio, sed si nobis communis dominus ob peccatorum multitudinem irascatur, his objectis*

Obadiah and John the Baptist are buried, and there she fell into fear and consternation at the many miracles, for she saw demons bellowing under various torments and howling before the sepulchres of the saints. She saw men in the likeness of wolves barking with the voice of dogs, roaring like lions, hissing as serpents and bellowing like bulls. Others of them made their heads rotate, or bend backwards until their heads touched the ground. Female figures too were hung up by their feet and yet their garments did not flow down over their faces.']

corporibus poterimus eum propitium reddere civitati.[9] This Oration was written at *Antioch*, while *Alexandria* was yet the Metropolis of the *East*, that is, before the year 381, in which *Constantinople* became the Metropolis: and it was a work of some years for the *Egyptians* to have distributed the miracle-working reliques of their Martyrs over all the world, as they had done before that year. *Egypt* abounded most with the reliques of Saints and Martyrs, the *Egyptians* keeping them embalmed upon beds even in their private houses; and *Alexandria* was eminent above all other cities for dispersing them, so as on that account to acquire glory with all men, and manifest

---

9   Edit. Frontonis Ducæi, Tom. 1. [Trans.: `Blessed be God that martyrs are appearing in Egypt: Egypt I say, that fought with the Lord and raged most wildly: Egypt, whence come impious lips and tongues that blaspheme. In this Egypt martyrs are honoured, and not only there or in the neighbouring regions, but everywhere on earth. And - to take a simile from the abundance of the grain supply - as when the inhabitants of the cities have seen that their harvest exceeds the possible home demand, they export it to foreign countries. This is first to show their courtesy and liberality, and secondly to employ the surplus in order to secure conveniently in return necessities which they lack. So it is in this spirit that the Egyptians have acted as regards the champions of religion. For when they saw that by the goodness of God they had a great host of martyrs in their land, far from confining that great gift of God to their own state, they poured out the wealth of their treasures unto all parts of the earth: and with a twofold purpose. Firstly it is to manifest their love to the brethren and then to honour the common Lord of all, and to win glory in the eyes of all for their state, which they thereby would declare to be the metropolis of the whole round earth. For the bodies of those martyred saints protect a city for us more securely than could any wall, however adamantine and impregnable, and like towering bulwarks, standing four-square, they ward off not merely those enemies which sense can grasp and eye can see; but also the unseen snares of demons, and all the deceits of Satan are by them overthrown and destroyed. But in truth it is not merely against the treachery of men or the deceit of demons that the possession of them is valuable to us: if our common Lord be wrathful against us for the multitide of our transgressions, by the mediations of these bodies we will immediately be enabled again to regain His favour for our state.']

herself to be the *Metropolis* of the world. *Antioch* followed the example of *Egypt*, in dispersing the reliques of the forty Martyrs:* and the examples of *Egypt* and *Syria* were soon followed by the rest of the world.

The reliques of the forty Martyrs at *Antioch* were distributed among the Churches before the year 373; for *Athanasius** who died in that year, wrote an Oration upon them. This Oration is not yet published, but *Gerard Vossius** saw it in MS. in the Library of Cardinal *Ascanius* in Italy, as he says in his commentary upon the Oration of *Ephræm Syrus** on the same forty Martyrs. Now since the Monks of *Alexandria* sent the reliques of the Martyrs of *Egypt* into all parts of the earth, and thereby acquired glory to their city, and declared her in these matters the Metropolis of the whole world, as we have observed out of *Chrysostom*;* it may be concluded, that before *Alexandria* recieved the forty Martyrs from *Antioch*, she began to send out the reliques of her own Martyrs into all parts, setting the first example to other cities. This practice therefore began in *Egypt* some years before the death of *Athanasius*. It began when the miracle-working bones of *John* the Baptist were carried into Egypt, and hid in the wall of a Church, *that they might be profitable to future generations*. It was restrained in the reign of *Julian* the Apostate: and then it spred from *Egypt* into all the Empire, *Alexandria* being the Metropolis of the whole world, according to *Chrysostom*, for propagating this sort of devotion, and *Antioch* and other cities soon following her example.

In propagating these superstitions, the ringleaders were the Monks, and *Antony** was at the head of them: for in the end of the life of *Antony*, *Athanasius* relates that these were his dying words to his disciples who then attended him. *Do you take care*, said *Antony, to adhere to* Christ *in the first place, and then to the Saints, that after death they may receive you as friends and acquaintance into the everlasting Taberbacles. Think upon these things, perceive these things; and if you have any regard to me, remember me as a father*. This being delivered in charge to the Monks by *Antony* at his death, A.C. 356, could not but inflame their whole body with devotion towards the Saints, as the ready way to be received by them into the eternal Taberbnacles after death. Hence came that noise about the miracles done by the reliques of the Saints in the time of *Constantius*:* hence came the dispersion of the miracle-working reliques into all the Empire; *Alexandria* setting the example, and being renowned for it above all other cites. Hence it came to pass in the days of *Julian*, A.C. 362, that *Athanasius* by a prophetic spirit, as *Ruffinus** tells us, hid the bones of *John* the Baptist from the Heathens, not in the ground to be forgotten, but in the hollow wall of a Church before proper witnesses, *that they might be profitable to future generations.* Hence also came the invocation of the Saints for doing such miracles, and for assisting men in their devotions, and mediating with God. For *Athanasius*, even from his youth, looked upon the dead Saints and Martyrs as mediators of our prayers: in his Epistle to *Marcellinus*,* written in the days of *Constantine* the Great, he saith that the words of the Psalms are not to he transposed or any wise changed, but to he recited and sung without any artifice, as they are written, *that the holy men who delivered them, knowing them to be their own words, may pray with us; or rather, that the Holy Ghost who spake in the holy men, seeing his own words with which he inspired them, may join* with them *in assisting us.*

Whilst *Egypt* abounded with Monks above any other country, the veneration of the Saints began sooner, and spred faster there than in other places. *Palladius** going into *Egypt* in the year 388 to visit the Monasteries and the sepulchres of *Apollonius* and other Martyrs of *Thebais** who had suffered under *Maximinus*, saith of them: *Iis omnibus Christiani fecereunt œdem unam, ubi nunc multœ virtutes peraguntur. Tanta autem fuit viri gratia, ut de iis quœ esset precatus statim exaudiretur, eum sic honorante servatore: quem etiam nos in martyrio precati vidimus, cum iis qui cum ipso fuerunt martyrio affecti; & Deum adorantes, eorum*

234

corpora salutavimus.[10] *Eunapius** also, a heathen, yet a competent witness of what was done in his own times, relating how the soldiers delivered the temples of *Egypt* into the hands of the Monks, which was done in the year 389, rails thus in an impious manner at the martyrs, as succeeding in the room of the old Gods of *Egypt*. *Illi ipsi, milites, Monachos Canobi quoque collocârunt, ut pro Diis qui animo cernuntur, servos & quidem flagitiosos divinis honoribus percolerent, hominum mentibus ad cultum ceremoniasque obligatis. Ii namque condita & salita eorum capita, qui ob scelerum multitudinem à judicibus extremo judicio fuerunt affecti, pro Divis ostentabant; iis genua submittebant, eos in Deorum numerum receptabant, ad illorum supulchra pulvere sordibusque conspurcati. Martyres igitur vocabantbur, & ministri quidem & legati arbitrique precum apud Deos; cum fuerint servilia infida & flagris pessimè subacta, quæ cicatrices scelerum ac nequitiæ vestigia corporibus circumferunt; ejusmodi tamen Deos fert tellus.*[11] By these instances we may understand the invocation of Saints was now of some standing in *Egypt*, and that it

---

10   [Trans.: `For all these martyrs the Christians have built a single temple, in which many deeds of healing are now performed. So great was the influence of Apollonius that his petition on any matter was immediately answered, this being the way in which his Saviour honoured him. We too, after prayer, beheld him in his shrine in company with those who were his fellows in martyrdom; and giving glory to God, we gave homage to their bodies.']

11   [Trans.: `These very soldiers stationed monks at Canopus also, in order that, instead of worshipping what is visible to the mind alone, they might pay divine honours to mere slaves and criminals, the minds of all men being addicted to ceremonial worship of some kind. They displayed as Gods the cured and salted heads of men who had suffered the final penalty of the law for the number of their crimes: to these they bowed to the knee; they received them into the number of their Gods, degrading themselves before their sepulchres with sack-cloth and ashes. Eventually they were called martyrs or mediators or ambassadors and censors of prayer at the Court of Heaven. In reality they had been faithless slaves, often flogged for their wickedness, and bore on their bodies the scars of their crimes and the marks of their profligacy. Yet such are the Gods that the land has to bear.']

was already generally received and practised there by the common people.

Thus *Basil*, a Monk, who was made Bishop of *Cæsarea* in the year 378, in his Oration on the Martyr *Mamas*, saith: *Be ye mindful of the Martyr; as many of you as have enjoyed him in your dreams, as many as in this place have been assisted by him in prayer, as many of you as upon invoking him by name have had him present in your works, as many as he has reduced into the way from wandering, as many as he has restored to health, as many as have had their dead children restored by him to life, as many have had their lives prolonged by him:* and a little after, he thus expresses the universality of this superstition in the regions of *Cappadocia* and *Bithynia*: *At the memory of the Martyr*, saith he, *the whole region is moved; at his festival the whole city is transported with joy. Nor do the kindred of the rich turn aside to the sepulchres of their ancestors, but all go to the place of devotion.* Again, in the end of the Homily he prays, that *God would preserve the Church, thus fortified with the great towers of the Martyrs*: and in his Oration on the forty Martyrs;* *These are they*, saith he, *who obtaining our country, like certain towers afford us safety against our enemies. Neither are they shut up in one place only, but being distributed are sent into many regions, and adorn many countries. — You have often endeavoured, you have often laboured to find one who might pray for you: here are forty emitting one voice of prayer. — He that is in affliction flies to these, he that rejoices has recourse to these: the first, that he may be freed from evil, the last that he may continue in happiness. Here a women praying for her children is heard; she obtains a safe return for her husband from abroad, and health for him in his sickness. — O ye common keepers of mankind, the best companions of our cares, suffragans and coadjutors of our prayers, most powerful embassadors to God*, &c. By all which is manifest, that before the year 378, the Orations and Sermons upon the Saints went much beyond the bounds of mere oratorical flourishes, and that the common people in the *East* were already generally corrupted by the Monks with Saint-worship.

*Gregory Nazianzen** a Monk, in his sixth Oration written A.C. 373, when he was newly made bishop of *Sasima*, saith: *Let us purify ourselves to the Martyrs, or rather to the God of the Martyrs*: and a little while after he calls the Martyrs *mediators of obtaining an ascension or divinity*. The same year, in the end of his Oration upon *Athanasius** then newly dead, he thus invokes him: *Do thou look down upon us propitiously, and govern this people, as perfect adorers of the perfect Trinity, which in the Father, Son and Holy Ghost, is contemplated and worshiped: if there shall be peace, preserve me, and feed my flock with me; but if of war, bring me home, place me by thyself, and by those that are like thee; however great my request.* And in the end of the funeral Oration upon *Basil,** written A.C. 378, he thus addressed him: *But thou, O divine and sacred Head, look down upon us from heaven; and by thy prayers either take away that thorn of the flesh which is given us by God for exercise, or obtain that we may bear it with courage, and direct all our life to that which is most fitting for us. When we depart this life, receive us there in your Tabernacles, that living together and beholding the holy and blessed Trinity more purely and perfectly, whereof we have now but an imperfect view, we may there come to the end of our desires, and receive this reward of the wars which we have waged or suffered*: and in his Oration upon *Cyprian*, not the Bishop of *Carthage,** but a *Greek*, he invokes him after the same manner; and tells us also how a pious Virgin named *Justina*, was protected by invoking the Virgin *Mary*, and how miracles were done by the ashes of *Cyprian*.

*Gregory Nyssen,** another eminent Monk and Bishop, in the life of *Ephræm Syrus,** tells us how a certain man returning from a far country, was in great danger, by reason all the ways were intercepted by the armies of barbarous nations; but upon invoking *Ephræm* by name, and saying *Holy* Ephræm *assist me*, he escaped the danger, neglected the fear of death, and beyond his hope got safe home. In the end of this Oration *Gregory* calls upon *Ephræm* after the following manner: *But thou, O*

Ephræm, assisting now at the divine altar, and sacrificing to the Prince of life, and to the most holy Trinity, together with the Angels; remember us all, and obtain for us pardon of our sins, that we may enjoy the eternal happiness of the kingdom of heaven. The same *Gregory*, in his oration on the Martyr *Theodorus* written A.C. 381, thus describes the power of that Martyr, and the practice of the people. *This Martyr,* saith he, *the last year quieted the barbarous tempest, and put a stop to the horrid war of the fierce and cruel Scythians. — If any one is permitted to carry away the dust with which the tomb is covered, wherein the body of the Martyr rests; the dust is accepted as a gift, and gathered to be laid up as a thing of great price. For to touch the reliques themselves, if any such prosperous fortune shall at any time happen; how great a favour that is, and not to be obtained without the most earnest prayers, they know well who have obtained it. For as a living and florid body, they who behold it embrace it, applying it to the eyes, mouth, ears, and all the organs of sense; and then with affection pouring tears upon the Martyr, as if he was whole and appeared to them: they offer prayers with supplication, that he would intercede for them as an advocate, praying to him as an Officer attending upon God, and invoking him as receiving gifts whenever he will.* At length *Gregory* concludes the Oration with this prayer: *O Theodorus, we want many blessings; intercede and beseech for thy country before the common King and Lord: for the country of the Martyr is the place of his passion, and they are his citizens, brethren and kindred, who have him, defend, adorn and honour him. We fear afflictions, we expect dangers: the wicked Scythians are not far off, ready to make war against us. As a soldier fight for us, as a Martyr use liberty of speech for thy fellow-servants. Pray for peace, that these publick meetings may not cease, that the furious and wicked barbarians may not rage against the temples and altars, that the profane and impious may not trample upon the holy things. We acknowledge it a benefit received from thee, that we are preserved safe and entire, we pray for freedom from danger in time to come: and if there shall be need of* *greater intercession and deprecation, call together the choir of thy brethren the Martyrs, and in conjunction with them all intercede for us.* Let the prayers of many just ones attone for the sins of the multitudes and the people; exhort Peter, excite Paul, *and also* John *the divine and beloved disciple, that they may be sollicitous for the Churches which they have erected, for which they have been in chains, for which they have undergone dangers and deaths; that the worship of idols may not lift up its head against us, that heresies may not spring up like thorns in the vineyard, that tares grown up may not choak the wheat, that no rock void of the fatness of true dew may be against us, and render the fruitful power of the word void of a root; but by the power of the prayers of thyself and thy companions, O admirable man and eminent among the Martyrs, the commonwealth of* Christians *may become a field of corn.* The same *Gregory Nyssen,* in his sermon upon the death of *Meletius* Bishop of *Antioch,* preached at *Constantinople* the same year, A.C. 381, before the Bishops of all the *East* assembled in the second general Council, spake thus of *Meletius. The Bridegroom,* saith he, *is not taken from us: he stands in the midst of us, tho we do not see him: he is a Priest in the most inward places, and face to face intercedes before God for us and the sins of the people.* This was no oratorical flourish, but *Gregory's* real opinion, as may be understood by what we have cited out of him concening *Ephræm* and *Theodorus*: and as *Gregory* preached this before the Council of *Constantinople,* you may thence know, saith *Baronius,*[12]* that he professed what the whole Council, and therewith the whole Church of those parts believed, namely, that the Saints in heaven offer prayers for us before God.

*Ephræm Syrus,** another eminent Monk, who was contemporary with *Basil,** and died the same year; in the end of his Encomium or Oration upon *Basil* then newly dead, invokes him after this manner: *Intercede for me, a very miserable man; and recal me by thy intercessions, O father; thou who art strong, pray for me who am*

---

[12]   Ad. an. 381, Sec. 41.

weak; thou who art diligent, for me who am negligent; thou who art chearful, for me who am heavy; thou who art wise, for me who am foolish. Thou who hast treasured up a treasure of all virtues, be a guide to me who am empty of every good work. In the beginning of his Encomium upon the forty Martyrs, written at the same time, he thus invokes them: *Help me therefore, O ye Saints, with your intercession; and O ye beloved, with your holy prayers; that* Christ *by his grace may direct my tongue to speak,* &c. and afterwards mentioning the mother of one of these forty Martyrs, he concludes the Oration with this prayer: *I entreat thee, O holy, faithful, and blessed woman, pray for me to the saints, saying; Intercede ye that triumph in* Christ, *for the most little and miserable Ephræm, that he may find mercy, and by the grace of* Christ *may be saved.* Again, in his second Sermon or Oration on the praises of the holy Martyrs of *Christ,* he thus addresses them: *We entreat you most holy Martyrs, to intercede with the Lord for us miserable sinners, beset with the filthiness of negligence, that he would infuse his divine grace into us*: and afterwards, near the end of the same discourse; *Now ye most holy men and most glorious Martyrs of God, help me a miserable sinner with your prayers, that in that dreadful hour I may obtain mercy, when the secrets of all hearts shall be made manifest. I am today become to you, most holy Martyrs of* Christ, *as it were an unprofitable and unskilful cup-bearer: for I have delivered to the sons and brothers of your faith, a cup of the excellent wine of your warfare, with the excellent table of your victory, replenished with all sorts of dainties. I have endeavoured, with the whole affection and desire of my mind, to recreate your fathers and brothers, kindred and relations, who daily frequent the table. For behold they sing, and with exultation and jubilee glorify God, who has crown'd your virtues, by setting on your most sacred heads incorruptible and celestial crowns; they with excessive joy stand about the sacred reliques of your martyrdoms, wishing for a blessing, and desiring to bear away holy medicines both for the body and the mind. As good disciples and faithful ministers of our benign*

Lord and Saviour, bestow therefore a blessing on them all: and on me also, tho weak and feeble, who having received strength by your merits and intercessions, have with the whole devotion of my mind, sung a hymn to your praise and glory before your holy reliques. Wherefore I beseech you stand before the throne of the divine Majesty for me Ephræm, *a vile and miserable sinner, that by your prayers I may deserve to obtain salvation, and with you enjoy eternal felicity by the grace and benignity and mercy of our Lord and Saviour* Jesus Christ, *to whom with the Father and Holy Ghost be praise, honour and glory for ever and ever.* Amen.

By what has been cited out of *Basil*, the *Gregories* and *Ephræm*, we may understand that Saint-Worship was established among the Monks and their admirers in *Egypt, Phoenicia, Syria* and *Cappadocia*, before the year 378, this being the year in which *Basil* and *Ephræm* died. *Chrysostom** was not much later; he preached at *Antioch* almost all the time of *Theodosius* the great, and in his Sermons are many exhortations to this sort of superstition, as may be seen in the end of his Orations on S. *Julia*, on St. *Pelagia*, on the Martyr *Ignatius*, on the *Egyptian* Martyrs, on Fate and Providence, on the Martyrs in general, on St. *Berenice* and St. *Prosdoce*, on *Juventinus* and *Maximus*, on the name of *Coemetery*, &c. Thus in his Sermon on *Berenice* and *Prosdoce: Perhaps,* saith he, *you are inflamed with no small love towards these Martyrs; therefore with this ardour let us fall down before their reliques, let us embrace their coffins. For the coffins of the Martyrs have great virtue, even as the bones of the Martyrs have great power. Nor let us only on the day of his festival, but also on other days apply to them, invoke them, and beseech them to be our patrons: for they have great power and efficacy, not only whilst alive, but also after death; and much more after death than before. For now they bear the marks or brands of Christ; and when they shew these marks, they can obtain all things of the King. Seeing therefore they abound with such efficacy, and have so much friendship with him; we also, when by continual attendance and perpetual visitation of them we* *have insinuated ourselves into their familiarity, may by their assistance obtain the mercy of God.*

Constantinople was free from these supersitions till *Gregory Nazianzen** came thither A.C. 379; but in a few years it was also inflamed with it. *Ruffinus** tells us, that when the Emperor *Theodosius* was setting out against the tyrant *Eugenius,* which was in the year 394, he went about with the Priests and people to all the places of prayer; lay prostrate before the shrines of the Martyrs and Apostles, and *pray'd for assistance by the intercession of the Saints.*[13] *Sozomen** adds, that when the Emperor was marched seven miles from *Constantinople* against *Eugenius,* he went into a Church which he had built to *John* the Baptist, and invoked the Baptist for his assistance.[14] *Chrysostom** says: *He that is clothed in purple, approaches to embrace these sepulchres; and laying aside his dignity, stands supplicating the Saints to intercede for him with God: and he who goes crowned with a diadem, offers his prayers to the tent-maker and the fisher-man as his Protectors.*[15] And in another place: *The cities run together to the sepulchres of the Martyrs, and the people are inflamed with the love of them.*[16]

This practice of sending reliques from place to place for working miracles, and thereby inflaming the devotion of the nations towards the dead Saints and their reliques, and setting up the religion of invoking their souls, lasted only till the middle of the reign of the Emperor *Theodosius* the great; for he then prohibited it by the following Edict: *Humatum corpus, nemo ad alterum locum transferat; nemo Martyrem distrahat, nemo mercetur: Habeant verò in potestate, si quolibet in loco*

---

[13]   Hist. Eccl. l. 2. c. 23.

[14]   L. 4. c. 24.

[15]   Hom. 66. ad populum. circa finem & Hom. 8, 27, in Matth. 42-43. in Gen. Hom. 1. in 1 Thess.

[16]   Exposit. in Psal. 114. sub finem.

sanctorum est aliquis conditus, pro ejus veneratione, quod Martyrium vocandum sit, addant quod voluerint fabricarum. Dat, iv. *Kal. Mart. Constantinople, Honorio nob. puero & Euodio Coss.* A.C. 386.[17] After this they filled the fields and high-ways with altars erected to Martyrs, which they pretended to discover by dreams and revelations: and this occasioned the making of the fourteenth Canon of the fifth Council of *Carthage,* A.C. 398. *Item placuit, ut altaria, quæ passim per agros aut vias, tanquam memoriæ Martyrum constituuntur, in quibus nullum corpus aut reliquiæ Martyrum conditæ probantur, ab episcopis, qui illis locis præsunt, si fieri potest, evertantur. Si autem hoc propter tumultus populares non finitur, plebes tamen admoneantur, ne illa loca frequentent, ut qui rectè sapiunt, nullâ ibi superstitione devincti teneantur. Et omnino nulla memoria Martyrum probabiliter acceptetur, nisi aut ibi corpus aut aliquæ certæ reliquiæ sint, aut ubi origo alicujus habitationis, vel possessionis, vel passionis fidelissima origine traditur. Nam quæ per somnia, & per inanes quasi revelationes quorumlibet hominum ubique constituuntur altaria, omnimodè reprobentur.*[18] These altars were for invoking the Saints or Martyrs buried or pretended to be buried under them. First they filled the Churches in all places with

---

[17]   [Trans.: `Once a corpse is buried, let no one transfer it to another place. Let no one retail a martyr or sell him for merchandise. Let power be granted however, if in any place there is a Martyr entombed, to raise there any building desired, for the purpose of doing him honour, the building to be called a Martyr's Shrine.']

[18]   [Trans.: `Also resolved: that the altars erected in the fields and highways as memorials to the martyrs, when no body or relics can be proved to repose therein, be demolished, if possible by the bishops of those parts. But if this be not permitted by reason of popular tumult, yet let the people be warned against frequenting such spots, so that men of good understanding may not there be held in the bonds of superstition. And let no memorial whatsoever of the martyrs be accepted as credible unless either the body or some genuine relics repose there, or unless tradition assert on incontrovertible grounds that a martyr lived there, held property or suffered there. These altars, which are being set up everywhere on the admonition of the dreams and futile revelations should be utterly disavowed.']

the reliques or pretended reliques of the Martyrs, for invoking them in the Churches; and then they filled the fields and high-ways with altars, for invoking them every where: and this new religion was set up by the Monks in all the *Greek* Empire before the expedition of the Emperor *Theodosius* against *Eugenius*, and I think before his above-mentioned Edict, A.C. 386.

The same religion of worshiping *Mahuzzims* quickly spread into the *Western Empire* also: but *Daniel* in his Prophecy describes chiefly the things done amongst the nations comprehended in the body of his third Beast.

PART II

OBSERVATIONS *UPON THE APOCALYPSE OF ST. JOHN*

CHAPTER I

Introduction, concerning the time when the Apocalypse was written.

Irenæus* introduced an opinion that the *Apocalypse* was written in the time of *Domitian*; but then he also postponed the writing of some others of the sacred books, and was to place the *Apocalypse* after them: he might perhaps have heard from his master *Polycarp** that he received this book from *John* about the time of *Domitian's* death; or indeed *John* might himself at that time have made a new publication of it, from whence *Irenæus* might imagine it was then but newly written. *Eusebius** in his *Chronicle* and *Ecclesiastical History* follows *Irenæus*; but afterwards[1] in his *Evangelical Demonstrations*, he conjoins the banishment of *John* into *Patmos*, with the deaths of *Peter* and *Paul*: and so do [2] *Tertullian** and *Pseudo-Prochorus*, as well

---

[1] Dem. Evang. l. 3. [given as note `a' - and subsequent notes similarly indicated in two alphabetical sequences]

[2] [b] Vide Pamelium in notis ad Tertull. de Pr'scriptionibus, p. 215. & Hieron. l. 1. contra Jovinianum, c. 14. Edit. Erasmi.

as the first author, whoever he was, of that very antient fable, that *John* was put by *Nero* into a vessel of hot oil, and coming out unhurt, was banished by him into *Patmos*. Tho this story be no more than a fiction, yet it was founded on a tradition of the first Churches, that *John* was banished into *Patmos* in the days of *Nero*. *Epiphanius** represents the *Gospel of John* as written in the time of *Domitian*, and the *Apoclaypse* even before that of *Nero*. *Arethas*[3] in the beginning of his Commentary quotes the opinion of *Irenæus* from *Eusebius*, but follows it not: for he afterwards affirms the *Apoclaypse* was written before the destruction of *Jerusalem*, and that former commentators had expounded the sixth seal of that destruction.

With the opinion of the first Commentators agrees the tradition of the Churches of *Syria*, preserved to this day in the title of the *Syriac* Version of the *Apocalypse*, which title is this: *The Revelation* which was made to John *the Evangelist by* God *in the Island Patmos, into which he was banished by Nero the Cæsar.* The same is confirmed by a story told by *Eusebius*[4] out of *Clemens Alexandrinus,** and other antient authors, concerning a youth, whom *John* some time after his return from *Patmos* committed to the care of the Bishop of a certain city. The Bishop educated, instructed, and at length baptized him; but then remitting of his care, the young man thereupon got into ill company, and began by degrees first to revel and grow vitious, then to abuse and spoil those he met in the night; and at last grew so desperate, that his companions turning a band of high-way men, made him their Captain: and, saith *Chrysostom,**[5] he continued their Captain a long time. At length *John* returning to that city, and hearing what was done, rode to the thief; and, when he out of reverence to his old master fled, *John* rode after him, recalled him, and restored him to the Church. This is a story of many years, and requires that *John*

---

[c] Areth.* c. 18-19.

[4] [d] Hist. Eccl. l. 3. c. 23.

[5] [e] Chrysost.* ad Theodorum lapsum.

should have returned from *Patmos* rather at the death of *Nero* than at that of *Domitian*; because between the death of *Domitian* and that of *John* there were but two years and a half; and *John* in his old age was[6] so infirm as to be carried to Church, dying above 90 years old, and therefore could not be then suppos'd able to ride after the thief.

This opinion is further supported by the allusions in the *Apocalypse* to the Temple and Altar, and holy City, as then standing; and to the *Gentiles*, who were soon after to tread under foot the holy City and outward Court. 'Tis confirmed also by the style of the *Apocalypse* itself, which is fuller of *Hebraisms* than his Gospel. For thence it may be gathered, that it was written when *John* was newly come out of *Judea*, where he had been used to the *Syriac* tongue; and that he did not write his Gospel, till by long converse with the *Asiatick* Greeks he had left off most of the *Hebraisms*. It is confirmed also by the many false *Apocalypses*, as those of *Peter, Paul, Thomas, Stephen, Elias* and *Cerinthus*,* written in imitation of the true one. For as the many false Gospels, false Acts, and false Epistles were occasioned by true ones; and the writing many false *Apocalypses*, and ascribing them to Apostles and Prophets, argues that there was a true Apostolic one in great request with the first *Christians*: so this true one may well be suppos'd to have been written early, that there may be room in the Apostolic age for the writing of so many false one afterwards, and fathering them upon *Peter, Paul, Thomas* and others, who were dead before *John. Caius*,* who was contemporary with *Tertullian*, tells[7] us that *Cerinthus* wrote his Revelations as a great Apostle, and pretended the visions were shewn him by Angels, asserting a *millennium* of carnal pleasures at *Jerusalem* after the resurrection; so that his *Apocalypse* was plainly written in imitation of *John's*: and

---

6   [f] Hieron. in Epist. ad Gal. l. 3. c. 6.

7   [g] Apud Euseb.* Eccl. Hist. l. 3. c. 28. Edit. *Valesii.*

248

yet he lived so early, that[8] he resisted the Apostles at *Jerusalem* in or before the first year of *Claudius*, that is, 26 years before the death of *Nero*, and[9] died before *John*.

These reasons may suffice for determining the time; and yet there is one more, which to considering men may seem a good reason, to others not. I'll propound it, and leave it to every man's judgment. The *Apocalypse* seems to be alluded to in the Epistles of *Peter* and that to the *Hebrews* and therefore to have been written before them. Such allusions in the Epistle to the Hebrews, I take to be the discourses concerning the High-Priest in the heavenly Tabernacle, who is both Priest and King, as was *Melchisedec*; and those concerning the *word of God*, with the *sharp two-edged sword*, the sabbatismos,[10] or *millennial* rest, the *earth whose end is to be burned*, suppose by the lake of fire, *the judgment and fiery indignation which shall devour the adversaries*, the *heavenly City which hath foundations whose builder and maker is God, the cloud of witnesses, mount* Sion, *heavenly* Jerusalem, *general assembly, spirits of just men made perfect, viz.* by the resurrection, and *the shaking of heaven and earth, and removing them, that the new heaven, new earth and new kingdom which cannot be shaken, may remain.* In the first of *Peter* occur these: *The Revelation of Jesus Christ,*[11] twice or thrice repeated; *the blood of* Christ *as of a lamb* foreordained before the foundation of the world;*[12] the *spiritual building* in heaven, 1 Pet. ii. 5. *an inheritance incorruptible and undefiled and that fadeth not away, reserved in heaven for us, who are kept unto the salvation, ready to be revealed in the last time,* 1, Pet. i. 4, 5.[13] the royal *Priesthood,*[14] the *holy*

---

[8]   [h] Epiphan.* Hæres. 28.

[9]   [i] Hieron. adv. Lucif.

[10]   [Sabbatismos originally given in Greek characters.]

[11]   [k] l. Pet. i. 7, 13. iv. 13. & v. 1.

[12]   [l] Apoc. xiii. 8.

[13]   [m] Apoc. xxi.

[14]   [n] Apoc. i. 6 & v. 10.

Priesthood,[15] the *judgement beginning at the house of God,*[16] and *the Church at Babylon.*[17] These are indeed obscurer allusions; but the second Epistle, from the 19th verse of the first Chapter to the end, seems to be a continued Commentary upon the *Apocalypse.* There, in writing to the *Churches in* Asia, to whom *John* was commanded to send this Prophecy, he tells them, they *have a more sure word of Prophecy,* to be heeded by them, *as a light that shineth in a dark place, until the day dawn, and the day-star arise in their hearts,* that is, until they begin to understand it: for *no Prophecy,* saith he, *of the scripture is of any private interpretation; the Prophecy came not in old time by the will of man, but holy men of God spake, as they were moved by the Holy Ghost. Daniel*[18] himself professes that he understood not his own *Prophecies*; and therefore the Churches were not to expect the interpretation from their Prophet *John,* but to study the Prophecies themselves. This is the substance of what *Peter* says in the first chapter; and then in the second he proceeds to describe, out of this *sure word of Prophecy,* how there should arise in the Church *false Prophets,* or false teachers, expressed collectively in the *Apocalypse* by the name of the false Prophet; who should *bring in damnable heresies, even denying the Lord that bought them,* which is the character of *Antichrist: And many,* saith he, *shall follow their lusts;*[19] they that dwell on the earth[20] shall be decieved by the false Prophet, and be made drunk with the wine of the Whore's fornication, *by reason of whom the way of truth shall be blasphemed;* for[21] the Beast is full of blasphemy: *and*

---

[15]   [o] Apoc. xx. 6.

[16]   [p] Apoc. xx. 4, 12.

[17]   [q] Apoc. xvii.

[18]   [a] Dan. viii. 15-16, 27. & xii. 8-9.

[19]   [b] aselgeias, in many of the best MSS [Trans.: lusts - aselgeias originally given in Greek characters].

[20]   [c] Apoc. xiii. 7, 12.

[21]   [d] Apoc. xiii. 1, 5-6.

thro' covetousness shall they with feigned words make merchandize of you; for these are the Merchants of the Earth, who trade with the great Whore, and their merchandize[22] is all things of price, with the bodies and souls of men: *whose judgment — lingreth not, and their damnation slumbreth*[23] not, but shall surely come upon them at the last day suddenly, as the flood upon the old world, and fire and brimstone upon *Sodom* and *Gomorrha*, when the just shall be delivered[24] like *Lot*; for *the Lord knoweth how to deliver the godly out of temptations, and to reserve the unjust unto the day of judgment to be punished*, in the lake of fire; *but chiefly them that walk after the flesh in the lust of uncleanness*, being[25] made drunk with the wine of the Whore's fornication; who *despise dominion, and are not afraid to blaspheme glories*; for the beast opened his mouth against God[26] to blaspheme his name and his tabernacle, and them that dwell in heaven. *These, as natural brute beasts*, the ten-horned beast and two-horned beast, or false Prophet, *made to be taken and destroyed*, in the lake of fire, *blaspheme the things they understand not*: — they count it pleasure to riot in the day-time — sporting themselves with their own deceivings, while they feast[27] with you, *having eyes full of an adulteress*[28]: for the kingdoms of the beast live deliciously with the great Whore, and the nations are made drunk with the wine of her fornication. *They are gone astray, following the way of* Balaam, *the son of* Beor, *who loved the wages of unrighteousness*, the false Prophet[29] who taught *Balak* to cast a stumbling block before the children of *Israel*. *These are*, not fountains

---

22   [e] Apoc. xviii. 12-13.

23   [f] Apoc. xix. 20.

24   [g] Apoc. xxi 3-4.

25   [h] Apoc. ix. 21 *and* xvii. 2.

26   [i] Apoc. xiii. 6.

27   [k] Apoc. xviii. 3, 7, 9.

28   [l] moichalidos [Trans.: adultery - moichalidos originally given in Greek characters].

29   [m] Apoc. ii. 14.

of living water, but *wells without water*; not such clouds of Saints as the two witnesses ascend in, *but clouds that are carried with a tempest*, &c. Thus does the author of this second Epistle spend all the second Chapter in describing the qualities of the *Apocalyptic* Beasts and false Prophet: and then in the third he goes on to describe their destruction more fully, and the future kingdom. He saith, that because the coming of *Christ* should be long deferred, they should scoff, saying, *where is the promise of his coming?* Then he describes the sudden, coming of the day of the Lord upon them, *as a thief in the night*, which is the *Apoclayptic* phrase; and the *millennium*, or *thousand years*, which *are with God but as a day*; the *passing away of the old heavens* and earth, by a conflagration in the lake of fire, and our *looking for new heavens and a new earth, wherein dwelleth righteousness*.

Seeing therefore *Peter* and *John* were Apostles of the cirumcision, it seems to me that they staid with their Churches in *Judea* and *Syria* till the *Romans* made war upon their nation, that is, till the twelfth year of *Nero*; that they then followed the main body of the flying Churches into *Asia*, and that *Peter* went thence by *Corinth* to *Rome*; that the *Roman* Empire looked upon those Churches as enemies, because *Jews* by birth; and therefore to prevent insurrections, secured their leaders, and banished *John* into *Patmos*. It seems also probable to me that the *Apocalypse* was there composed, and that soon after the Epistle to the *Hebrews* and those of *Peter* were written to these Churches, with reference to this Prophecy as what they were particularly concerned in. For it appears by these Epistles, that they were written in times of general affliction and tribulation under the heathens, and by consequence when the Empire made war upon the *Jews*; for till then the heathens were at peace with the *Christian Jews*, as well as with the rest. The Epistle to the *Hebrews*, since it mentions *Timothy* as related to those *Hebrews*, must be written to them after their flight into *Asia*, where *Timothy* was Bishop; and by consequence after the war began, the *Hebrews* in Judea being strangers to *Timothy*. *Peter* seems also to call *Rome*

Babylon, as well with respect to the war made upon *Judea*, and the approaching captivity, like that under old *Babylon*, as with respect to that name in the *Apocalypse*: and in writing *to the strangers scattered thro 'out* Pontus, Galatia, Cappadocia, Asia *and* Bithynia, he seems to intimate that they were the strangers newly scattered by the *Roman* wars; for those were the only strangers there belonging to his care.

This account of things agrees best with history when duly rectified. For *Justin*[30]* and *Irenæus*[31]* say, that *Simon Magus* came to *Rome* in the reign of *Claudius*, and exercised juggling tricks there. *Pseudo-Clemens** adds, that he endeavoured there to fly, but broke his neck thro' the prayers of *Peter*. Whence *Eusebius*,[32]* or rather his interpolator *Jerom*,* has recorded that *Peter* came to *Rome* in the second year of *Claudius*: but *Cyril*[33]* Bishop of *Jerusalem*, *Philastrius*,* *Sulpitius*,* *Prosper*,* *Maximus Taurinensis*,* and *Hegesippus** junior, place this victory of *Peter* in the time of *Nero*. Indeed, the antienter tradition was, that *Peter* came to *Rome* in the days of this Emperor, as may be seen in *Lactantius*.[34]* *Chrysostom*[35]* tells us, that the Apostles continued long in *Judea*, and that then being driven out by the *Jews*, as *Josephus** tells us, began to be tumultious and violent in all places. For all agree that the Apostles were dispersed into several regions at once; and *Origen** has set down the time, telling[36] us that in the beginning of the *Judaic* war, the Apostles and disciples of our Lord were scattered into all nations; *Thomas* into *Parthia*, *Andrew* into *Scythia*, *John* into *Asia*, and *Peter* first into *Asia*, where he

---

[30]   [n] Apol. ad Antonin Pium.

[31]   [o] Hæres. l. 1. c. 20. Vide etiam Tertullianum, Apol. c. 13.

[32]   [p] Euseb. Chron.

[33]   [q] Cyril.* Catech. 6. Philastr. de h'res. cap. 30. Sulp. Hist. l. 2. Prosper de promiss. dimid. temp. cap. 13. Maximus serm. 5. in Natal. Apost. Hegesip. l. 2. c. 2.

[34]   [r] Lactant.* de mortib. Persec. c. 2.

[35]   [s] Hom. 70. in Matt. c. 22.

[36]   [t] Apud Euseb. Eccl. Hist. l. 2. c. 25.

preacht to the dispersion, and thence into *Italy*. *Dionysius Corinthius*[37]* saith, that *Peter* went from *Asia* by *Corinth* to *Rome*, and all antiquity agrees that *Peter* and *Paul* were martyred there in the end of *Nero's* reign. *Mark* went with *Timothy* to *Rome*, 2 *Tim*. iv. 11. *Colos*. iv. 10. *Sylvanus* was *Paul's* assistant; and by the companions of *Peter*, mentioned in his first Epistle, we may know that he wrote from *Rome*; and the Antients generally agree, that in this Epistle he understood *Rome* by *Babylon*. His second Epistle was writ to the same dispersed strangers with the first, 2 *Pet*. iii. 1. and therein he saith, that *Paul* had writ of the same things to them, and also in his other Epistles, *ver*. 15, 16. Now as there is no Epistle of *Paul* to these strangers besides that to the *Hebrews*, so in this Epistle, chap. x. 11, 12. we find at large all those things which *Peter* had been speaking of, and here refers to; particularly the *passing away of the old heavens and earth*, and *establishing an inheritance immoveable*, with an exhortation to grace, because God, to the wicked, *is a consuming fire*, Heb. xii, 25, 26, 28, 29.

Having determined the time of writing the *Apocalypse*, I need not say much about the truth of it, since it was in such request with the first ages, that many endeavoured to imitate it, by feigning *Apocalypses* under the Apostles names; and the Apostles themselves, as I have just now shewed, studied it, and used its phrases; by which means the style of the Epistle to the *Hebrews* became more mystical than that of *Paul's* other Epistles, and the style of *John's* Gospel more figurative than that of the other Gospels. I do not apprehend that *Christ* was called the word of God in any book of the New Testament written before the *Apocalypse*; and therefore am of opinion, the language was taken from this Prophecy, as were also many other phrases in this Gospel, such as those of *Christ's* being *the light which enlightens the world, the lamb of God which taketh away the sins of the world, the bridegroom, he that testifieth, he that came down from heaven, the Son of God*, &c. *Justin Martyr*,* who

---

[37]   [v] Euseb. Hist. l. 2. c. 25.

within thirty years after *John's* death became a *Christian*, writes expressly *that a certain man among the* Christians *whose name was* John, *one of the twelve Apostles of* Christ, *in the Revelation which was shewed to him, prophesied that those who believed in* Christ *should live a thousand years at* Jerusalem. And a few lines before he saith: *But I, and as many as are* Christians, *in all things right in their opinions, believe both that there shall be a resurrection of the flesh, and a thousand years life at* Jersualem *built, adorned and enlarged.* Which is as much to say, that all true *Christians* in that early age received this Prophecy: for in all ages, as many believed the thousand years, received the *Apocalypse* as the true foundation of their opinion: and I do not know one instance to the contrary. *Papias* Bishop of *Hierapolis*, a man of the Apostolic age, and one of *John's* own disciples, did not only teach the doctrine of the thousand years, but also[38] asserted the *Apocalypse* as written by divine inspiration. *Melito*,* who flourished next after *Justin*,[39]* wrote a commentary upon this Prophecy; and he, being Bishop of *Sardis* one of the seven Churches, could neither be ignorant of their tradition about it, nor impose upon them. *Irenæus*,* who was contemporary with *Melito*, wrote much upon it, and said, that *the number 666 was in all the antient and approved copies; and that he had it also confirmed to him by those who had seen* John *face to face*, meaning no doubt his master *Polycarp** for one. At the same time[40] *Theophilus* Bishop of *Antioch* asserted it, and so did *Tertullian*,* *Clemens Alexandrinus*,* and *Origen** soon after; and their contemporary *Hippolytus** the Martyr, Metropolitan of the *Arabians*,[41] wrote a commentary upon it. All these were antient men, flourishing within a hundred and twenty years after *John's* death, and of greatest note in the Churches of those times. Soon after did

---

[38]   [w] Arethas in Proæm. comment in Apoc.

[39]   [x] Euseb. Hist. l. 4. cap. 26. Hieron.

[40]   [y] Euseb. Hist. l. 4. c. 24.

[41]   [z] Hieron.

*Victorinus Pictaviensis** write another commentary upon it; and he lived in the time of *Dioclesian*. This may surely suffice to shew how the *Apocalypse* was received and studied in the first ages: and I do not indeed find any other book of the New Testament so strongly attested, or commented upon so early as this. The Prophecy said: *Blessed is he that readeth, and they that hear the words of this Prophecy, and keep the things which are written therein*. This animated the first *Christians* to study it so much, till the difficulty made them remit, and comment more upon the other books of the New Testament. This was the state of the *Apocalypse*, till the thousand years being misunderstood, brought a prejudice against it: and *Dionysius of Alexandria*,* noting how it abounded with barbarisms, that is with *Hebraisms*, promoted that prejudice so far, as to cause many *Greeks* in the fourth century to doubt of the book. But whilst the *Latins*, and a great part of the *Greeks*, always retained the *Apocalypse*, and the rest doubted only out of prejudice, it makes nothing against its authority.

This Prophecy is called *the Revelation*, with respect to *the scripture of truth*, which *Daniel* was commanded to *shut up and seal, till the time of the end. Daniel*[42] sealed it *until the time of the end*; and until that time comes the Lamb is opening the seals: and afterwards the two Witnesses prophesy out of it a long time in sack-cloth, before they ascend up to heaven in a cloud. All which is as much to say, that these Prophecies of *Daniel* and *John* should not be understood till the time of the end: but then some should prophesy out of them in an afflicted and mournful state for a long time, and that but darkly, so as to convert but few. But in the very end, the Prophecy should be so far interpreted as to convince many. *Then*, saith Daniel, *many shall run to and fro, and knowledge shall be encreased*. For the Gospel must be preached in all nations before the great tribulation, and end of the world. The palm-bearing multitude, which came out of this great tribulation, cannot be innumerable out of all

---

[42]   Dan. x. 21. xii. 4, 9.

nations, unless they be made so by the preaching of the Gospel before it comes. There must be a stone cut out of a mountain without hands, before it can fall upon the toes of the Image, and become a great mountain and fill the earth. An Angel must fly thro' the midst of heaven with the everlasting Gospel to preach to all nations, before *Babylon* falls, and the Son of man reaps his harvest. The two Prophets must ascend up to heaven in a cloud, before the kingdoms of this world become the kingdoms of *Christ*. 'Tis therefore a part of this Prophecy, that it should not be understood before the last age of the world; and therefore it makes for the credit of the Prophecy, that it is not yet understood. But if the last age, the age of opening these things, be now approaching, as by the great successes of late interpreters it seems to be, we have more encouragement than ever to look into these things. If the general preaching of the Gospel be approaching, it is to us and our posterity that those words mainly belong: *In the time of the end the wise shall understand, but none of the wicked shall understand.*[43] *Blessed is he that readeth, and they that hear the words of this Prophecy, and keep those things which are written therein.*[44]

The folly of Interpreters has been, to foretel times and things by this Prophecy, as if God designed to make them prophets. By this rashness they have not only exposed themselves, but brought the Prophecy also into contempt. The design of God was much otherwise. He gave this and the Prophecies of the Old Testament, not to gratify men's curiosities by enabling them to foreknow things, but that after they were fulfilled they might be interpreted by the event, and his own Providence, not to the Interpeters, be then manifested thereby to the world. For the event of things predicted many ages before, will then be a convincing argument that the world is governed by providence. For as the few and obscure Prophecies concerning *Christ's* first coming were for setting up the *Christian* religion, which all nations have since

---

[43]   Dan. xii. 4, 10.

[44]   Apoc. i. 3.

corrupted; so the many and clear Prophecies concerning the things to be done at *Christ's* second coming, are not only for predicting but also for effecting a recovery and re-establishment of the long-lost truth, and setting up a kingdom wherein dwells righteousness. The event will prove the *Apocalypse*; and this Prophecy, thus proved and understood, will open the old Prophets, and all together will make known the true religion, and establish it. For he that will understand the old Prophets, must begin with this; but the time is not yet come for understanding them perfectly, because the main revolution predicted in them is not yet come to pass. *In the days of the voice of the seventh Angel, when he shall begin to sound, the mystery of God shall be finished, as he hath declared to his servants the Prophets*: and then *the kingdoms of this world shall become the kingdoms of our* Lord *and his* Christ, *and he shall reign for ever*, Apoc. x. 7. xi. 15. There is already so much of the Prophecy fulfilled, that as many as will take pains in this study, may see sufficient instances of God's providence: but then the signal revolutions predicted by all the holy Prophets, will at once both turn mens eyes upon considering the predictions, and plainly interpret them. Till then we must content ourselves with interpreting what hath already been fulfilled.

Amongst the Interpreters of the last age there is scarce one of note who hath not made some discovery worth knowing; and thence I seem to gather that God is about opening these mysteries; The success of others put me upon considering it; and if I have done any thing which may be useful to following writers, I have my design.

CHAPTER II

Of the relation which the Apocalypse of John hath to the Book of the Law of Moses, and to the worship of God in the Temple.

The *Apocalypse* of John is written in the same style and language with the Prophecies of *Daniel*, and hath the same relation to them which they have to one another, so that all of them together make but one complete Prophecy; and in like manner it consists of two parts, an introductory Prophecy, and an interpretation thereof.

The Prophecy is distinguish'd into seven successive parts, by the opening of the seven seals of the book which *Daniel* was commanded to seal up: and hence it is called the *Apocalypse* or *Revelation* of *Jesus Christ*. The time of the seventh seal is sub-divided into eight successive parts by the silence in heaven for half and hour, and the sounding of seven trumpets sucessively: and the seventh trumpet sounds to the battle of the great day of God Almighty, *whereby the kingdoms of this world become the kingdoms of the Lord and of his Christ*, and those are destroyed that destroyed the earth.

The Interpretation begins with the words, *And the temple of God was opened in heaven, and there was seen in his temple the Ark of his Testament*: and it continues to the end of the Prophecy. The Temple is the scene of the visions, and the visions in the Temple relate to the feast of the seventh month: for the feasts of the *Jews* were typical of things to come. The Passover related to the first coming of *Christ*, and the feasts of the seventh month to his second coming: his first coming being therefore over before this Prophecy was given, the feasts of the seventh month are here only alluded unto.

On the first day of that month, in the morning, the High-Priest dressed the lamps: and in allusion hereunto, this Prophecy begins with a vision of one like *the Son of man* in the High-Priest's habit, appearing as it were in the midst of the seven golden candlesticks, or over against the midst of them, dressing the lamps, which appeared like a rod of seven stars in his right hand: and this dressing was perform'd by the sending seven Epistles to the Angels or Bishops of the seven Churches of *Asia*, which in the primitive times illuminated the Temple or Church Catholick. These Epistles contain admonitions against the approaching Apostacy, and therefore relate to the times when the Apostacy began to work strongly, and before it prevailed. It began to work in the Apostles days, and was to continue working *til the man of sin should be revealed.* It began to work on the disciples of *Simon, Menander, Carpocrates, Cerinthus*, and such sorts of men as had imbibed the metaphysical philosophy of the *Gentiles* and *Cabalistical Jews*, and were thence called *Gnosticks. John* calls them *Antichrists*, saying that in his days there were many *Antichrists*. But these being condemned by the Apostles, and their immediate disciples, put the Churches in no danger during the opening of the first four seals. The visions at the opening of these seals relate only to the civil affairs of the heathen *Roman* Empire. So long the Apostolic traditions prevailed, and preserved the Church in its purity: and therefore the affairs of the Church do not begin to be considered in this prophecy until the opening of the fifth seal. She began then to decline, and to want admonitions; and therefore is admonished by these Epistles, till the Apostacy prevailed and took place, which was at the opening of the seventh seal. The admonitions therefore in these seven Epistles relate to the state of the Church in the times of the fifth and sixth seals. At the opening of the fifth seal, the Church is purged from hypocrites by a great persecution. At the opening of the sixth, that which letted* is taken out of the way, namely the heathen *Roman* Empire. At the opening of the seventh, the man of sin is revealed. And to these times the seven Epistles relate.

The seven Angels, to whom these seven Epistles were written, answer to the seven *Amarc-holim*, who were Priests and chief Officers of the Temple, and had jointly the keys of the gates of the Temple, with those of the Treasurers, and the direction, appointment and oversight of all things in the Temple.

After the lamps were dressed, *John* saw *the door of the* Temple *opened*; and by *the voice as it were of a trumpet*, was called up to the eastern gate of the great court, to see the visions: and *behold a throne was set, viz.* the mercy-seat upon the Ark of the Testament, which the *Jews* respected as *the throne of God between the* Cherubims, *Exod.* xxv. 2. *Psal.* xcix. 1. *And he that sat on it was to look upon like* Jasper *and Sardine* stone, that is, of an olive colour, the people of *Judea* being of that colour. *And*, the Sun being then in the *East, a rainbow was about the throne*, the emblem of glory. *And round about the throne were four and twenty seats*; answering to the chambers of the four and twenty princes of the Priests, twelve on the south side, and twelve on the north side of the Priests Court. *And upon the seats were four and twenty Elders sitting, clothed in white rayment, with crowns on their heads*; representing the Princes of the four and twenty courses of the Priests clothed in linen. *And out of the throne proceeded lightnings and thunderings, and voices, viz.* the flashes of the fire upon the Altar at the morning-sacrifice, and the thundering voices of those that sounded the trumpets, and sung at the Easter gate of the Priests Court; for these being between John and the throne appeared to him as proceeding from the throne. *And there were seven lamps of fire burning*, in the Temple, *before the throne, which are the seven spirits of God*, or Angels of the seven Churches, represented in the beginning of this Prophecy by seven stars. *And before the throne was a sea of glass clear as crystal*; the brazen sea between the porch of the Temple and the Altar, filled with clear water. *And in the midst of the throne, and round about the throne, were four beasts full of eyes before and behind*: that is, one Beast before the throne and one behind it, appearing to *John* as in the midst of the throne, and one on either side in the circle about it, to represent the multitude of their eyes the people standing in the four sides of the peoples court. *And the first Beast was like a lion and the second was like a calf, and the third had the face of a man, and the fourth was like a flying eagle.* The people of *Israel* in the wilderness encamped round about the tabernacle, and on the east side were three tribes under the standards of *Judah*, on the west were three tribes under the standard of *Ephraim*, on the south were three tribes under the standard of *Reuben*, and on the north were three tribes under the standard of *Dan, Numb.* ii. And the standard of *Judah* was a Lion, that of *Ephraim* an Ox, that of *Reuben* a Man, and that of *Dan* an Eagle, as the *Jews* affirm. Whence were framed the hieroglyphicks of *Cherubims* and *seraphims*, to represent the people of *Israel*. A *Cherubim* had one body with four faces, the faces of a Lion, Ox, a Man and an Eagle, looking to four winds of heaven, without turning about, as in *Ezekiel's* vision, chap. i. And four *Seraphims* had the same four faces with four bodies, one face to every body. The four Beasts are therefore four *Seraphims* standing in the four sides of the peoples court; the first in the eastern side with the head of a Lion, the second in the western side with the head of an Ox, the third in the southern side with the head of a Man, the fourth in the northern side with the head of an Eagle: and all four signify together the twelve tribes of *Israel*, out of whom the hundred forty and four thousand were sealed, *Apoc.* vii. 4. *And the four beasts had each of them six wings*, two to a tribe, in all twenty and four wings, answering to the twenty and four stations of the people. And they were full of eyes within, or under their wings. *And they rest not day and night*, or at the morning and evening-sacrifices, *saying holy, holy, holy Lord God Almighty which was, and is, and is to come.* These animals are therefore the

Seraphims, which appeared to *Isaiah* in a vision like this of the *Apocalypse.*[1] For there also the Lord sat upon a throne in the temple; and the *Seraphims* each with six wings cried, *Holy, holy holy Lord God of hosts. And when those animals give glory and honour and thanks to him that sitteth upon the throne, who liveth for ever and ever, the four and twenty Elders* go into the Temple, and there *fall down before him that sitteth on the throne, and worship him that liveth for ever and ever, and cast their crowns before the throne, saying, Thou art worthy, O Lord, to receive glory and honour and power: for thou has created all things, and for thy pleasure they are and were created.* At the morning and evening-sacrifices, so soon as the sacrifice was laid upon the Altar, and the drink-offering began to be poured out, the trumpets sounded, and the *Levites* sang by course three times; and every time when the trumpets sounded, the people fell down and worshiped. Three times therefore did the people worship; to express which number, the Beasts cry *Holy, holy, holy*: and the song being ended, the people prayed standing, till the solemnity was finished. In the mean time the Priests went into the Temple, and there fell down before him that sat upon the throne, and worshiped.

And John *saw, in the right hand of him that sat upon the throne, a book written within and on the backside, sealed with seven seals, viz.* the book which *Daniel* was commanded to seal up, and which is here represented by the prophetic book of the Law laid up on the right of the Ark, as it were in the right hand of him that sat on the throne: for the festivals and ceremonies of the Law prescribed to the people in this book, adumbrated those things which were predicted in the book of *Daniel*; and the writing within and on the backside of this book, relates to the synchronal Prophecies. *And none was found worthy to open the book* but the Lamb of God. *And lo, in the midst of the throne and of the four Beasts, and in the midst of the Elders*, that is, at the foot of the Altar, *stood a lamb as it had been slain*, the morning-

---

[1]   Isa. vi.

sacrifice; *having seven horns*, which are the seven Churches, *and seven eyes, which are the seven spirits of God sent forth into all the earth. And he came, and took the book out of the right hand of him that sat on the throne: And when he had taken the book, the four Beasts and four and twenty Elders fell down before the Lamb, having every one of them harps, and golden vials full of odours, which are the prayers of saints. And they sung a new song, saying, Thou art worthy to take the book, and to open the seals thereof: for thou wast slain, and hast redeemed us to God by thy blood out of every kindred and tongue, and people, and nation; and hast made us, unto our God, Kings and Priests, and we shall reign on the earth.* The Beasts and Elders therefore represent the primitive *Christians* of all nations; and the worship of these *Christians* in their Churches is here prepresented under the form of worshiping God and the Lamb in the Temple: God for his benefaction in creating all things, and the Lamb for his benefaction in redeeming us with his blood: God as sitting upon the throne and living for ever, and the Lamb as exalted above all by the merits of his death. *And I heard*, saith John, *the voice of many Angels round about the throne, and the Beasts and the Elders: and the number of them was ten thousand times ten thousand, and thousands of thousands; saying with a loud voice, Worthy is the Lamb that was slain to receive power, and riches, and wisdom, and strength, and honour, and glory, and blessing. And every creature which is in heaven, and on the earth, and under the earth, and such as are in the sea, and all that are in them, heard I, saying Blessing, honour, glory, and power be unto him that sitteth upon the throne, and unto the Lamb for ever and ever. And the four Beasts said,* Amen. *And the four and twenty Elders fell down and worshiped him that liveth for ever and ever.*[2] This was the worship of the primitive *Christians.*

It was the custom for the High-Priest, seven days before the fast of the seventh month, to continue constantly in the Temple, and study the book of the Law,

---

[2]   Apoc.vi.

that he might be perfect in it against the day of expiation; wherein the service, which was various and intricate, was wholly to be performed by himself; part of which service was reading the Law to the people: and to promote his studying it, there were certain Priests appointed by the *Sanhedrin** to be with him those seven days in one of his chambers in the Temple, and there to discourse with him about the Law, and read it to him, and put him in mind of reading and studying it himself. This his opening and reading the Law those seven days, is alluded unto in the Lamb's opening the seals. We are to conceive that those seven days begin in the evening before each day; for the *Jews* began their day in the evening, and that the solemnity of the fast begins in the morning of the seventh day.

The seventh seal was therefore opened on the day of expiation, and then *there was silence in heaven for half an hour. And an Angel*, the High-Priest, *stood at the Altar, having a golden Censer*, and *there was given him much incense, that he should offer it with the prayers of all Saints, upon the golden Altar which was before the throne*. The custom was on other days, for one of the Priests to take fire from the great Altar in a silver Censer; but on this day, for the High Priest to take fire from the great Altar in a golden Censer: and when he was come down from the great Altar, he took incense from one of the Priests who brought it to him, and went with it to the golden Altar: and while he offered the incense, the people prayed without in silence, which is the silence in heaven for half an hour. When the High-Priest had laid the incense on the Altar, he carried a Censer of it burning in his hand, into the most holy place before the Ark. *And the smoke of the incense, with the prayers of the Saints, ascended up before God out of the Angel's hand.* On other days there was a certain measure of incense for the golden Altar: on this day there was a greater quantity for both the Altar and the most holy Place, and therefore it is called *much incense*. After this *the Angel took the Censer, and filled it with fire from the* great *Altar, and cast it into the earth*; that is, by the hands of the Priests who belong to his mystical body, he cast it to the earth without the Temple, for burning the Goat which was the Lord's lot. And at this and other concomitant sacrifices, until the evening-sacrifice was ended, *there were voices, and thundrings, and lightnings, and an earthquake*; that is, the voice of the High-Priest reading the Law to the people, and other voices and thundrings from the trumpets and temple-musick at the sacrifices, and lightnings from the fire of the Altar.

The solemnity of the day of expiation being finished, the seven Angels sound their trumpets at the great sacrifices of the seven days of the feast of tabernacles; and at the same sacrifices, the seven thunders utter their voices, which are the musick of the Temple, and singing of the *Levites*, intermixed with the sounding of the trumpets: and the seven Angels pour out their vials of wrath, which are the drink-offerings of those sacrifices.

When six of the seals were opened, *John* said: *And after these things*, that is, after the visions of the sixth seal, *I saw four Angels standing on the four corners of the earth, holding the four winds of the earth, that the wind should not blow on the earth, nor on the sea, nor on any tree. And I saw another Angel ascending from the* East, *having the seal of the living God: and he cried with a loud voice to the four Angels, to whom it was given to hurt the earth and the sea, saying, Hurt not the earth, nor the sea, nor the trees, till we have sealed the servants of our God in their foreheads.*[3] This sealing alludes to a tradition of the *Jews*, that upon the day of expiation all the people of *Israel* are sealed up in the books of life and death. For the *Jews* in their *Talmud* tell us,[4] that in the beginning of every new year, or first day of the month *Tisri*, the seventh month of the sacred year, three books are opened in judgment; the book of life, in which the names of those are written who are perfectly just; the book of death, in which the names of those are written who are Atheists or

---

[3] Apoc. vii.

[4] Buxtorf* in Synagoga Judaica, c. 18, 21.

very wicked; and a third book, of those whose judgment is suspended until the day of expiation, and whose names are not written in the book of life or death before that day. The first ten days of this month they call the penitential days; and all these days they fast and pray very much, and are very devout, that on the tenth day their sins may be remitted, and their names may be written in the book of life; which day is therefore called the day of expiation. And upon this tenth day, in returning home from the Synagogues, they say to one another, *God the creator seal you to a good year.* For they conceive that the books are now sealed up, and that the sentence of God remains unchanged henceforward to the end of the year. The same thing is signified by the two Goats, upon whose foreheads the High-Priest yearly, on the day of expiation, lays the two lots inscribed, *For God* and *For Azazel;** God's lot signifying the people who are sealed with the name of God in their foreheads; and the lot *Azazel,* which was sent into the wilderness, representing those who receive the mark and name of the Beast, and go into the wilderness with the great Whore.

The servants of God being therefore sealed in the day of expiation, we may conceive that this sealing is synchronal to the visions which appear upon opening the seventh seal; and that when the Lamb had opened six of the seals and seen the visions relating to the inside of the sixth, he looked on the backside of the seventh leaf, and then saw *the four Angels holding the four winds of heaven, and another angel ascending from the* East *with the seal of God.* Conceive also, that the Angels which held the four winds were the first four of the seven Angels, who upon opening the seventh seal were seen standing before God; and that upon their holding the winds, *there was silence in heaven for half an hour;* and that while the servants of God were sealing, the Angel with the golden Censer offered their prayers with incense upon the golden Altar, and read the Law: and that so soon as they were sealed, the winds hurt the earth at the sounding of the first trumpet, and the sea at the sounding of the second; these winds signifying the wars, to which the first four trumpets sounded. For as the first four seals are distinguished from the three last by the appearance of four horsemen towards the four winds of heaven; so the wars of the first four trumpets are distinguished from those of the three last, by representing these *by four winds*, and the others by *three great woes.*

In one of *Ezekiel's* visions, when the *Babylonian* captivity was at hand, *six men* appeared *with slaughter-weapons; and a seventh,* who appeared *among them clothed in white linen and a writer's ink-horn by his side, is commanded to go thro' the midst of* Jerusalem, *and set a mark upon the foreheads of the men that sigh and cry for all the abominations done in the midst thereof:*[5] and then the six men, like the Angels of the first six trumpets, are commanded to slay those men who are not marked. Conceive therefore that the hundred forty and four thousand are sealed, to preserve them from the plagues of the first six trumpets; and that at length by the preaching of the everlasting gospel, they grow into a *great multitude, which no man could number, of all nations, and kindreds, and peoples and tongues*: and at the sounding of the seventh trumpet come out of the great tribulation *with Palms in their hands: the kingdoms of this world,* by the war to which that trumpet sounds, *becoming the kingdoms of God and his Christ.* For the solemnity of the great *Hosannah* was kept by the *Jews* upon the seventh or last day of the feast of tabernacles; the *Jews* upon that day carrying Palms in their hands, and crying *Hosannah.*

After six of the Angels, answering to the six men with slaughter-weapons, had sounded their trumpets, the Lamb* in the form of *a mighty Angel came down from heaven clothed with a cloud, and a rainbow was upon his head, and his face was as it were the Sun, and his feet as pillars of fire, the shape in which Christ* appeared in the beginning of this Prophecy; *and he had in his hand a little book open,* the book which he had newly opened; for he received but one book from him that

---

[5]   Ezek. ix.

sitteth upon the throne, and he alone was worthy to open and look upon this book. *And he set his right foot upon the sea and his left foot upon the earth, and cried with a loud voice, as when a lion roareth.* It was the custom for the High-Priest on the day of expiation, to stand in an elevated place in the peoples court, at the Eastern gate of the Priests court, and read the Law to the people, while the Heifer and the Goat which was the Lord's lot, were burning without the Temple, We may therefore suppose him standing in such a manner, that his right foot might appear to *John* as it were standing on the sea of glass, and his left foot on the ground of the house; and that he cried with a loud voice, in reading the Law on the day of expiation. *And when he had cried, seven thunders uttered their voices.* Thunders are the voice of a cloud, and a cloud signifies a multitude; and this multitude may be the *Levites*, who sang with thundering voices, and played with musical instruments at the great sacrifices, on the seven days of the feast of Tabernacles: at which times the trumpets also sounded. For the trumpets sounded, and the *Levites* sang alternately, three times at every sacrifice. The Prophecy therefore of the seven thunders is nothing else than a repetition of the Prophecy of the seven trumpets in another form. *And the Angel which I saw stand upon the sea and upon the earth, lifted up his hand to heaven, and sware by him that liveth for ever and ever, that after the seven* thunders *there should be time no longer; but in the days of the voice of the seventh Angel, when he shall begin to sound, the mystery of God should be finished, as he hath declared to his servants the Prophets.* The voices of the thunders therefore last to the end of this world, and so do those of the trumpets.

And the voice which I heard from heaven, saith John, *spake unto me again and said, Go and take the little book,* &c. *And I took the little book out of the Angel's hand, and ate it up; and it was in my mouth sweet as honey, and as soon as I had eaten it, my belly was bitter. And he said unto me, Thou must prophesy again before many peoples, and nations, and tongues, and kings.* This is an introduction to a new

Prophecy, to a repetition of the Prophecy of the whole book; and alludes to *Ezekiel's* eating a roll or book spread open before him, and written within and without full of lamentations and mourning and woe, but sweet in his mouth. Eating and drinking signify acquiring and possessing; and eating the book is becoming inspired with the Prophecy contained it. It implies being inspired in a vigorous and extraordinary manner with the Prophecy of the whole book, and therefore signifies a lively repetition of the whole Prophecy by way of interpretation, and begins not till the first Prophecy, that of the seals and trumpets is ended. It was sweet in *John's* mouth, and therefore begins not with the bitter Prophecy of the *Babylonian* captivity, and the *Gentiles* being in the outward court of the Temple, and treading the holy city under foot; and the prophesying of the *two witnesses* in sackcloth, and their smiting the earth with all plagues, and being killed by the Beast: but so soon as the Prophecy of the trumpets is ended, it begins with the sweet Prophecy of the glorious *Woman in heaven*, and the victory of *Michael** over the Dragon; and after that, it is bitter in *John's* belly, by a large description of the times of the great Apostacy.

And the Angel stood, upon the earth and sea, *saying, Rise and measure the Temple of God and the Altar, and them that worship therein*, that is, their courts with the buildings thereon, *viz.* the square court of the Temple called the separate place, and the square court of the Altar called the Priests *court*, and the court of them that worship in the Temple called the new court: *but the great new court which is without the Temple, leave out, and measure it not, for it is given to the* Gentiles, *and the holy city shall they tread under foot forty and two months*. This measuring hath reference to *Ezekiel's* measuring the Temple of *Solomon*: there the whole Temple, including the outward court, was measured, to signify that it should be rebuilt in the latter days. Here the courts of the Temple and Altar, and they who worship therein, are only measured, to signify the building of a second Temple, for those that are sealed out of all the twelve tribes of *Israel*, and worship in the inward court of sincerity and truth:

but *John* is commanded to leave out the outward court, or outward form of religion and Church-government, because it is given to the *Babylonian Gentiles*. For the glorious woman in heaven, the remnant of whose seed kept the commandments of God, and had the testimony of *Jesus*, continued the same woman in outward form after her flight into the wilderness, whereby she quitted her former sincerity and piety, and became the great Whore. She lost her chastity, but kept her outward form and shape. And while the *Gentiles* tread the holy city underfoot, and worship in the outward court, the two witnesses, represented perhaps by the two feet of the Angel standing on the sea and earth, prophesied against them, and *had power*, like *Elijah* and *Moses, to consume their enemies with fire proceeding out of their mouth, and to shut heaven that it rain not the in the days of their Prophecy, and to turn the waters into blood, and to smite the earth with all plagues as often as they will*, that is, with the plagues of the trumpets and vials of wrath; and at length they are slain, rise again from the dead, and ascend up to heaven in a cloud; and then the seventh trumpet sounds to the day of judgment.

The Prophecy being finished, *John* is inspired anew by the eaten book, and begins the Interpretation thereof with these words, *And the Temple of God was opened in heaven, and there was seen in his Temple the Ark of the Testament*. By the Ark, we may know that this was the first Temple; for the second Temple had no Ark. *And there were lightnings, and voices and thundrings, and an earthquake, and great hail*. These answer to the wars in the *Roman* Empire, during the reign of the four horsemen, who appeared upon opening the first four seals. *And there appeared a great wonder in heaven, a woman clothed with the Sun*. In the *Prophecy*, the affairs of the Church begin to be considered at the opening of the fifth seal; and in the Interpretation, they begin at the same time with the vision of the Church in the form of a woman in heaven: there she is persecuted, and here she is pained in travail. The Interpretation proceeds down first to the sealing of the servants of God, and marking the rest with the mark of the Beast; and then to the day of judgement, represented by a harvest and vintage. Then it returns back to the times of opening the seventh seal, and interprets the Prophecy of the seven trumpets by the pouring out of seven vials of wrath. The Angels who pour them out, come out of the *Temple of the Tabernacle*; that is, out of the second Temple, for the Tabernacle had no outward court. Then it returns back again to the times of measuring the Temple and Altar, and of the *Gentiles* worshipping in the outward court, and of the Beast killing the witnesses in the streets of the great city; and interprets these things by the vision of *a woman sitting on the Beast, drunken with the blood of the Saints*; and proceeds in the Interpretation downwards to the fall of the great city and the day of judgment.

The whole Prophecy of the book, represented by the book of the Law, is therefore repeated, and interpreted in the visions which now follow those of sounding the seventh trumpet, and begin with that of the Temple of God opened in heaven. Only the things, which the seven thunders uttered, were not written down, and therefore not interpreted.

CHAPTER III

Of the relation which the Prophecy of John hath to those of Daniel; and of the Subject of the Prophecy.

The whole scene of sacred Prophecy is composed of three principal parts: the regions beyond *Euphrates*, represented by the two first Beasts of *Daniel*; the Empire of the *Greeks* on this side of *Euphrates*, represented by the Leopard and by the He-Goat; and the Empire of the *Latins* on this side of *Greece*, represented by the Beast with ten horns. And to these three parts, the phrases of the *third part of the earth, sea, rivers, trees, ships, stars, sun, and moon*, relate. I place the body of the fourth Beast on this side of Greece, because the three first of the four Beasts had their lives prolonged after their dominion was taken away, and therefore belong not to the body of the fourth. He only stamped them with his feet.

By the *earth*, the *Jews* understood the great continent of all *Asia* and *Africa*, to which they had access by land: and by the Isles of the *sea*, they understood the places to which they sailed by sea, particularly all *Europe*: and hence in the Prophecy, the *earth* and sea are put for the nations of the *Greek* and *Latin* Empires.

The third and fourth Beasts of *Daniel* are the same with the Dragon and ten-horned Beast of *John*, but with this difference: *John* puts the Dragon for the whole *Roman* Empire while it continued entire, because it was entire when that Prophecy was given; and the Beast he considers not till the Empire became divided: and then he puts the Dragon for the Empire of the *Greeks*, and the Beast for the Empire of the

Latins. Hence it is that the Dragon and Beast have common heads and common horns: but the Dragon hath crowns only upon his heads, and the Beast only upon his horns; because the Beast and his horns reigned not before they were divided from the Dragon: and when the Dragon gave the Beast his throne, the ten horns received powers as Kings, the same hour with the Beast. The heads are seven successive Kings. Four of them were the four horsemen which appeared at the opening of the first four seals. In the latter end of the sixth head, or seal, considered as present in the visions, it is said, *five* of the seven Kings *are fallen, and one is, and another is not yet come; and the Beast that was and is not*, being wounded to death with a sword, *he is the eighth, and of the seven*: he was therefore a collateral part of the seventh. The horns are the same with those of *Daniel's* fourth Beast, described above.

The four horsemen which appear at the opening of the first four seals, have been well explained by Mr. *Mede*; excepting that I had rather continue the third to the end of the reign of the three *Gordians* and *Philip* the *Arabian*, those being Kings from the *South*, and begin the fourth with the reign of *Decius*, and continue it till the reign of *Dioclesian*. For the fourth horseman *sat upon a pale horse, and his name was Death; and hell followed with him; and power was given them to kill unto the fourth part of the earth, with the sword, and with famine, and with the plague, and with the Beasts of the earth*, or armies of invaders and rebels: and as such were the times during all this interval. Hitherto the *Roman* Empire continued in an undivided monarchical form, except rebellions; and such it is represented by the four horsemen. But *Dioclesian* divided it between himself and *Maximianus*, A.C. 285; and it continued in that divided state, till the victory of *Constantine* the great over *Licinius* A.C. 323, which put an end to the heathen persecutions set on foot by *Dioclesian* and *Maximianus*, and described at the opening of the fifth seal. But this division of the Empire was imperfect, the whole still being under one and the same Senate. The same victory of *Constantine* over *Licinius* a heathen persecutor, began the fall of the heathen Empire, described at the opening of he sixth seal: and the visions of this seal continue till after the reign of *Julian* the Apostate, he being a heathen Emperor, and reigning over the whole *Roman* Empire.

The affairs of the Church begin to be considered at the opening of the fifth seal, as was said above. Then she is represented by *a woman* in the Temple of heaven, *clothed with the sun* of righteousness, *and the moon of Jewish* ceremonies *under her feet, and upon her head a crown of twelve stars* relating to the twelve Apostles and to the twelve tribes of *Israel*. When she fled from the Temple into the wilderness, she left in the Temple *a remnant of her seed, who kept the commandments of God, and had the testimony of Jesus Christ*; and therefore before her flight she represented the true primitive Church of God, tho afterwards she degenerated like *Ahola* and *Aholibah*. In *Dioclesian's* persecution *she cried, travelling in birth, and pained to be delivered*. And in the end of that persecution, by the victory of *Constantine* over *Maxentius* A.C. 312, *she brought forth a man-child*, such a child as *was to rule all nations with a rod of Iron*, a *Christian* Empire. *And her child*, by the victory of *Constantine* over *Licinius*, A.C. 322, *was brought up unto god and to his throne. And the woman*, by the division of the *Roman* Empire into the *Greek* and *Latin* Empires, *fled* from the first Temple *into the wilderness*, or spiritually barren Empire of the *Latins*, where she is found afterwards sitting upon the Beast and upon the seven mountains; and is called *the great city which reigneth over the Kings of the earth*, that is, over the ten Kings who give their kingdom to her Beast.

But before her flight there was war in heaven between *Michael** and the Dragon, the *Christian* and the heathen religions; and the Dragon, *that old serpent, called the Devil and Satan, who deceiveth the whole world, was cast out to the earth, and his Angels were cast out with him*. And *John heard a voice in heaven, saying, Now is come salvation and strength, and the kingdom of our God, and the power of his* Christ: *for the accuser of our brethren is cast down. And they overcame him by* *the blood of the Lamb, and by the sword of their testimony. And they loved not their lives unto the death. Therefore rejoice, ye heavens, and ye that dwell in them. Woe be to the inhabiters of the earth and sea,* or people of the *Greek* and *Latin* Empires, *for the devil is come down amongst you, having great wrath, because he knoweth that he hath but a short time.*

And when the Dragon saw that he was cast down from the *Roman* throne, and the man-child caught up thither, he *persecuted the woman which brought forth the man-child; and to her,* by the division of the *Roman* Empire between the cities of *Rome* and *Constantinople* A.C. 330, *were given two wings of a great eagle,* the symbol of the *Roman* Empire, *that she might flee* from the first Temple *into the wilderness of Arabia, to her place at Babylon* mystically so called. *And the serpent,* by the division of the same Empire between the sons of *Constantine* the Great, A.C. 337, *cast out of his mouth water as a flood,* the *Western* Empire, *after the woman; that he might cause her to be carried away by the flood. And the earth,* or *Greek* Empire, *helped the woman, and the earth opened her mouth, and swallowed up the flood,* by the victory of *Constantius* over *Magnentius,* A.C. 353, and thus the Beast was wounded to death with a sword. *And the Dragon was wroth with the woman,* in the reign of *Julian the Apostate* A.C. 361, *and,* by a new division of the Empire between *Valentinian* and *Valens,* A.C. 364, *went* from her into the *Eastern* Empire *to make war with the remnant of her seed,* which she left behind her when she fled: and thus the Beast revived. By the next division of the Empire, which was between *Gratian* and *Theodosius* A.C. 379, the *Beast* with ten horns rose out of the sea, and the *Beast* with two horns out of the earth: and by the last division thereof, which was between the sons of *Theodosius,* A.C. 395, *the Dragon gave the Beast his power and throne, and great authority.* And the ten horns *received power as Kings, the same hour with the Beast.*

At length the woman arrived at her place of temporal as well as spiritual dominion upon the back of the Beast, where she is nourished *a time, and times, and half a time, from the face of the serpent*; not in his kingdom, but at a distance from him. She is nourished by *the merchants* of the earth, three times or years and an half, or 42 months, or 1260 days: and in these Prophecies days are put for years. During all this time the Beast acted, and *she sat upon him*, that is, reigned over him, and over the ten Kings *who gave their power and strength*, that is, their kingdom *to the Beast*; and she was *Drunken with the blood of the Saints*. By all these circumstances she is the eleventh horn of *Daniels's* fourth Beast, who reigned with a *look more stout than his fellows*, and was of a different kind from the rest, and had eyes *and a mouth* like the woman; *and made war with the saints, and prevailed against them*, and *wore them out*, and *thought to change times and laws*, and had them *given into his hand, until a time, and times, and a half time*. These characters of the woman, and little horn of the Beast, agree perfectly: in respect of her temporal dominion, she was a horn of the Beast; in respect of her spiritual dominion, she rode upon him in the form of a woman, and was his Church, and committed fornication with the ten kings.

The second Beast, which *rose up out of the earth*, was the Church of the *Greek* Empire: for it *had two horns like those of the Lamb*, and therefore was a Church; and it *Spake as the Dragon*, and therefore was of his religion; and it *came up out of the earth*, and by consequence in his kingdom. It is called also *the false Prophet* who wrought miracles before the first Beast, by which he deceived them that received his mark, and worshiped his image. When the Dragon went from the woman to make war with the remnant of her seed, this Beast arising out of the earth assisted in that war, and *caused the earth and them which dwell therein to worship* the authority of *the first Beast, whose mortal wound was healed*, and to *make an Image to him*, that is, to assemble a body of men like him in point of religion. He had also *power to give life* and authority *to the Image*, so that it could *both speak*, and by dictating *cause that all* religious bodies of men, *who would not worship* the authority of the *Image, should be* mystically killed. *And he causeth all men to receive* a mark in their right hand or in their forehead, and that no man might buy or sell save he that had the mark, or the name of the Beast, or the number of his name; all the rest being excommunicated by the Beast with two horns. His mark is ✠✠✠, and his name LATEINOS,[1] and the number of his name 666.

Thus the Beast, after he was wounded to death with a sword and revived, was deified, as the heathens used to deify their Kings after death, and had an Image erected to him; and his worshipers were initiated in this new religion, by receiving the mark or name of the new God, or the number of his name. By killing all that will not worship him and his Image, the first Temple, illuminated by the lamps of the seven Churches, is demolished, and a new Temple, or outward form of a Church, is given to the *Gentiles*, who worship the Beast and his Image: while they who will not worship him, are sealed with the name of God in their forheads, and retire into the inward court of this new Temple. These are the 144000 sealed out of all the twelve tribes of *Israel*, and called the two *Witnesses*, as being derived from the two wings of the woman while she was flying into the wilderness, and represented by two of the seven candlesticks. These appear to *John* in the inward court of the second Temple, standing on mount *Sion* with the Lamb, as it were on the sea of glass. These are *the Saints of the most High*, and *the host of heaven, and the holy people* spoken of by *Daniel*, as worn out and trampled under foot, and destroyed in the latter times by the little horns of his fourth Beast and He-Goat.

While the *Gentiles* tread the holy city under foot, God *gives power to his two Witnesses, and they prophesy a thousand two hundred and threescore days clothed in sackcloth*. They are called *the two Olive-trees*, with relation to the two Olive-trees, which in *Zechary's* vision, chap. iv stand on either side of the golden candlestick to supply the lamps with oil: and Olive-trees, according to the Apostle *Paul*, represent

---

[1]   [LATEINOS originally given in Greek characters.]

Churches, *Rom.* xi. They supply the lamps with oil, by maintaining teachers. They are also called *the two candlesticks*; which in this Prophecy signify Churches, the seven Churches of *Asia* being represented by seven candlesticks. Five of these Churches were found faulty, and threatned if they did not repent; the other two were without fault, and so their candlesticks were fit to be placed in the second Temple. These were the Churches in *Smyrna* and *Philadelphia*. They were in a state of tribulation and persecution, and the only two of the seven in such a state: and so their candlesticks were fit to represent the Churches in affliction in the times of the second Temple, and the only two of the seven that were fit. The *two Witnesses* are not new Churches: they are the posterity of the primitive Church, the posterity of the two wings of the woman, and so are fitly represented by two of the primitive candlesticks. We may conceive therefore, that when the first Temple was destroyed, and a new one built for them who worship in the inward court, two of the seven candlesticks were placed in this new Temple.

The affairs of the Church are not considered during the opening of the first four seals. They begin to be consider'd at the opening of the fifth seal, as was said above; and are further considered at the opening of the sixth seal; and the seventh seal contains the times of the great Apostacy. And therefore I refer the Epistles to the seven Churches unto the times of the fifth and sixth seals: for they relate to the Church when she began to decline, and contain admonitions against the great Apostacy then approaching.

When *Eusebius** had brought down his *Ecclesiastical History* to the reign of *Dioclesian*, he thus describes the state of the Church: *Qualem quantamque gloriam simul ac libertatem doctrina veræ erga supremum Deum pietatis à Christo primùm hominibus annunciata, apud omnes Græcos pariter & barbaros ante persecutionem nostrâ memoriâ excitam, consecuta sit, nos certè pro merito explicare non possumus. Argumento esse possit Imperatorum benignatis erga nostros: quibus regendas etiam* *provincias committebant, omni sacrificandi metu eos liberantes ob singularem, qua in religionem nostram affecti erant, benevolentiam.* And a little after: *Jam vero quis innumerabilem hominum quotidiè ad fidem Christi confugientium turbam, quis numerum ecclesiarum in singulis urbibus, quis illustres populorum concursus in ædibus sacris, cumulatè possit describere? Quo factum est, ut priscis ædificiis jam non contenti, in singulis urbibus spatiosas ab ipsis fundamentis extruerent ecclesias. Atque hæc progressu temporis increscentia, & quotidiè in majus & melius proficiscentia, nec livor ullus attetere, nec malignitis dæmonis fascinare, nec hominum insidæ prohibere unquam potuerunt, quamdie omnipotentis Dei dextra populum suum, utpote tali dignum præsidio, texit atque custodiit. Sed cum ex nimia libertate in negligentiam ac defendiam prolapsi essemus; cum alter alteri invidere atque obtrectare cæpisset; cum inter nos quasi bella intestina gereremus, verbis, tanquam armis quibusdam hastisque, nos mutuò vulnerantes; cum Antistites adversus Antistites, popoli in populos collisi, jurgia ac tumultus agitarent; denique cum fraus & simulatio ad summum malitiæ culmen adolevisset: tum divina ultio, levi brachio ut solet, integro adhuc ecclesiæ statu, & fidelium turbis liberè convenientibus, sensim ac moderatè in nos cæpit animadvertere; orsâ primùm persecutionem ab iis qui militabant. Cum verò sensu omni destituti de placando Dei numine ne cogitaremus quidem; quin potius instar impiorum quorundam res humanas nullâ providentiâ gubernari rati, alia quotidiè criminia aliis adjiceremus: cum Pastores nostri spretâ religionis regulâ, mutuis inter se contentionibus decertarent, nihil aliud quam jurgia, minas, æmulationem, odia, ac mutuas inimicitias amplificare studentes; principatum quasi tyrannidem quandam contentissimè sibi vindicantes: tunc demùm juxta dictum Hieramiæ, obscuravit Dominis in ira sua filiam Sion, & dejecit de cælo gloriam Israel, — per Ecclesiarum scilicet subversionem, &c.*[2] This was the state of the

---

[2]   [Trans.: 'Truly we could never adequately describe the nature and extent of the glory and liberty, which the doctrine of true piety towards the God of Heaven (a doctrine first

Church just before the subversion of the Churches in the beginning of *Dioclesian's*

---

proclaimed to all by Christ) secured for itself everywhere, both among the Greeks and barbarians, prior to the persecution which began within my own recollection. But we might point to the kindness of the emperors towards our brethren: they even entrusted to them the government of whole provinces and freed them from all fear of having to sacrifice to idols, such was the remarkable good will displayed by them towards our religion. (And a little after:) But further, who could ever give a detailed account of the innumerable hosts of men who daily found refuge in belief in Christ, of the numbers of Churches in every city, or the distinguished congregations that gathered in the sacred edifices. The result of this enthusiasm was that, becoming dissatisfied with the ancient buildings, in every city they reared Churches on a grandiose scale from the very foundations. In the process of time these buildings were enlarged and every day grew to something greater and better: nor could they be harmed by envy, nor bewitched by the spite of the Evil One, nor hindered in their progress by the unbelief of men, so long as the right arm of God Almighty shielded and guarded His people, and while His people merited such protection. But in time our absolute freedom led us into negligence and sloth: men began to envy and abuse their neighbours. We used to wage war against ourselves: a kind of civil war, wounding each other, blow for blow, with words instead of arms and spears; priests against priests, peoples against peoples, and feuds and tumults were stirred up. In short, deceit and hypocrisy reached the highest pitch of wickedness. Then at last divine vengeance gradually and gently began to stir against us, but lightly at first and the status of the Church remained unimpaired. The masses of the faithful were still at liberty to assemble, for the persecution first began against the militant party. But in our folly, we did not give a thought to appeasing the Majesty of God. Rather, imagining like infidels that providence did not control the affairs of men, day by day we added fresh sin to that of the past. Our pastors spurned the ordinances of religion, strove and quarreled with each other. They set themselves to nothing else than to widen the disputes, to increase their threats and to intensify the rivalry, passions and enmity they bore to one another. With the utmost vehemence they claimed for themselves the Primacy, as though it were by a kind of tyrany. Then it was that in the words of Jeremiah, "The Lord covered the daughter of Zion with a cloud in his anger and cast down from heaven unto earth the beauty of Israel," that is by the overthrow of the Churches.']

persecution: and to this state of the Church agrees the first of the seven Epistles to the Angel of the seven Churches, that to the Church in *Ephesus. I have something against thee*, saith *Christ* to the Angel of that Church, *because thou hast left thy first love. Remember therefore from whence thou art fallen, and repent, and do the first works; or else I will come unto thee quickly, and will remove thy candlestick out of its place, except thou repent: But this thou hast, that thou hatest the deeds of the* Nicolaitans,[3] *which I also Hate.*[4] The *Nicolaitans* are the *Continentes* above described, who placed religion in abstinence from marriage, abandoning their wives if they had any. They are here called *Nicolaitans*, from *Nicholas* one of the seven deacons of the primitive Church of *Jerusalem*; who having a beautiful wife, and being taxed with uxoriousness, abandoned her, and permitted her to marry whom she pleased, saying that we must disuse the flesh; and thenceforward lived a single life in continency, as his children also. The *Continentes* afterwards embraced the doctrine of *Æons** and Ghosts male and female, and were avoided by the Churches till the fourth century; and the Church of *Ephesus* is here commended for hating their deeds.

The persecution of *Dioclesian* began in the year of *Christ* 302, and lasted ten years in the *Eastern* Empire and two years in the *Western*. To this state of the Church the second Epistle, to the Church of *Smyrna*, agrees. *I know*, saith *Christ, thy works, and tribulation, and poverty, but thou art rich; and I know the blasphemy of them, which say they are* Jews *and are not, but are the synagogue of Satan. Fear none of those things which thou shalt suffer: Behold, the Devil shall cast some of you into prison, that ye may be tried; and ye shall have tribulation ten days. Be thou faithful*

---

3   [The Nicolaitans have an uncertain history, and may not have had any real existence as a sect. They are mentioned in the New Testament only in Revelation; although a few early writers refer to the existence of such a sect.]

4   Apoc. ii. 4, &c.

unto death, and I will give thee a crown of life.[5] The tribulation of ten days can agree to no other persecution than that of *Dioclesian*, it being the only persecution which lasted ten years. By *the blasphemy of them which say they are* Jews *and are not, but are the synagogue of Satan*, I understand the Idolatry of the *Nicolaitans*, who falsly said they were *Christians*.

The *Nicolaitans* are complained of also in the third Epistle, as men that *held the doctrine of* Balaam,* *who taught Balac to cast a stumbling-block before the children of* Israel, *to eat things sacrificed to Idols, and to commit* spiritual *fornication.*[6] For *Balaam* taught the *Moabites* and *Midianites* to tempt and invite *Israel* by their women to commit fornication, and to feast with them at the sacrifices of their Gods.[7] The Dragon therefore began now to come down among the inhabitants of the earth and sea.

The *Nicolaitans* are also complained of in the fourth Epistle, under the name of the *woman* Jezabel,* *who calleth herself a Prophetess, to teach and to seduce the servants of* Christ *to commit fornication, and to eat things sacrificed to Idols*. The woman therefore began now to fly into the wilderness.

The reign of *Constantine* the great from the time of his conquering *Licinius*, was monarchical over the whole *Roman* Empire. Then the Empire became divided between the sons of *Constantine*: and afterwards it was again united under *Constantius*, by his victory over *Magnentius*. To the affairs of the Church in these three successive periods of time, the third, fourth and fifth Epistles, that is, those to the Angels of the Churches in *Pergamus*, *Thyatira*, and *Sardis*, seem to relate. The next Emperor was *Julian* the Apostate.

In the sixth Epistle, to the Angel of the Church in *Philadelphia*, *Christ* saith:

---

[5]   Apoc. ii, 9-10.

[6]   Ver. 14.

[7]   Numb. xxv. 1-2, 18. & xxxi. 16.

Because in the reign of the heathen Emperor *Julian, thou hast kept the word of my patience, I also will keep thee from the hour of temptation, which* by the woman's flying into the wilderness, and the Dragon's making war with the remnant of her seed, and the killing of all who will not worship the Image of the Beast, *shall come upon all the world, to try them that dwell upon the* earth, and to distinguish them by sealing the one with the name of God in their foreheads, and marking the other with the mark of the Beast. *Him that overcometh, I will make a pillar in the Temple of my God; and he shall go no more out* of it. *And I will write upon him the name of my* God in his forehead.[8] So the *Christians* of the Church of *Philadelphia*, as many of them as overcome, are sealed with the seal of God, and placed in the second Temple, and go no more out. The same is to be understood of the Church in *Smyrna*, which also kept the word of God's patience, and was without fault. These two Churches, with their posterity, are therefore the *two Pillars*, and the *two Candlesticks*, and the *two Witnesses* in the second Temple.

After the reign of the Emperor *Julian*, and his successor *Jovian* who reigned but five months, the Empire became again divided between *Valentinian* and *Valens*. Then the Church Catholick, in the Epistle to the Angel of the Church of *Laodicea*, is reprehended as *lukewarm*, and threatened to be *spewed out of* Christ's *mouth*. She said, that she was *rich and increased with goods, and had need of nothing*, being in outward prosperity; *and knew not that she was inwardly wretched, and miserable, and poor, and blind, and naked*.[9] She is therefore *spewed out of* Christ's *mouth* at the opening of the seventh seal: and this puts an end to the times of the first Temple.

About one half of the *Roman* Empire turned *Christians* in the time of *Constantine* the great and his sons. After *Julian* had opened the Temples, and restored the worship of the heathens, the Emperors *Valentinian* and *Valens* tolerated

---

[8]   Apoc. iii. 10, 12.

[9]   Apoc. iii. 16-17.

it all their reign; and therefore the Prophecy of the sixth seal was not fully accomplished before the reign of their successor *Gratian*. It was the custom of the heathen Priests, in the beginning of the reign of every sovereign Emperor, to offer him the dignity and habit of the *Pontifex Maximus*.* This dignity all Emperors had hitherto accepted: but *Gratian* rejected it, threw down the idols, interdicted the sacrifices, and took away their revenues with the salaries and authority of the Priests. *Theodosius* the great followed his example; and heathenism afterwards recovered itself no more, but decreased so fast, that *Prudentius*,* about ten years after the death of *Theodosius*, called the heathens, *vix pauca ingenia & pars hominum rarissima.*[10] Whence the affairs of the sixth seal ended with the reign of *Valens*, or rather with the beginning of the reign of *Theodosius*, when he, like his predecessor *Gratian*, rejected the dignity of *Pontifex Maximus*. For the *Romans* were very much infested by the invasions of foreign nations in the reign of *Valentinian* and *Valens*: *Hoc tempore,* saith *Ammianus*,* *velut per universum orbem Romanum bellicum canentibus buccinis, excitæ gentes sævissimæ limites sibi proximos persultabant: Gallias Rhætiasque simil Alemanni populabantur: Sarmatæ Pannonias & Quadi: Picti, Saxones, & Scoti & Attacotti, Brittanos ærumnis vexavare continuis: Austoriani, Mauricæque alæ gentes Africam solito acriùs incursabant: Thracias diripiebant prædatorii globi Gotthorum: Persarum Rex manus Armeniis injectabat.*[11] And whilst

---

[10]   [Trans.: `merely a few intellectuals and a minute fraction of mankind'.]

[11]   [Trans.: `At this time (saith Ammianus) you might have thought that through the whole Roman world, trumpets were blowing for war, and that, excited by that sound, the fiercest tribes were leaping across the frontiers that lay nearest to them. The Gallic and Rhaetian provinces were simultaneously ravaged by the Alemanni, the provinces of Pannonia by the Sarmatae and Quadi; while the Britons were being constantly harassed and raided by the Picts, Saxons, Scots and Attacotti. The Austorians and the other Moorish tribes made deeper incursions than usual into the province of Africa. The Thracian provinces were plundered by marauding bands of Goths, and the King of Persia was always sending his forces against

the Emperors were busy in repelling these enemies, the *Hunns* and *Alans* and *Goths* came over the *Danube* in two bodies, overcame and slew *Valens*, and made so great a slaughter of the *Roman* army, that *Ammianus* saith: *Nec ulla Annalibus præter Cannensem ita internecionem res ligitur gesta.*[12] These wars were not fully stopt on all sides till the beginning of the reign of *Theodosius*, A.C. 379 & 380: but henceforward the Empire remained quiet from foreign armies, till his death. A.C. 395. So long the four winds were held: and so long there was silence in heaven. And the seventh seal was opened when this silence began.

Mr. *Mede* hath explained the Prophecy of the first six trumpets not much amiss: but if he had observed, that the Prophecy of pouring out the vials of wrath is synchronal to that of sounding the trumpets, his explanation would have been yet more complete.

The name of *Woes* is given to the wars to which the three last trumpets sound, to distinguish them from the wars of the four first. The sacrifices on the first four days of the feast of Tabernacles, at which the first four trumpets sound, and the first four vials of wrath are poured out, are slaughters in four great wars; and these wars are represented by four winds from the four corners of the earth. The first was an east wind, the second a west wind, the third a south wind, and the fourth a north wind, with respect to the city of *Rome*, the metropolis of the old *Roman* Empire. These four plagues fell upon the *third part of the Earth, Sea, Rivers, Sun, Moon and Stars*; that is, upon the Earth, Sea, Rivers, Sun, Moon and Stars of the third part of the whole scene of these Prophecies of *Daniel* and *John*.

The plague of the eastern wind at the sounding of the first trumpet,[13] was to

---

the Armenians.']

[12] [Trans.: `No action in history, with the exception of Cannae,* was ever carried to a bloodier finish than this.']

[13] Apoc. viii. 7, &c.

fall upon the *Earth*, that is, upon the nations of the *Greek* Empire. Accordingly, after the death of *Theodosius* the great, the *Goths, Sarmatians, Hunns, Isaurians*, and *Austorian Moors* invaded and miserably wasted *Greece, Thrace, Asia minor, Armenia, Syria, Egypt, Lybia*, and *Illyricum*, for ten or twelve years together.

The plague of the western wind at the founding of the second trumpet, was to fall upon the Sea, or Western Empire, by means of *a great mountain burning with fire* cast into it, and *turning it to blood*. Accordingly in the year 407, that Empire began to be invaded by the *Visigoths, Vandals, Alans, Sueves, Burgundians, Ostrogoths, Heruli, Quadi, Gepides*; and by these wars it was broken into ten kingdoms, and miserably wasted: and *Rome* itself, the burning mountain, was besieged and taken by the *Ostrogoths*, in the beginning of these miseries.

The plague of the southern wind at the sounding of the third trumpet, was to cause *a great star, burning as it were a lamp, to fall from heaven upon the rivers and fountains of waters*, the *Western* Empire now divided into many kingdoms, and to turn them to *wormwood* and *blood*, and make them *bitter*. Accordingly *Genseric*, the King of the *Vandals* and *Alans* in Spain, A.C. 427, enter'd *Africa* with an army of eighty thousand men; where he invaded the *Moors*, and made war upon the *Romans*, both there and on the sea-coasts of *Europe*, for fifty years together, almost without intermission, taking *Hippo* A.C. 431, and *Carthage* the capital of *Africa* A.C. 439. In A.C. 455, with a numerous fleet and an army of three hundred thousand *Vandals* and *Moors*, he invaded *Italy*, took and plundered *Rome, Naples, Capua*, and many other cities; carrying thence their wealth with the flower of the people into *Africa*: and the next year, A.C. 456, he rent all *Africa* from the Empire, totally expelling the *Romans*. Then the *Vandals* invaded and took the Islands of *the Mediterranean, Sicily, Sardinia, Corsica, Ebusus, Majorca, Minorca*, &c and *Ricimer* besieged the Emperor *Anthemius* in Rome, took the city, and gave his soldiers the plunder, A.C. 472. The *Visigoths* about the same time drove the *Romans* out of *Spain*: and now the *Western*

Emperor, *the great star which fell from heaven, burning as it were a lamp*, having by all these wars gradually lost almost all his dominions, was invaded, and conquered in one year by *Odoacer* King of the *Heruli* A.C. 476. After this the *Moors* revolted A.C. 477, and weakened the *Vandals* by several wars, and took *Mauritania* from them. These wars continued till the *Vandals* were conquered by *Belisarius*, A.C. 534. and by all these wars *Africa* was almost depopulated, according to *Procopius*,* who reckons that above five millions of men perished in them. When the *Vandals* first invaded *Africa*, that country was very populous, consisting of about 700 bishopricks, more than were in all *France*, *Spain* and *Italy* together: but by the wars between the *Vandals*, *Romans* and *Moors*, it was depopulated to that degree, that *Procopius* tells us, it was next to a miracle for a traveller to see a man.

In pouring out the third vial it is said: *Thou art righteous, O Lord, — because thou hast judged thus: for they have shed the blood of thy Saints and Prophets, and thou hast given them blood to drink, for they are worthy.*[14] How they shed the blood of Saints, may be understood by the following Edict of the Emperor *Honorius*, procured by four bishops sent to him by a Council of *African* Bishops, who met at *Carthage* 14 June, A.C. 410.

Impp. Honor. & Theod. AA. Heracliano Com. Afric. Oraculo penitus remote, quo ad ritus suos hæreticæ superstitionis obrepserant, sciant omnes sanctæ legis imimici, plectentdos se poena & proscriptionis & sanguinis, si ultra convenire per publicum, execrandâ sceleris sui temeritate temptaverint. Dat. viii. Kal. Sept. Varano V.C. Cons. A.C. 410.[15]

---

[14]   Apoc. xvi 5-6.

[15]   [Trans.: `The Emperors Honorius and Theodosius to Heraclianus Governor of Africa. Now that the shrine - whither they stole to practise their rites of heretical superstition - has been utterly demolished, let all enemies of the Holy Law take notice that they will henceforth

Which Edict was five years after fortified by the following.

Impp. Honor. & Theod. AA. Heracliano Com. Afric. Sciant cuncti qui ad ritus suos hæresis superstitionibus obrepserant sacrosanctæ legis inimici, plectandos se poenâ & proscriptionis & sanguinis, si ultra convenire per publicum exercendi sceleris sui temeritate temptaverint: ne quâ vera divinaque reverentia contagione temeretur. Dat. viii. Kal. Sept. Honorio x. & Theod. vi. AA. Coss. A.C. 415[16].

These Edicts being directed to the governor of Africa, extended only to the Africans. Before these there were many severe ones against the *Donatists*,* but they did not extend to blood. These two were the first which made their meetings, and the meetings of all dissenters, capital: for by *hereticks* in these Edicts are meant all dissenters, as is manifest by the following against *Euresius* a *Luciferan** Bishop.

Impp. Arcad. & Honor. AA. Aureliano Proc. Africæ. Hæreticorum vocabulo continentur, & latis adversus eos sanctionibus debent succumbere, qui vel levi argumento à judicio Cathlicæ religionis & tramite detecti fuerint deviare: ideoque experientia tua Euresium hæreticum esse congnoscat. Dat. iii. Non. Sept. Constantinop. Olymbrio & Probino Coss. A.C. 395.[17]

---

suffer the punishment of both outlawry and of blood if, in their accursed and criminal insolence, they attempt to assemble in public. Given on the 25th August in the Consulship of Veranus. A.C. 410.']

[16]   [Trans.: `The Emperors Honorius and Theodosius to Heraclianus Governor of Africa. Let all enemies of the Holy Law, who in heretical superstition have crept to the performance of their rites, take notice that they must suffer the punishment both of outlawry and of blood, if henceforth they impudently assemble in public to practise this abomination. This we command lest anywhere reverence for the true God should be defiled by contagion with them. Given on the 25th August, in the Consulship of Honorius and Theodosius, A.C. 415.']

[17]   [Trans.: `The Emperors Arcadius and Honorius to Aurelianus, Procurator of Africa. All who

The *Greek* Emperor *Zeno* adopted *Theodoric* King of the *Ostrogoths* to be his son, made him master of the horse and *Patricius*, and Consul of *Constantinople*; and recommending to him the Roman people and Senate, gave him the *Western* Empire, and sent him into *Italy* against *Odoacer* King of the *Heruli*. *Theodoric* thereupon led his nation into *Italy*, conquered *Odoacer*, and reigned over *Italy, Sicily, Rhœtia, Noricum, Dalmatia, Liburnia, Istria* and part of *Suevia, Pannonia* and *Gallia*. Whence *Ennodius** said, in a *Panegyric* to *Theoderic*: *Ad limitem suum regna remeâsse.*[18] *Theoderic* reigned with great prudence, moderation and felicity; treated the *Romans* with singular benevolence, governed them by their own laws, and restored their government under their Senate and Consuls, he himself supplying the place of Emperor, without assuming the title. *Ita sibi parentibus præfuit, saith Procopius,* ut vere Imperitori conveniens decus nullum ipsi abesset: Justitiæ magnus ei cultus, legumque diligens custodia: terras à barbaris servavit intactas,*[19] &c. Whence I do not reckon the reign of this King, amongst the plagues of the four winds.

The plague of the northern wind, at the sounding of the fourth trumpet, was to cause *the Sun, Moon, and Stars*, that is the King, kingdom and Princes of the *Western* Empire, *to be darkened*, and to continue some time in darkness. Accordingly *Belisarius*, having conquered the *Vandals*, invaded *Italy* A.C. 535, and made war upon the *Ostrogoths* in *Dalmatia, Liburnia, Venetia, Lombardy, Tuscany*, and other regions northward from *Rome*, twenty years together. In this war many cities were

---

have even on trivial evidence been found to dissent from the judgment of the Catholic Church and to deviate from its course, are within the meaning of the term "heretic" and must come under the laws enacted against them.']

[18] [Trans.: `He restored the Roman Empire to its ancient frontiers.']

[19] [Trans.: `So far did he excel his predecessors (saith Procopius*), that in truth he lacked no glory fitting of an emperor. He had a great love of justice and was constant in the protection he afforded to the law, and preserved his territory intact from the neighbouring barbarians.']

taken and retaken. In retaking *Millain* from the *Romans*, the *Ostrogoths* slew all the males young and old, amounting, as *Procopius* reckons, to three hundred thousand, and sent the women captives to their allies the *Burgundians*. *Rome* itself was taken and retaken several times, and thereby the people were thinned; the old government by a Senate ceased, the nobles were ruined, and all the glory of the city was extinguish'd: and A.C. 552, after a war of seventeen years, the kingdom of the *Ostrogoths* fell; yet the remainder of the *Ostrogoths*, and an army of *Germans* called in to their assistance, continued the war three or fours years longer. Then ensued the war of the *Heruli*, who, as *Anastasius** tells us, *perimebant cunctam Italiam*, slew all *Italy*. This was followed by the war of the *Lombards*, the fiercest of all the *Barbarians*, which began A.C. 568, and lasted for thirty eight years together; *factâ tali clade, saith Anastasius, qualem à sæcolo nullis meminit;*[20] ending at last in the Papacy of *Sabinian*, A.C. 605, by a peace then made with the *Lombards*. Three years before this war ended, *Gregory* the great, then Bishop of *Rome*, thus speaks of it: *Qualiter enim & quotidianis gladiis & quantis Longobardorum incursionibus, ecce jam per triginta quinque annorum longitudinem premimur, nullis explere vocibus suggestionis valemus:*[21] and in one of his Sermons to the people, he thus expresses the great consumption of the *Romans* by these wars: *Ex illa plebe innumerabili quanti remanseritis aspicitis, & tamen adhuc quotidiè flagella urgent, repentini casus opprimunt, novæ res & improvisæ clades affligunt.*[22] In another Sermon he thus describes the desolations: *Destructæ urbes, eversa sunt castra, depopulati agri, in*

---

[20] [Trans.: `with slaughter (saith Anastasius) such as cannot be recalled in the past.']

[21] [Trans.: `In no words of description can we fully tell how for a period now of 35 years, we have been harassed with daily fighting and numerous incursions of the Longobards.']

[22] [Trans.: `Your own eyes behold how few of you remain out of a once countless people, and even yet, day after day, one scourge and another harries us, sudden misfortunes overwhelm us, new and unforseen disasters crush us.']

solitudinem terra redacta est. Nullus in agris incola, penè nullus in urbibus habitator remansit. Et tamen ipsæ parvæ generis humani reliquiæ adhuc quotidiè & sine cessatione feriuntur, & finem non habent flagella coelistis justutiæ. Ipsa autem quæ aliquando mundi Domina esse videbantur, qualis remansit Roma conspicimus innumeris doloribus multipliciter attrita, desolatione civium, impressione hostium, frequentiâ ruinarum. — Ecce jam de illa omnes hujus sæculi potentes ablati sunt. — Ecces populi defecerunt. — Ubi enim Senatius? Ubi jam populus? Contabuerunt ossa, consumptæ sunt carnes. Omnis enim sæcularium dignitatum ordo extinctus est. & tamen ipsos nos paucos qui remansimus, adhuc quotidiè gladii, adhuc quotidiè innumeræ tribulationes premunt. — Vacua jam ardet Roma. Quid autem ista de hominibus dicimus? Cum ruinis crebrescentibus ipsa quoque destrui ædificia videmus. Postquam defecerunt homines etiam parietes cadunt. Jam ecce desolata, ecce contrita, ecce gemitibus oppressa est, &c.[23] All this was spoken by *Gregory* to the people of *Rome*, who were witnesses of the truth of it. Thus by the plagues of the four winds, the Empire of the *Greeks* was shaken, and the Empire of the *Latins* fell;

---

[23]   [Trans.: 'Our cities are destroyed: our armaments are overthrown, our fields laid waste, our land made a wilderness. None now live in the country, and there is hardly a single person left in the cities. And yet these small remnants of the human race, endlessly, day by day, are still under the lash: the scourging of divine wrath knows no end. Rome that was once thought the mistress of the world, our eyes see all that is left of it, wasted in countless ways by countless sorrows, by the desolations of its citizens, the violence of the foe, and the recurrence of disasters. — Thus, all the powerful men of this generation have been swept away from it. See, the peoples are in revolt. Where is the Senate? Where are the people? Their bones have wasted away and their flesh has smouldered. For the whole order of lay dignitaries is extinct. And yet we few who survive, day by day we are threatened by the sword and by countless tribulations. — A tenantless Rome is in agony. But why speak such words of men only, when we see the very houses tumbling down as disasters multiply? Even the walls fall when men forsake them: Rome is desolate, broken, overwhelmed with sorrow, &c.']

and *Rome* remained nothing more than the capital of a poor dukedom, subordinate to *Ravenna*, the seat of the Exarchs.[24]

The fifth trumpet sounded to the wars, which the *King of the South*, as he is called by *Daniel*, made *in the time of the end*, in *pushing at the King who did according to his will*. This plague began with the *opening of the bottomless pit*, which denotes the letting out of a false religion: *the smoke which came out of the pit*, signifying the multitude which embraced that religion; and the *locusts which came out of the smoke*, the armies which came out of the multitude. This pit was opened, to let out smoke and locusts into the regions of the four monarchies, or some of them. *The King of these locusts* was the *Angel of the bottomless pit*, being chief governor as well as in religious as in civil affairs, such as was the *Caliph* of the *Saracens*. Swarms of locusts often arise in *Arabia fælix*,* and from thence infest the neigbouring nations: and so are a very fit type of the numerous armies of *Arabians* invading the *Romans*. They began to invade them A.C. 634, and to reign at *Damascus* A.C. 637. They built *Bagdad* A.C. 766, and reigned over *Persia, Syria, Arabia, Egypt, Africa* and *Spain*. They afterwards lost *Africa* to *Mahades*, A.C. 910; *Media, Hircania, Chorasan*, and all *Persia*, to the *Dailamites*, between the years 927 and 935; *Mesopotamia* and *Miafarekin* to *Nasiruddaulas*, A.C. 930; *Syria* and *Egypt* to *Achsjid*, A.C. 935. and now being in great distress, the *Caliph* of *Bagdad*, A.C. 936, surrendered all the rest of temporal power to *Mahomet*, the son of *Rajici*, King of *Wasit* in *Chaldea*, and made him Emperor of Emperors. But *Mahomet* within two years lost *Bagdad* to the *Turks*; and thenceforward *Bagdad* was sometimes in the hands of the *Turks*, and sometimes in the hands of the *Saracens*, till *Togrul-Beig*, called also *Togra, Dogrissa, Tangrolipix*, and *Sadoc*, conquered *Chorasan* and *Persia*; and A.C. 1055, added *Bagdad* to his Empire, making it the seat thereof. His successors *Olub-Arslan* and *Melechschah*, conquered the regions upon *Euphrates*;

---

[24] [The exarch was responsible to Constantinople.]

and these conquests, after the death of *Melechschah*, brake into the kingdoms of *Armenia*, *Mesopotamia*, *Syria*, and *Cappadocia*. The whole time that the *Caliphs* of the *Saracens* reigned with a temporal dominion at *Damascus* and *Bagdad* together, was 300 years, *viz.* from the year 637 to the year 936 inclusive. Now locusts live but five months; and therefore, for the decorum of the type, these locusts are said to *hurt men five months and five months*, as if they had lived about five months at *Damascus*, and again about five months at *Bagdad*; in all ten months, or 300 prophetic days, which are years.

The sixth trumpet sounded to the wars, which *Daniel's* King of the *North* made against the King above-mentioned, *who did according to his will*. In these wars the King of the *North*, according to *Daniel*, conquered the Empire of the *Greeks*, and also *Judea, Egypt, Lybia*, and *Ethiopia*: and by these conquests the Empire of the *Turks* was set up, as may be known by the extent thereof. These wars commenced A.C. 1258, when the four kingdoms of the *Turks* seated upon *Euphrates*, that of *Armenia* major seated at *Miyapharekin*, *Megarkin* or *Martyropolis*, that of *Mesopotamia* seated at *Mosul*, that of all *Syria* seated at *Aleppo*, and that of *Cappadocia* seated at *Iconium*, were invaded by the *Tartars* under *Hulacu*, and driven into the western parts of *Asia minor*, where they made war upon the *Greeks*, and began to erect the present Empire of the *Turks*. Upon the sounding of the sixth trumpet, *John heard a voice from the four horns of the golden Altar which is before God, saying to the sixth Angel which had the Trumpet, Loose the four Angels which are bound at the great river* Euphrates. *And the four Angels were loosed, which were prepared for an hour and a day, and a month and a year, for to slay the third part of men.*[25] By the four horns of the golden Altar, is signified the situation of the head cities of the said kingdoms, *Miyapharekin, Mosul, Aleppo*, and *Iconium*, which were in a quadrangle. They slew the third part of men, when they conquered the *Greek*

---

[25]   Apoc. ix. 13, &c.

Empire and took *Constantinople*, A.C. 1453. and they began to be prepared for this purpose, when *Olub-Arslan* began to conquer the nations upon the *Euphrates*, A.C. 1063. The interval is called an hour and a day, and a month and year, or 391 prophetic days, which are years. In the first thirty years, *Olub Arslan* and *Melechschah* conquered the nations upon *Euphrates*, and reigned over the whole. *Melechschah* died A.C. 1092, and was succeeded by a little child; and then this kingdom broke into the four kingdoms above mentioned.

ADVERTISEMENT

The last pages of these Observations having been differently drawn up by the Author in another copy of his Work; they are here inserted as they follow in that copy, after the 22nd line of the 261st page foregoing.

And none was found worthy to open the book till the Lamb of God appeared; the great High-Priest represented by a lamb slain at the foot of the Altar in the morning-sacrifice. *And he came, and took the book out of the hand of him that sat upon the throne.* For the High-Priest, in the feast of the seventh month, went into the most holy place, and took the book of the law out of the right side of the Ark, to read it to the people: and in order to read it well, he studied it seven days, that is, upon the fourth, fifth, sixth, seventh, eight, ninth and tenth days, being attended by some of the priests to hear him perform. These seven days are alluded to, by the Lamb's opening of the seven seals successively.

Upon the tenth day of the month, a young bullock was offered for a sin-offering for the High-Priest, and a goat for a sin-offering for the people: and lots were cast upon two goats to determine which of them should be God's lot for the sin-offering; and the other goat was called *Azazel,** the scape-goat. The High-Priest in his linen garments, took a censer* full of burning coals of fire from the Altar, his hand being full of sweet incense beaten small; and went into the most holy place within the veil, and put the incense upon the fire, and sprinkled the blood of the bullock with his finger upon the mercy-seat and before the mercy-seat seven times: and then he killed the goat which fell to God's lot, for a sin-offering for the people, and brought his blood within the veil, and sprinkled it also seven times upon the mercy-seat and before the mercy-seat. Then he went out to the Altar, and sprinkled it also seven times with the blood of the bullock, and as often with the blood of the goat. *After this he laid both his hands upon the head of the live goat; and confessed over him all the iniquities of the children of* Israel, *and all their transgressions in all their sins, putting them upon the head of the goat; and sent him away into the wilderness by the hands of a fit man: and the goat bore upon him all their iniquities into a land not inhabited,* Levit. chap. iv. & chap. xvi. While the High-Priest was doing these things in the most holy place and at the Altar, the people continued at their devotion quietly and in silence. Then the High-Priest went into the holy place, put off his linen garments, and put on other garments; then came out, and sent the bullock and the goat of the sin-offering to be burnt within the camp, with a fire taken in a censer from the Altar: and as the people returned home from the Temple, they said to one another, *God seal you to a good new year.*

In allusion to all this, *when he had opened the seventh seal, there was silence in heaven about the space of half an hour. And an Angel stood at the Altar having a golden Censer, and there was given unto him much incense, that he should offer it with the prayers of all Saints, upon the golden Altar which was before the throne. And the smoke of the incense with the prayers of the Saints ascended up before God out of the Angel's hand. And the Angel took the Censer, and filled it with fire of the Altar, and cast it to the earth,* suppose without the camp, for sacrificing the goat which fell to God's lot. For the High-Priest being Christ himself, the bullock is omitted. At this sacrifice *there were voices and thundrings,* of the musick of the Temple, *and lightnings* of the sacred fire, *and an earthquake*: and synchronal to these things was the sealing of *the 144000 out of all the twelve tribes of the children of Israel with the seal of God in their foreheads,* while the rest of the twelve tribes received the mark of the Beast, and the Woman fled from the Temple into the wilderness to her place upon this Beast. For this sealing and marking was represented by casting lots upon the two goats, sacrificing God's lot on mount *Sion,* and sending the scape-goat into the wilderness loaden with the sins of the people.

Upon the fifteenth day of the month, and the six following days, there were very great sacrifices. And in allusion to the sounding of trumpets, and singing with thundring voices, and pouring out drink-offerings at those sacrifices, *seven trumpets are sounded,* and *seven thunders utter their voices,* and *seven vials of wrath are poured out.* Wherefore the sounding of the *seven trumpets,* the voices of the *seven thunders,* and the pouring out of the *seven vials of wrath,* are synchronal, and relate to one and the same division of the time of the seventh seal following the silence, into seven successive parts. The seven days of this feast were called the feast of the Tabernacles; and during these seven days the children of *Israel* dwelt in booths, and rejoiced with palm-branches in their hands. To this alludes *the mulititude with palms in their hands,* which appeared after the sealing of the 144000, and *came out of the great tribulation* with triumph at the battle of the great day, to which the seventh trumpet sounds. The visions therefore of the 144000, and of the palm-bearing multitude, extend to the sounding of the seventh trumpet, and therefore are synchronal to the times of the seventh seal.

When the 144000 *are sealed out of all the twelve tribes of* Israel, and the rest receive *the mark of the Beast,* and thereby the first temple is destroyed, *John* is bidden to *measure the temple and the altar,* that is, their courts, *and them that worship therein,* that is, the 144000 standing on mount *Sion* and on the sea of glass: *but the court that is without the temple,* that is, the peoples court, to *leave out and measure it not, because it is given to the* Gentiles, those who receive the mark of the

Beast; *and the holy city they shall tread under foot forty and two months*, that is, all the time that the Beast acts under the woman *Babylon*: and *the two witnesses prophesy* 1260 *days*, that is, all the same time, *clothed in sackcloth. These have power*, like *Elijah, to shut heaven that it rain not*, at the sounding of the first trumpet; and like *Moses, to turn the waters into blood* at the sounding of the second; *and to smite the earth with all plagues*, those of the trumpets, as often as they will. These prophesy at the building of the second temple, like *Haggai* and *Zechary*. These are *the two Olive-trees*, or Churches, which *supplied the lamps with oil, Zech.* iv. These are *the two candlesticks*, or Churches, *standing before the God of the earth*. Five of the seven Churches of *Asia*, those in prosperity, are found fault with, and exhorted to repent, and threatned to be *removed out of their places*, or *spewed out of* Christ's *mouth*, or *punished with the sword of* Christ's *mouth*, except *they repent*: the other two, the Churches of *Smyrna* and *Philadelphia*, which were under persecution, remain in a state of persecution, to illuminate the second temple. When the primitive Church catholick, represented by the *woman in heaven*, apostatized, and became divided into two corrupt Churches, represented by the *whore* of Babylon and the *two-horned Beast*, the 144000 *who were sealed out of all the twelve tribes*, became the *two Witnesses*, in opposition to those two false Churches: and the name of *two Witnesses* once imposed, remains to the true Church of God in all times and places to the end of the Prophecy.

In the interpretation of this prophecy, *the woman in heaven clothed with the sun*, before she flies into the wilderness, represents the primitive Church catholick, illuminated with the *seven lamps* in the *seven golden candlesticks*, which are the *seven Churches of Asia*. The Dragon signifies the same Empire with *Daniel's* He-goat in the reign of the last horn, that is, the whole *Roman* Empire, until it became divided into the *Greek* and *Latin* Empires; and all the time of that division it signifies the *Greek* Empire alone: and the Beast is *Daniel's* fourth Beast, that is, the Empire of the *Latins*. Before the division of the *Roman* Empire into the *Greek* and *Latin* Empires, the Beast is included in the body of the Dragon; and from the time of that division, the Beast is the *Latin* Empire only. Hence the Dragon and the Beast have the same heads and horns; but the heads are crowned upon the Dragon, and the horns upon the Beast. The horns are ten kingdoms, into which the Beast becomes divided presently after his separation from the Dragon, as hath been described above. The heads are seven successive dynasties, or parts, into which the *Roman* Empire becomes divided by the opening of the seven seals. Before the woman fled into the wilderness, *she being with child* of a Christian Empire, *cried travelling, viz.* in the ten years persecution of *Dioclesian*, and pained to be delivered: and the Dragon, the heathen *Roman* Empire, *stood before her, to devour her child as soon as it was born. And she brought forth a man child, who at length was to rule all nations with a rod of iron. And her child was caught up unto God, and to his throne* in the Temple, by the victory of *Constantine* the great over *Maxentius: and the woman fled from the Temple into the wilderness* of *Arabia* to *Babylon, where she hath a place* of riches and honour and dominion, upon the back of the Beast, *prepared of God, that they should feed her there 1260 days. And there was war in heaven*, between the heathens under *Maximinus* and the new Christian Empire; *and the great Dragon was cast out, that old serpent, which deceiveth the whole world*, the spirit of heathen idolatry; *he was cast out* of the throne *into the earth. And they overcame him by the blood of the Lamb, and by the word of their testimony; and they loved not their lives unto the death.*

And when the Dragon saw that he was cast unto the earth, he persecuted the woman which brought forth the man child, stirring up a new persecution against her in the reign of *Licinius. And to the woman*, by the building of *Constantinople* and equalling it to *Rome, were given two wings of a great eagle, that she might flee into the wilderness into her place* upon the back of her Beast, *where she is nourished for a time, and times, and half a time, from the face of the serpent. And the serpent,* upon the death of *Constantine* the great, *cast out of his mouth water as a flood, viz.* the *Western* Empire under *Constantine junior* and *Constans, after the woman: that he might cause her to be carried away by the flood. And the earth,* the nations of *Asia* now under *Constantinople, helped the woman;* and by conquering the *Western* Empire, now under *Magnentius, swallowed up the flood which the Dragon cast out of his mouth. And the Dragon was wroth with the woman, and went to make war with the remnant of her seed, which keep the commandments of God, and have the testimony of* Jesus Christ, *which in that war were sealed out of all the twelve tribes of Israel,* and remained upon mount *Sion* with the Lamb, being in number 144000, and having their father's name written in their foreheads.

When the earth had swallowed up the flood, and the Dragon was gone to make war with the remnant of the woman's seed, *John stood upon the sand of the sea, and saw a Beast rise out of the sea, having seven heads and ten horns. And the Beast was like unto a Leopard, and his feet were as the feet of a Bear, and his mouth as the mouth of a Lion. John* here names *Daniel's* four Beasts in order, putting his Beast in the room of *Daniel's* fourth Beast to shew that they are the same. *And the Dragon gave this Beast his power and his seat and great authority,* by relinquishing the *Western* Empire to him. *And one of his heads,* the sixth, was *as it were wounded to death, viz.* by the sword of the earth, which swallowed up the waters cast out of the mouth of the Dragon; *and his deadly wound was healed,* by a new division of the Empire between *Valentinian* and *Valens, An.* 364. *John* saw the Beast rise out of the sea, at the division thereof between between *Gratian* and *Theodosius, An.* 379. The Dragon gave the Beast his power, and his seat and and great authority, at the death of *Theodosius,* when *Theodosius* gave the *Western* Empire to his son *Honorius.* After which the two Empires were no more united: but the *Western* Empire became presently divided into ten kingdoms, as above; and these kingdoms at length united in religion under the woman, and reign with her *forty and two months.*

And I beheld, saith *John, another Beast coming up out of the earth.* When the woman fled from the Dragon into the kingdom of the Beast, and became his Church, this other Beast rose up out of the earth, to represent the Church of the Dragon. *For he had two horns like the Lamb,* such as were the bishopricks of *Alexandria* and *Antioch: and he spake as the Dragon* in matters of religion: and *he causeth the earth,* or nations of the Dragon's kingdom, *to worship the first Beast, whose deadly wound was healed,* that is, to be of his religion. *And he doth great wonders, so that he maketh fire come down from heaven on the earth in the sight of men*; that is, he excommunicateth those who differ from him in point of religion: for in pronouncing their excommunications, they used to swing down a lighted torch from above. *And he said to them that dwell on the earth, that they should make an image to the Beast, which had the wound by a sword, and did live*; that is, that they should call a Council of men of the religion of this Beast. *And he had power to give life unto the image of the Beast, that the image of the Beast should both speak, and cause that as many as would not worship the image of the Beast should be killed,* viz. mystically, by dissolving their Churches. *And he causeth all both small and great rich and poor, free and bond, to receive a mark in their right hand or in their foreheads, and that no man might buy or sell, save he that had the mark, or the name of the Beast, or the number of his name*; that is the mark ✠, or the name LATEINOS,[1] or the number thereof, 666.[2] All others were excommunicated.

When the seven Angels had poured out the seven vials of wrath, and *John* had described them all in the present time, he is called up from the time of the seventh vial to the time of the sixth seal, to take a view of the woman and her Beast,

---

[1]   [LATEINOS originally given in Greek characters.]

[2]   [666 originally provided in both Arabic and Greek numerals.]

who were to reign in the times of the seventh seal. In respect of the latter part of time of the sixth seal, then considered as present, the Angel tells *John: The Beast that thou sawest, was and is not, and shall ascend out of the abyss, and go into perdition*; that is, he was in the reign of *Constans* and *Magnentius*, and re-united the *Western* Empire to the *Eastern*. He is not during the re-union, and he shall ascend out of the abyss or sea at a following division of the Empire. The Angel tells him further: *Here is the mind which hath wisdom: the seven heads are seven mountains, on which the woman sitteth*; *Rome* being built upon seven hills, and thence called the seven-hilled city. *Also there are seven Kings: five are fallen, and one is, and the other is not yet come; and when he cometh, he must continue a short space: and the Beast that was and is not, even he is the eighth and is of the seven, and goeth into perdition*. Five are fallen, the times of the five first seals being past; and one is, the time of the sixth seal being considered as present; and another is not yet come, when he cometh, which will be at the opening of the seventh seal, he must continue a short space: and the Beast that was and is not, even he is the eighth, by means of the division of the *Roman* Empire into two collateral Empires; and is of the seven, being one half of the seventh, and shall go into perdition. The words, *five are fallen, and one is, and the other is not yet come*, are usually referred by interpreters to the time of *John* the Apostle, when the Prophecy was given: but it is to be considered, that in this Prophecy many things are spoken of as present, which were not present when the Prophecy was given, but which would be present with respect to some future time, considered as present in the visions. Thus where it is said upon pouring out the seventh vial of wrath, that great Babylon *came in remembrance before God, to give unto her the cup of the wine of the fierceness of his wrath*; this relates not to the time of *John* the Apostle, but to the time of pouring out the seventh vial of wrath. So where it is said, *Babylon is fallen, is fallen; and thrust in thy sickle and reap, for the time is come for thee to reap; and the time of the dead is come, that they should be judged*; and again, *I saw the dead small and great stand before God*: these sayings relate not to the days of *John* the Apostle, but to the latter times considered as present in the visions. In like manner the words, *five are fallen, and one is, and the other is not yet come, and the Beast that was and is not, he is the eighth*, are not to be referred to the age of *John* the Apostle, but relate to the time when the Beast was to be wounded to death with a sword, and shew that this wound was to be given him in his sixth head: and without this reference we are not told in what head the Beast was wounded. *And the ten horns which thou sawest, are ten Kings, which have received no kingdom as yet, but receive power as Kings one hour with the Beast. These have one mind*, being all of the whore's religion, *and shall give their power and strength unto the Beast. These shall make war with the Lamb*, at the sounding of the seventh trumpet; *and the Lamb shall overcome them: for he is Lord of Lords and King of Kings; and they that are with him are called and chosen and faithful. And he saith unto me, the waters which thou sawest where the whore sitteth, are peoples and multitudes and nations and tongues*, composing her Beast. *And the ten horns which thou sawest upon the Beast, these shall hate the whore, and shall make her desolate and naked, and shall eat her flesh, and burn her with fire*, at the end of the 1260 *days. For God hath put in their hearts to fulfil his will, and to agree and give their kingdom unto the Beast, until the words of God shall be fulfilled. And the woman which thou sawest, is that great city which reigneth over the Kings of the earth*, or the great city of the *Latins*, which reigneth over the ten kings till the end of those days.

GLOSSARY, ABBREVIATIONS AND CALENDAR
CONVENTIONS

N.B. Dates given are AD unless stated BC.

Aeons	*Semi-divine spiritual intermediaries emanating from God; a concept present in the thought of Valentinian* Gnostics.*
Ammianus	*Marcellanus (c. 330 d. 395), historian of Roman history.*
Anastasium (or Anastasius)	*Anastasius Bibliothecarius (9th cent.), Roman scholar and librarian to the pope.*
Anno Urbis	*from the founding of the City of Rome (see also below in Calendar Conventions section).*
Antiochus Epiphanes	*(d. 163 BC), King of Syria from 175 BC.*
Antony	*of Eygpt (251?-356), a hermit, closely associated with Athanasius in the Arian* controversy.*
Apollinaris	*Bishop of Laodicea (310-c. 390).*
Arabia fælix	*this is a variant spelling of Arabia felix, which is the archaic term for Arabia.*
Arethas	*6th century Archbishop of Caesaria in Cappadocia, he wrote a commentary on the Apocalypse.*
Arianism	*Arians maintained that the Son of God was not eternal but created by God from nothing; therefore the Son was not God by nature, but a changeable creature dependent on the will of God.*
Athanasius	*Bishop of Alexandria (c. 296-373), considered by Newton as the great exponent of the Trinitarian corruption of the Church.*

Azazel	*In Old Testament theology (Leviticus 16:1-28) the demon (originally probably a goat-deity) dwelling in the desert; elsewhere (Enoch 6, 8, 10) he is the leader of the fallen angels and the author of all sin.*
Balaam	*A non-Israelite prophet mentioned in the Old Testament (Num. 22-24).*
Basil	*the Great (c. 330-79), monk, hermit and Bishop of Caesarea; one of the three Cappadocian Fathers.*
Baronius	*Cesare (1538-1607), Catholic ecclesiastical historian who wrote the <u>Annales Eclesiastici a Christo nato ad annum 1198</u> (12 vols, Rome, 1588-1607).*
Beda	*`The Venerable Bede' (c. 673-735) biblical scholar and `father of English history'.*
Book of Jasher	*an ancient book of national songs, quoted from in the Old Testament.*
Bucher	*Urbain Godefroi (fl. 1710s-1720s), German historian.*
Buxtorf	*John (1564-1629), German Hebraist.*
Caius	*or Gaius (early 3rd cent.) Roman presbyter.*
Camden	*William (1551-1623), English antiquary and pioneer of historical method.*
Cannae	*site of Hannibal's victory over the Romans, 216 BC.*
Cassiodorus	*Flavius Magnus Aurelius (c. 485-c. 580), Roman senator, author and monk.*
Cataphrygians (ie. from Phrygia)	*2nd century heretics, followers of Montanus, otherwise termed Montanists.*
Censer	*another name for thurible, the vessel for the ceremonial burning of incense.*
Cerinthus	*(fl. c. 100) Gnostic heretic.*
Chrysostom	*John (c. 347-407), theologian, hermit and Bishop of Constantinople.*
Clem. Alex.	*see next entry.*
Clemens Alexandrinus	*Clement of alexandrina (c. 150-c. 215), theologian.*
Commodus	*Roman Emperor (177-192).*

Constantius	*Emperor Constantius Chlorus (293-306).*
Cyprian	*Bishop of Carthage (d. 258).*
Cyprian	*(c. 300) `not the Bishop of Carthage, but a Greek' (Observations, p.236 [221]). There is no definite evidence this Cyprian, or indeed Justina, ever existed; they were perhaps only inventions of the fourth century.*
Cyril	*Patriarch of Alexandria (d. 444), wrote in defence of Christianity against Emperor Julian the Apostate.*
Dedication, feast of	*feast to commemorate the purification of the Temple and its altar after their defilement by Antiochus Epiphanes.*
Dioclesian	*Roman Emperor (284-305).*
Diodorus	*Siculus, 1st century BC Greek historian.*
Dionysius of Alexandria	*(d. c. 264) Bishop of Alexandria, theologian.*
Dionysius Corinthius	*(c. 170) Bishop of Corinth.*
Dionysius Exiguus	*a Scythian monk who lived in Rome c. 500-550.*
Donatists	*a schismatic body in the African Church.*
Encratites	*A title given to several groups of early Christians who carried their ascetic practice and doctrine to extremes and which were usually considered heretical.*
Ennodius	*Magnus felix (c. 473-521) Christian rhetorician and Bishop of Pavia.*
Ephræm Syrus	*(c. 306-73), Syrian biblical exegete and ecclesiastical writer.*
Epiphanius	*(c. 315-403) Bishop of Salamis.*
Eunapius	*(b. 347) Greek sophist and historian.*
Eusebius	*Bishop of Caesarea (c. 260-c. 340) `Father of Church History'.*
Forty Martyrs	*The Forty Martyrs of Sebaste, forty Christian soldiers martyred at Sebaste in Lesser Armenia during the Licinian persecution (c. 320).*
Fredigarius (Fredigario)	*Fredegar (d. 643), Frankish chronicler.*
Funccius	*Christianus (1659-1729), German theologian.*

Gerard Vossius	*Gerhard Jan Voss (1577-1649), Dutch humanist theologian.*
Gregory Bishop of Neocæsarea	*Gregory Thaumaturgus (c.213-c. 270), Greek Church Father.*
Gregory Nazianzen	*Gregory of Nazianzus (329-89), the `theologian', one of the Cappadocian Fathers; adopted the monastic life.*
Gregory Nyssen	*Gregory of Nyssa (c. 330-c. 395), Cappadocian Father*
Gregorii Turonensis	*Gregory of Tours (c. 540-94), Bishop of Tours and historian of the Franks.*
Grotius	*Hugo (1583-1645), Dutch jurist and theologian.*
Hegesippus	*(2nd cent.) Church historian.*
Herodotus	*(b. 484 BC) earliest Greek historian.*
Hilarion	*(c. 291-371), founder of the anchoritic (hermitic) life in Palestine.*
Hilary	*Bishop of Poitiers (c. 315-67), theologian and historian.*
Hippolytus	*(c. 170-c. 236) the most important 3rd century theologian of the Roman Church.*
Holpen	*helped.*
Holstenius	*Holste, Lucas (1596-1661), Vatican librarian.*
Idacius	*(or Idatius or Ithacius; fl. 2nd half of 5th century) Gallician historian, probably an ecclesiastic.*
Intercalary	*day, days or month inserted in the calendar to complete the solar year.*
Irenæus	*Bishop of Lyons (c. 130-c. 200), his chief work was his <u>Adversus omnes haereses</u>.*
Isidorus	*Bishop Isidore of Seville (c. 560-636), who wrote the <u>Historia de regibus Gothorum, Vandalorum et Suevorum</u>, the principal source of the history of these peoples.*
Ivo Cartonensis	*Bishop Ivo of Chatres (c. 1040-1115).*
Jerome	*(c. 342-420), successively hermit, priest and monk; noted for his biblical scholarship and as the continuator of the Chronicle of Eusebius.* *

Jezabel (also Jezebal)	*(d. c. 843 BC) in the Old Testament (Kings 1-2), the wife of King Ahab who, by her actions, provoked the internecine strife which was to enfeeble Israel for decades. She has traditionally been seen as the archetype of the wicked woman.*
Jornandes	*6th century Goth and historian.*
Josephus	*Flavius (c. 37-c. 100), Jewish (Palestinian) historian.*
Julian Period	*See under Calendar Conventions section below.*
Julius Africanus	*Sextus (c. 160-c. 240), Christian writer and historian.*
Justin (the Martyr)	*Justin (c. 100-c. 165), Christian apologist.*
Labbe	*Philippe (1607-67) Church historian.*
Lactantius	*(c. 240-c. 320) Christian apologist.*
Lamb	*usually signifying Jesus (and his suffering).*
Law, Book of	*The Five Books of Moses or Pentateuch.*
letted	*that which impedes or hinders.*
Luciferan	*a supporter of the tenets of the schismatic Bishop Lucifer of Cagliari (d. 370 or 371).*
Macchiavel	*Niccolò Machiavelli (1469-1527), Florentine statesman and political philsopher.*
Mahuzzims	*Newton uses this term to denote the invocation of the saints in medieval Christianity: `the worship of the images and souls of dead men, here called Mahuzzims' (Observations part 1, ch. 13, p. 195).*
Manesses	*or Manasseh, the first born son of Joseph.*
Manichees	*Manichaeans, followers of the third-century dualist heresy of Manes.*
Marcellinus	*Comes (fl. late 5th-early 6th cent.), a native of Illyricum.*
Marcione	*Marcion (d. c. 160), heretical leader of the Marcionite sect.*
***Maximus* (Taurinensis)**	*Bishop of Turin (d. 408/23), little is known of his life and there has been some confusion with another Bishop Maximus who died after 465.*
Melito	*Bishop of Sardis (d. c. 190).*

Michael	*St Michael the Archangel.*
Montanus	*founder of the Montanists, an apocalyptic movement of the latter half of the second century, which soon developed ascetic traits.*
mulcts	*compulsory payments.*
Nabonassar	*8th century BC king of Babylon; see also under Calendar Conventions section below.*
Nennius	*(fl. 796) English historian.*
Olympiad	*in reference to the dates of Olympic Games (see also below in Calendar Conventions section).*
Olympiodorus	*5th century historian, native of Thebes; he took up his historical account from about the period at which Eunapius* had ended his own account.*
Ordericus Vitalis	*(1075-?1142) Anglo-Norman historian.*
Origen	*(c. 185-c. 254) Alexandrian biblical critic, exegete, theologian and spiritual writer.*
Orosius	*Paulus, early fifth-century historian.*
Ovid	*(b. 43 BC) Italian writer.*
Palladius	*(c. 365-425) historian of early monasticism, who spent several years with the monks of Egypt.*
parabolical	*expressed by parable.*
Paul the Eremite	*Paul of Thebes (d. c. 340), traditionally the first Christian hermit.*
Paulus Diaconus	*Paul the Deacon (b. c. 720), Lombard historian and poet, his <u>Historia Longobardorum</u> is the principle source of information on the Lombards.*
Paulus Warnefridus	*(or Paulus Diaconus), see under Paulus Diaconus.*
Pelagians	*from the name of the late 4th and early 5th century English theologian and exegete Pelagius, who founded a lay, aristocratic, ascetic movement.*
Pentateuch	*the Five Books of Moses.*
Petavius	*Dionysius Petavius or Denis P, tau (1583-1652), Jesuit historian and theologian.*
Peter's Pence	*an ecclesiastical tax in England paid to the pope, first paid by King Offa (d. 796).*
Philastrius	*Philaster or Filaster (d. c. 397), Bishop of Brescia.*

Platina	*Bartolomeo (1421-81), Italian humanist and historian of the popes.*
Plutarch	*(b. c. 46 AD) biographer and author.*
Polycarp	*Bishop of Smyrna (c. 69-c. 155), a leading Christian figure in 2nd century Roman Asia.*
Pontifex Maximus	*Supreme Pontiff, originally a pagan title of the chief priest at Rome.*
Priscillianists	*from the fourth-century Gnostic heresy of Priscillian.*
promulging	*exposing to public view, publishing.*
Prosper	*of Aquitaine (c. 390-c. 463) theologian.*
Procopius, of Caesaria (mid	*6th cent.), Byzantine historian.*
Prudentius	*Aurelius Clemens (348-c. 410) Spanish Christian writer.*
Pseudo-Clemens	*Clementine literature: the many apocryphal writings which circulated in the early Church under the name of St Clement of Rome (fl. c. 96).*
Ptol.	*Ptolemy, of Megalopolis, 3rd century BC historian.*
Regifuge	*the flight or expulsion of the kings from Rome.*
Rhenanus	*Beatus Rhenanus (1485-1547, a German humanist.*
Rolevinc or Rolewinck	*Werner (1425-1502), of Chartreux, chronicler.*
Ruffinus	*Tyrannius Rufinus (c. 345-410), Italian monk, historian and translator.*
Rutilius	*Claudius Namatianus, 5th century Latin Poet.*
St Austin	*St Augustine, first archbishop of Canterbury (d. 604/5).*
Sanhedrin	*the supreme council and highest court of justice at Jerusalem in New Testament times.*
Saturnino	*Saturninus, 2nd century Syrian Gnostic.*
Seventh General Council	*Council of Nicea, 2nd (787).*
Shishak	*the founder of the royal Egyptian Shishak dynasty.*
Sidonius	*Apollinaris (c. 423-c. 480), statesman, author and Bishop of Clermont.*
Sigebert	*of Gembloux (c. 1030-1112), Benedictine monk and chronicler.*

Sigonius	*Charles (1524-1584), Italian historian.*
Socrates	*'Scholasticus' (c. 380-450), Greek Church historian.*
Sozomen	*Salmaninius, early fifth-century Church historian.*
Sulpitius	*Sulpicius Severus (c. 360-c. 420), historian and hagiographer.*
Tatian	*(c. 160) Christian apologist and rigorist.*
Tertullian	*Quintus Septimus Florens (c. 160-c. 225), African Church Father, author of many apologetic, theological, controversial and ascetic works.*
Theodoret	*Bishop of Cyrrhus (c. 393-c. 466), theologian.*
Thebais	*the Thebaid (a region named after its capital, Thebes), the upper part of the Nile valley, the cradle of Christian monasticism.*
Thucydides	*(b. c. 460-d. c.404 BC) the greatest of all ancient Greek historians.*
Urbes Conditæ	*See below in Calendar Conventions section.*
Valentinus	*2nd century Gnostic theologian, founder of the sect of Valentinians.*
Victorinus Pictaviensis	*(d. c. 304) Bishop of Pettau (Poetovio) in Pannonia.*
Vigilantius	*(fl. c. 400), a presbyter of Aquitaine. He was attacked in Jerome's* <u>Contra Vigilantium</u> (406), a defence of monasticism, clerical celibacy and certain practices connected with the cult of the martyrs.*
Xenophon	*(431-?355 BC), Greek general and historian.*
Zosimus	*fifth-century Greek historian.*

Calendar Conventions and Newton's Abbreviations for them.

A.U.C. (ad urbe condita)	*from the founding of the city of Rome - understood as 754 BC; therefore the year of the birth of Christ is 754*
Anno Urbes Conditæ	*as above, dates reckoned from the founding of Rome.*
A.C.	*Anno Christo, Year of Christ.*
Cos.(or Coss. or Cons.)	*in the (ancient Roman) consulship of ...*
An.	*anno = year.*
An. Olymp.	*dates reckoned by dates of the ancient Olympic Games, with a four year period between each set of games (thus expressed An. 4 Olymp. 88); the first set considered to have been in the year 776 BC.*
Anno Nabonass. (or anno Nabonassar)	*the accession of Nabonassar to the throne of Babylon is given by the ancients as 747 BC, which date provided the beginning of the Era of Nabonassar, considered as the starting point of Babylonian chronology. In astronomical calculations, the Era of Nabonassar served a similar function as the Greek civil calendar based on the Olympiads (see preceding entry). Hence `Anno Nabonass. 580' (Observations, p. 30) is the equivalent of 167 BC.*
J.P.	*Julian Period, that is to say a date calculated from the beginning of the first Julian Period, Jan. 1st 4713 BC. (the Julian period is a cycle of 7,980 years).*

SELECTED BIBLIOGRAPHY

Seventeenth Century

Boyle, Robert,
The Christian Virtuoso: shewing, that by being addicted to experimental philosophy, a man is rather assisted than indisposed to be a good Christian (London, 1690).

Mede, Joseph,
Clavis Apocalyptica (Cantabrigiae, 1627).

More, Henry,
The Antidote Against Idolatry, (1st edn 1669), in *A Brief Reply to a Late Answer to Dr. Henry More and his Antidote Against Idolatry* (London, 1672).

More, Henry,
Apocalypsis apocalypseos; or the Revelation of St John Unveiled (1680).

More, Henry,
A Plain and Continued Exposition of the several Prophecies or Divine Visions of the Prophet Daniel (London, 1681).

Ormerod, Oliver,
The Picture of a Papist ... Whereunto is annexed a Certain Treatise, intituled Pagano-Papismus: wherein is proved ... that Papisme is flat Paganisme (London, 1606).

Eighteenth Century

Anon.,
A Short Explication of the Apocalypse of St. John, and part of Daniel's Prophecy (London, 1757).

Brown, John,
A General History of the Christian Church from the Birth of our Saviour to the Present Time (Edinburgh, 1771).

Brown, John,
The Harmony of Scripture Prophecies, and the History of their Fulfilment (Glasgow, 1784).

Dennis, John,
Priestcraft distinguished from Christianity (London, 1715).

Howard, Robert,
The history of Religion. As it has been manag'd by Priestcraft (London, 1709).

Newton, Isaac,   *Observations upon the Prophecies of Daniel and the Apocalypse of St.John* (London, 1733).

Newton, Isaac,   *The Chronology of Ancient Kingdoms Amended* (London, 1728).

Nisbet, Patrick,   *An Abridgement of Ecclesiastical History* (London, 1776).

Priestley, Joseph,   *A General History of the Christian Church from the Fall of the Western Empire to the Present time* (Northumberland U.S.A., 1802).

Priestley, Joseph,   *An Answer to Mr. Paine's Age of Reason, being a Continuation of Letters to the Philosophers and Politicians of France on the Subject of Religion* (London, 1795 - but originally Northumberland U.S.A., 1794).

Priestley, Joseph,   *The Present State of Europe compared with Antient Prophecies* (Phildelphia, 1794).

Trenchard, John,   *The Natural History of Superstition* (London, 1709).

Toland, John,   *Christianity not Mysterious* (London, 1696).

Walmesley, Charles,   *A General history of the Christian Church. Chiefly deduced from the Apocalypse of St. John the Apostle* (London? 1771).

Nineteenth Century

Brewster, David,   *Memoirs of ... Sir isaac Newton* (Edinburgh, 1855).

318

Twentieth Century

Barker, M.,

The Gate of Heaven, History and Symbolism in the New Testament (SPCK, 1991).

Barker, M.,

On Earth as it is in Heaven, Temple Symbolism in the New Testament (Edinburgh, 1995).

Barnett, S.,

'The Prophetic Thought of Sir Isaac Newton, its Origin and Context', in *Prophecy*, Eds B. Taithe and T. Thornton (Sutton Press, 1997).

Barnett, S.,

Idol Temples and Crafty Priests: The Origins of Enlightenment Anticlericalism (London, 1998).

Brooke, John,

'The God of Isaac Newton', in J. Fauvel, R. Flood, M. Shortland, R. Wilson (eds), *Let Newton Be!* (New York, 1989).

Dawson, Jane A,

'The apocalytic thinking of the Marian exiles', in *Prophecy and Eschatology, Studies in Church History*, Subsidia 10, ed. Michael Wilks (Oxford, 1994).

Finegan, J.,

Handbook of Biblical Chronology (Princeton University Press, 1964).

Funkenstein, A.,

Theology and the Scientific Imagination from the Middle Ages to the Seventeenth Century (Princeton, 1986).

Goodman, D.C. (ed.).

Science and Religious Belief 1600-1900 (Dorchester, 1973).

Hall, Rupert,

Isaac Newton. *Adventurer in Thought* (Cambridge, 1996 - 1st edn 1992).

Hankins, T.,

Science and the Enlightenment (Cambridge University Press, 1995; 1st edn 1985).

Harrison, John,

The Library of Isaac Newton (Cambridge, 1978).

Hayward, C. T. R.,

The Jewish Temple, a Non-biblical Source book (London, 1996).

Headley, J. M.,

Luther's view of Church History (New Haven and London, 1963).

Hill, Christopher,

The World Turned upside down. Radical Ideas during ·the English Revolution' (Harmondsworth, 1975).

Hill, Christopher,

The Antichrist in Seventeenth Century England (London, 1971).

Hutton, Sarah,   'More, Newton, and the Language of Biblical Prophecy', in E. Force and R. Popkin (eds), *The Books of Nature and Scripture: Recent Essays on Natural Philosohy, Theology, and Biblical Criticism in the Netherlands of Spinoza's time and the British Isles of Newton's time* (Dordrecht, 1994).

Iliffe, Rob,   '" Making a Shew" : Apocalyptic Hermeneutics and the Sociology of Christian Idolatry in the work of Isaac Newton and Henry More', in E. Force and R. Popkin (eds), *The Books of Nature and Scripture: Recent Essays on Natural Philosohy, Theology, and Biblical Criticism in the Netherlands of Spinoza's time and the British Isles of Newton's time* (Dordrecht, 1994).

Inch, Morris A.,   *Understanding Bible Prophecy* (New York, London, 1977).

Jacob, M. C.,   *The Newtonians and the English Revolution* 1689-1720 (Hassocks, 1976).

Kochavi, Matania Z.,   'One Prophet Interprets Another: Sir Isaac Newton and Daniel', in E. Force and R. Popkin (eds), *The Books of Nature and Scripture: Recent Essays on Natural Philosohy, Theology, and Biblical Criticism in the Netherlands of Spinoza's time and the British Isles of Newton's time* (Dordrecht, 1994).

Mandlebrote, Scott,   'A Duty of the Greatest Moment: Isaac Newton and the Writing of Biblical Criticism', in *The British Journal for the History of Science*, 26 (1993).

Manuel, Frank E.,   *A Portrait of Isaac Newton* (Cambridge, Mass., 1968).

Manuel, Frank E.,   *Isaac Newton Historian* (Cambridge, 1963).

Manuel, Frank, E.,   *The Religion of Isaac Newton* (Oxford, 1974.

Moyise, S.,   *An Introduction to Biblical Studies* (London, 1998).

Popkin, Richard, H.,   'The Third Force in Seventeenth Century Philosophy: Scepticism, Science and Biblical Prophecy', *in Nouvelles de la Republique des Lettres* (1, 1983).

320

Popkin, Richard H.,   'Divine Causality: Newton, the Newtonians and Hume', in *Greene Centennial Studies: Essays Presented to Donald Greene in the Centennial year of the University of South California* (Charlottesville, 1984).

Reedy, Gerard,   *The Bible and Reason: Anglicans and Scripture in Late Seventeenth-Century England* (Phildelphia, 1985).

Reventlow, Henning Graf,   *The Authority of the Bible and the Rise of the Modern World* (London, 1984).

Rattansi, Piyo,   'Newton and the Wisdom of the Ancients', in J. Fauvel, R. Flood, M. Shortland, R. Wilson (eds), *Let Newton Be!* (New York, 1989).

Southern, R. W.,   'Aspects of the European Tradition of Historical Writing: 3. History as Prophecy', *in Transactions of the Royal Historical Society*, 5th ser., 22 (1972).

Thomas, Keith,   *Religion and the Decline of Magic. Studies in Popular Beliefs in Sixteenth- and Seventeenth-Century England* (London, 1991).

Westfall, Richard S.,   'Isaac Newton in Cambridge: The Restoration University and Scientific Creativity', in Zagorin, Perez. (ed) *Culture and Politics from Puritanism to the Enlightenment* (Berkeley, 1980).

Westfall, Richard S.,   *The Life of Isaac Newton* (Cambridge, 1994).

White, Michael,   Isaac Newton, *The Last Sorcerer* (London, 1997).

Whitla, William,   *Sir Isaac Newton's Daniel and the Apocalypse* (London, 1922).

Williams, Ann (ed),   *Prophecy and Millenarianism. Essays in honour of Marjorie Reeves* (Harlow, 1980).

INDEX

322

MELLEN CRITICAL EDITIONS AND TRANSLATIONS